THE CONSULTATION CHART

To Cathryn
Best wishes
Wanda Sellar
20th July 2014

Other titles by Wanda Sellar

The Directory of Essential Oils
Frankincense and Myrrh (with Martin Watt)

Other titles from The Wessex Astrologer

The Essentials of Vedic Astrology by Komilla Sutton
Astrolocality Astrology by Martin Davis
You're not a person - just a birth chart by Paul F. Newman
Pattens of the Past by Judy Hall

The No Nonsense Guide to Astrology: *Aspects*
(various authors)   *Transits*
                                                                       Elements and Modes
                                                                       Progressions

Coming Soon

The Lunar Nodes - Crisis and Redemption by Komilla Sutton
Karmic Connections by Judy Hall

The Consultation Chart

A Guide to What it is and How to use it

by Wanda Sellar

Published in England in 2001 by
The Wessex Astrologer Ltd
PO Box 2751
Bournemouth
BH6 3ZJ
England

www.wessexastrologer.com

© Wanda Sellar 2000

Wanda Sellar asserts the moral right to be identified as the author
of this work

ISBN 978-1-902405-08-7

Cover art © Paul F. Newman 2000

Printed and bound in the UK by Biddles Ltd.,
Kings Lynn, Norfolk

A catalogue record for this book is available
at the British Library

No part of this book may be reproduced or used in any form
or by any means without the written permission of the publisher.
A reviewer may quote brief passages

Dedication

With heartfelt thanks to Janet Augustine, Elena Dramchini, Maurice McCann and Olivia Barclay for the support and encouragement they have given me throughout the years.

Contents

Chapter 1
The Rising Sign 1

Chapter 2
Prognostication: What May Happen 16

Chapter 3
The Personal Planets 22

Chapter 4
The Social Planets 60

Chapter 5
All Change: The Outer Planets 76

Chapter 6
The Magic Dragon and the Wounded Healer 89

Chapter 7
All Around the Houses 93

Case Histories 151

Conclusion 213

Bibliography 215

Astrological Schools and Organisations 217

Index 223

Introduction

THE MEETING OF TWO MINDS

Accompanying the client into the consultation room are his hopes, dreams and aspirations. He hopes that the astrologer will shed light on his problems and direct him towards a happier, more fulfilling path in life. Sometimes he wants to have a direct answer to his questions: what will happen in his relationship, will he get the job or should he move house? Sometimes he wants to look more deeply into his psyche and examine his inner drives in order to ponder upon the historic basis to his problems. In either case, the consultation chart can be an invaluable tool for delineation.

A chart drawn up for the moment the astrologer and client meet reflects not only the present but holds the past and the future within its grasp. To some extent, the consultation chart can substitute for a natal chart if an accurate birth-time is not available. It can also be used in conjunction with the natal chart in order to gain greater insight into the client's life and loves.

The immediacy of the consultation chart helps both client and astrologer establish an empathic rapport very quickly. Almost instantly, the astrologer enters into the client's frame of reference and thereby gains his trust. The client hears his most pressing issues outlined in detail, something not always possible using the natal chart. Indeed, the natal chart, whilst useful in depicting the larger canvas of clients' lives, does not always describe their present dilemma. However, the two charts used together can be a powerful tool for counselling. The consultation chart is an entirely practical way of dealing with client's problems and more importantly, his potential. It can show why the client has elected to consult an astrologer and as example charts will show, there are very few areas of life that cannot be described within the planetary pattern. Relationships, health, career and even descriptions of the dear departed come within its province of delineation.

Interpretation of charts in this book is by the most basic rules of delineation but any techniques that the astrologer finds useful can be employed. Ultimately, I believe, that rules of delineation serve only to prompt the intuition in divulging unconscious processes.

People bring similar problems into the consultation room; lost love, work difficulties, exam nerves, home buying, existential crises, family and health problems. Yet all people differ in their level of consciousness, in their understanding of psychological processes and the soul aspect of life. The more the individual feels that he is driven by higher ideals and less by personal desires, the more he is in contact with his soul. Of course, this is not an idea espoused by all, either astrologers or clients, therefore the process of delineation varies widely. The client's feedback in a consultation is therefore, of tremendous importance as in this way the astrologer can gain insight into the client's level of consciousness and understanding. It is not always a matter of intelligence. Some highly educated people for instance may be less willing to view their life circumstances as lessons and opportunities for growth than perhaps those whose lives may not have been so privileged.

Some people may only be interested in the form aspect of life, maybe in events and the satisfaction of personal needs, whilst others are interested in their growth and enrichment through their response to environmental pressures. Whatever the client's motives, the objective of the consultation chart, as well as the natal chart, is to give the client some hope even when the situation at that moment looks bleak. This can sometimes only be gained by looking for the meaning behind the events, which naturally takes chart interpretation into psychological and sometimes, spiritual realms.

Esoteric thought posits that the entire story of evolution is the story of consciousness from the microscopic interest of the self-conscious individual towards the divine consciousness of the universal mind. In an attempt to encompass all three levels of understanding, the signs, houses and planets will therefore be described from a physical, psychological and spiritual viewpoint, as far as possible. Where the astrologer and client choose to pitch the level of their consultation is obviously a decision made tacitly between them.

I see both the consultation chart and the natal chart as a voyage of adventure shared with the client, exploring his thoughts and feelings so that he can eventually make more informed decisions. Prediction can be a part of the delineation and judgement, which then turns the consultation chart into a horary chart, especially if the client asks definite questions. In horary charts the client is referred to as the querent, and the thing or person he or she wants to know about is the quesited. In this book we shall keep to the word client to emphasis the fact that we are looking at a consultation chart, rather than specifically at questions.

I have used the Placidus house system because it was convenient to do so at the time - not because I find it superior to others. To me the chart is a way to understand the psyche of the client and the symbols in front of me open my consciousness to something more intangible. The method which helps me to arrive at judgements may suit me but perhaps it does not suit others and I believe we have to find our own path.

Some astrologers are uncertain whether to use the client's co-ordinates or their own when taking telephone consultations. I do not hold firm opinions about this either but I tend to use my own co-ordinates as I am the one erecting the chart.

Please note that for the sake of convenience the client will always be referred to by the male gender, except where example charts are used, and no offence is intended towards the feminine sex.

1

The Rising Sign

Naturally, every astrologer ultimately devises their own method of chart interpretation, but a guide is always useful. Initial steps at delineation should first consider the 'message' of the rising sign. In the consultation chart the rising sign will probably be different to that in the natal chart, and its effect more transient in the client's life. However, if it duplicates the sign rising in the natal chart, this points to current issues having a deeper significance. The rising sign will therefore be indicative of the main area of interest at the present time. For instance, Gemini rising suggests that the client has to deal with many conflicting issues at this moment in time; Scorpio rising indicates changes, probably of an oppressive nature, occurring in the client's life; Sagittarius rising reveals expansive urges within the client's psyche defined perhaps through travel or studies. Ultimately, the rising sign is only an indication of psychological and material possibilities. Obviously, it is necessary to examine the whole chart, and particularly the Ascendant ruler for further indications.

Split rulership

If the rising sign also cusps the twelfth house, this should be included in the delineation. It may be that the problematic issues of the twelfth house impinge upon the client's life at this time. He may find difficulty in pursing his plans straightforwardly and needs more time to reflect upon his present circumstances. If the rising sign also rules the second house, financial and considerations are part of the client's concern just now.

Descriptions of Rising Signs

The following descriptions of the signs should be looked upon as food for thought and possibly as inspiration for intuition. Not every quality of the sign will apply to each client. It should be noted that when early degrees rise, the issues depicted by the rising sign are perhaps embryonic and probably just unfolding; middle degrees indicate that the client is embroiled in some life situation which he is still trying to understand through overcoming various obstacles and challenges; the last degrees of the rising sign put the client at the end of a cycle. He is now assimilating the lessons of the sign and is ready to move on to the next stage of his life's journey.

Aries

A cardinal/fire sign, Aries has great energy and enthusiasm. Regarded as the sign giving impetus to new ideas, a fresh cycle of activity always beckons. Inspiration flows unimpeded with many thoughts occurring of future possibilities, and courage to carry out new enterprises is certainly not lacking. Such a new burst of energy may be expressed selfishly, thinking only of personal satisfaction. Alternatively, it can inspire leadership for the benefit of others. Aries will pass through tumultuous storms creating a sheltered path for those who follow.

In the consultation chart, Aries rising indicates that one phase of life has ended for the client and a new one beckons. The client, recently lacking in motivation and direction, suddenly finds a new burst of energy at his disposal. This impels him to seek an alternative life-style. At this point ideas may still be in the conceptual and planning stage so it will be important not to lose sight of goals should obstacles arise. Enthusiasm should be accompanied by hard work. A new path in life will of course bring its own crop of difficulties because the client may be sailing into uncharted waters. Uncertainty is always part and parcel of any new enterprise, yet a new direction is just what the client needs at this moment. It is possible that this new cycle will bring a new level of awareness in partnerships, career and family life, and certain adjustments may have to be made in these areas. The client may have to decide whether the promised changes are worth sacrificing the familiar, if stale, ground he has trodden up till now. Embarking on a new way of life tends to bring with it a feeling of renewal and a fresh zest for life. Confidence and positive thinking are the qualities needed most right now.

Taurus

A fixed/earth sign, Taurus endeavours to strive for material and emotional security. Desire for personal satisfaction and experience is very pronounced. Taurus forges the instruments of constructive living, bestowing the ability to manipulate matter towards high achievement. This may be expressed through financial acumen. Inner illumination and inspiration may act as a spur to great feats within the creative arts. Alternatively, physical desires may be very strong; eating and drinking to excess resulting in inertia and indolence.

In a consultation chart, Taurus rising suggests that the client has been working hard to put all his knowledge and wisdom into a constructive form. Improved finances may be the result of perseverance and strict dedication to his goals. Dealing with money on all levels may be part of his life at this time. His experiences with the material world will give rise to profound consideration as to what he really values in his life. He may gradually come to realise that some things he thought important are no longer so meaningful. Change however, will come gradually.

This heralds a time when the client begins to explore his creative abilities: a new interest in beauty, art and gardening may be developing. Perhaps hobbies once carried out purely for pleasure will now bring him a new source of revenue. Life may also become more settled which could indicate a tendency towards self-indulgence, especially in matters to do with food and putting on weight could be a possibility. Business interests in catering could be a source of real profit. There may also be thoughts of taking up some form of complementary therapy which deal with the body such as massage and shiatsu. Hard work and a sense of responsibility will help him towards achieving success.

Gemini

A mutable/air sign, Gemini has the quality of diversity and change. There is a strong sense of duality which may bring conflict when making decisions. The client begins to sense that there are alternatives to his present life-style but this may initially only serve to confuse him. New ideas occur but they may be difficult to carry through. Gradually through many different experiences, he learns to pull together all the different strands of his life.

When Gemini ascends in a consultation chart, many opportunities begin to arise for the client. At first this may make choices difficult and initially it may be an unsettling period in his life. He has to explore many different avenues of experience before finally deciding which course to take. Indeed, the client will often be in two minds when making decisions or torn in two different directions.

He may sometimes feel there are not enough hours in the day to accommodate all that he needs to do. It is also possible that many projects begun will remain unfinished. New people are likely to enter his life and his social life could greatly improve. This may be quite an exciting time. Slowly, ideas will emerge which will have important future implications and he learns how to accommodate these, becoming adept at communicating them to others. All types of communication become important. Short distance travel may feature more often in his life and this may involve buying a new car. A course of study or training in some field will be advantageous if contemplating a new career. The ability to deal with people from all walks of life will help the client along the road to success. With so much happening around him there may be a strain on the nervous system, so adequate rest is necessary.

Cancer

A cardinal/water sign, the characteristics of Cancer suggest that life's experiences flow in an undulating rhythm rather than in a straight stream. Deep experiences attest to the swelling tide of strong emotion. As Cancer is the sign of mass consciousness, it also bestows the ability to merge with the feelings of others developing a high measure of empathy in the process. An instinctive awareness of subtle environmental nuances gives enormous potential for reflecting mass needs and gaining popularity.

When Cancer rises in the consultation chart, there may be a keen desire to build a new foundation. This may involve buying and selling property or making substantial alterations to the home and garden.

Demands made by the family right now may make the client feel that he has little time for himself, and his fine qualities of caring and compassion will be at full stretch at this time. This may involve looking after an aged parent, or perhaps the addition of a new family member brings extra work. It is possible that someone from the past will be reappearing in the client's life. Restructuring the conditions of work and relationships may also be necessary. Emotions are likely to resemble a roller-coaster at this time and life will appear burdensome. Ultimately, the client will have greater confidence in himself when dealing with family issues. Letting go of past problems will help him develop more stable relationships.

His caring qualities may involve the concerns of the community, and environmental issues become important. Responsibilities thrust upon him could ultimately bring a sense of fulfilment and greater self-esteem. The client's instinctive awareness of other people's needs may act as a spur towards developing psychic abilities. This will deepen his involvement with people outside the family circle.

Leo

A fixed/fire sign, Leo seeks to harness creative ideas. Thought is translated into action. Leo is the sign of individual consciousness and initially therefore, ambitions tend to be self-serving; however, understanding and wisdom are acquired through the trials of experience and self reliance turns into knowledge of self. He gradually learns tolerance and responsibility for others. Qualities of organisation and leadership emerge.

When Leo rises in a consultation chart the client begins to develop confidence in his own abilities. Events occur which enable him to emerge from the crowd as an individual thinker. He begins to see possibilities that were not clear to him before. He learns to organise and maximise his talents into a coherent whole. Now he gains a much wider perspective of life and develops trust and faith in future possibilities.

The force of his personality is paramount in impressing his ideas on the environment. It is now time to assert his individuality though initially it may seem uncomfortable to push himself forward in such a forthright manner. This is not the time for modesty since circumstances arise where his dynamic style will be needed. He may even find himself appearing before the public in some way and leadership may be thrust upon him.

Up until now the client may have been quite happy to side with prevailing thought, seeing no reason for change, but the growing feeling of discontentment will signal that a change in self-expression is imminent. He now needs to become more in control of his life and not look to others for guidance and direction. Becoming aware of his own power may bring him into collaboration with others, perhaps becoming a leading light in some humanitarian group concern. Here he will have to learn how to merge his own talents with those of others. This may see him guiding the young, as children may begin to play an important role in his life. With growing enthusiasm and foresight into future possibilities his life becomes more complete.

Virgo

A mutable/earth sign, Virgo has to deal with the tides of change and renewal. He is only too aware of environmental discord, and struggles to perfect all contrary elements around him. Worry and anxiety accompany his path through life as he endeavours to restore coherence in his world. His excellent reasoning ability gradually controls his wayward emotions. Slowly he learns to focus on what is useful and what is superfluous in his life. Inner changes will reveal to him the true purpose of his life and this will bring him happiness.

When Virgo rises in the consultation chart, the client may feel that his daily routine no longer seems to have much purpose. At first, this may bring confusion and a lack of direction. His career may no longer be entirely satisfactory. For so long now he may have been working quietly behind the scenes that communicating his thoughts and feelings openly may seem difficult. A change of job is the most likely expression of such discontent, but a conflict arises between finding work which gives more fulfilment against adequate remuneration. Since returning to college may be a requisite of a change of lifestyle, money becomes more of an issue. Failure to resolve this conflict could result in ill-health, albeit temporarily. Paradoxically, it is when he takes time out through illness that he may be able to find the answers to some of his problems. Part of the client's difficulty may be a lack of confidence in his own abilities as well as low self-esteem, although this is not an opinion shared by those around him: he needs a great deal of encouragement now to push aside the trivial concerns that obscure his true light.

Rewards may not be quickly apparent but he needs to press on as opportunities will occur which cater for his talents. This is a time of putting in the spade-work which eventually will lead to recognition. His ability to focus on what is real and what is possible will help him to achieve mastery of his self-doubts.

Libra

A cardinal/air sign, Libra represents the point of balance between spirit and matter. Libra seeks inner alignment and a sense of wholeness initially within relationships. However, the search for 'the other' to make life meaningful may result in disappointment. He has to become complete within himself rather than rely too heavily on someone else to make life meaningful. Someone who complements his talents rather than someone he can lean on brings the most happiness.

When Libra rises in a consultation chart, the focus is primarily upon relationships. Without a partner, the client feels empty. It might be helpful to discuss with the client what else they could do with their lives to make themselves feel whole. Do they need to sort out past problems with the family or find a career that best uses their talents? If the client is not receptive to this idea life may become meaningless until he finds that perfect partner. Difficulties may arise in existing relationships at this time. It may be necessary to ask if the outer crisis masks other unresolved issues between the couple. If so, this might be the time to confront them and hopefully, save the relationship. Eventually the client may find that the answers to his problems lie in relating to others with love and detachment.

It is possible that at this moment in time the client has reached a crossroads in his life. Inwardly he knows that the next step may be a difficult one and that if any progress is going to be made, hard work must be the order of the day. This is the quiet before the storm. He must now summon up his reserves of strength to face the challenges ahead.

Getting the balance right can also be expressed through the legal profession which may indicate that affairs of a legal nature may need to be sorted out. This might involve divorce, real estate or probate.

Scorpio

A fixed/water sign, Scorpio has great emotional depth which can bring inner turmoil or perfect peace. Life experiences feel like a descent into the abyss, yet a new light and a new sense of purpose arises from these difficulties. Points of crisis occur in order to facilitate a re-orientation towards developing a new attitude. It is a sign of struggle, tests and trials, usually in the area of money, power and love.

When Scorpio rises in the consultation chart, it indicates a period of enforced changes that may be painful and upsetting. There may be a feeling of oppression and resistance to change but the greater the struggle to keep things as they are, the less things run smoothly. A new path in life beckons, but the process of adapting to fresh ideas and circumstances is often a difficult one. Leaving cherished notions and loved ones behind will be an effort.

There is usually a big decision to be made: whether to stay tied to the past or to move forward into uncharted territory. The past may be more descriptive of entrenched feelings, rather than physical circumstances. Such feelings may include resentment, hatred, jealousy and anger. Holding on to these feelings are likely to limit the client's vision of future possibilities.

This might be a time when the client finds it hard to tread the middle way and experiences extremes of emotions. He feels at the mercy of his life's circumstances and for a while he may seem helpless. Struggles may take place in the area of shared resources, power conflicts and within the sexual arena. Nevertheless, this can be a time of growth, because once the trials and tests have been overcome, there is renewed vigour. Interest may grow in areas of psychology, the occult and in the law. Slowly the mind begins to control the emotions and a knowledge that one can direct one's own life. Greater insight occurs into problems of others.

Sagittarius

This is a mutable/fire sign indicating change and inspiration. Goals to achieve something new are invariably in sight urging a feeling of restlessness and expectancy. Fresh challenges are welcomed as they invite a desire for expansion and growth. Old traditions are readily cast aside and a new vision of the future arises. Sometimes there is a certain lack of attention given to present issues because new objectives seem more exciting.

When Sagittarius rises in the consultation chart, the client feels that life has become a little stale and it is time for taking part in activities of a more stimulating nature. He begins to welcome new diversions and feels it is now time to embrace new concepts and ideas. The old way of doing things has become a little tiresome and the client may want to push his boundaries farther than he has before. This may be expressed through education and travel. Perhaps it involves taking up an important new course of study which may pave the way for a different and more fulfilling career. Interests may develop in the fields of philosophy and religion as well as publishing. Perhaps the client feels he should write his memoirs. Whether these are published or not, it will nevertheless lead to greater insight regarding his life. This feeling of freedom and expansion may become detrimental to existing relationships. It may be necessary to pursue activities without present partners, albeit temporarily. The client may not be satisfied to live only in the present and wants to concentrate more on the future. He may feel that it is time to synthesise his knowledge into some practical enterprise.

It may be a time in the client's life when he needs to concentrate upon important objectives to the exclusion of less significant factors in the life, although there may be a tendency to over extend himself. This should be an exciting time for the client as a fresh impetus for living will attract new and interesting people into his life.

Capricorn

Capricorn is a cardinal/earth sign indicating that material ambition is usually very pronounced. There is normally a strong drive to reach the top whatever the area of interest. Capricorn is a sign often involved with matters concerning power and authority as it is not afraid to shoulder responsibility. Plans are carefully construed and tasks and challenges are undertaken that others would find daunting. Capricorn can also be a sign of extremes expressing the best and worst in human nature.

When Capricorn rises in the consultation chart, it is possible that the client is in a state of prevarication as he tries to make the best possible decision regarding his future. If he has been involved in any kind of project or enterprise, he may feel that further progress is impossible because there are too many obstacles to overcome. He may even feel that he wants to give up and could easily succumb to depression, yet usually at his bleakest moments, just when he thinks that things are unlikely to get better, somehow the situation improves. He may have suffered some humiliating occurrence such as redundancy at work or a failure to do his duty in some area. He feels imprisoned by his own depressing thoughts. He then finds he is able to press on with life regardless of pain and unhappiness and discovers that he is loved despite everything.

He now has the chance to rise from the ashes and go on to greater heights than before. He is able to take on even more responsibility, especially on behalf of others. He learns the virtue of patience and becomes more understanding.

Success is measured in both material and spiritual terms. At this time, the client has the chance to fulfil many of his ambitions through hard work.

Aquarius

A fixed/air sign, Aquarius often succeeds in putting his ideas into practice. He is sensitive to humanitarian issues as he has an acute awareness of the inner bonds that unite humanity. He works to bring new conditions into materialisation, thereby improving the fate of others. In some ways, he feels that he has a universal mission. The welfare of humanity may, however, be the highest expression of the Aquarius energy. Sometimes the urge to right the wrongs of humanity becomes an acceptable evasion from dealing with one's own problems.

When Aquarius rises in a consultation chart, the urge to unite with others is more likely to be a desire for convivial company. There will be a need to mix with friends and groups of common interest and it will be a time for increased social activity. It is possible that until now, the client has detached himself from intimate relationships and close friendships because of problems he may have experienced in the past. Now is the time to re-enter the social scene but there may be difficulties in making that first move. Emotions are not easy to express, and he fears losing his freedom, but he faces a dilemma since he really does not like to be alone. He enjoys exchanging ideas with others. Alternatively, the client may be facing a confrontational situation with a group of people. Differences of opinion within teamwork of a professional kind may occur, or he may find that the values he once shared with his friends are no longer viable. Outer changes mask a growing inner turmoil that drives him towards finding his true niche in the world. Facing loneliness may be part of the changes he now faces.

The highest expression of the Aquarian energy indicates a growing conviction in the client that it is time to serve humanity in some way. His communicative abilities and sense of fairness will be of enormous help to him in this field.

Pisces

A mutable/water sign, Pisces is indicative of a fluid and sensitive temperament which is open to all experiences. There is a particular attraction to healing, clairvoyance or the arts. Alternatively, the oppressive qualities of the real world can sometimes be too much to bear and he may escape into retirement or even oblivion. Pisces, the last sign, can indicate the end of a cycle or experience.

When Pisces rises in a consultation chart, it may be that a certain phase of life is drawing to a close. Existing patterns of living are breaking up and this becomes a period of uncertainty. The client stands alone, unsupported and unable to lean on anyone. Instead he finds that he is often called to offer a comforting shoulder for others to cry on. The client could well be in the process of learning about unselfishness and compassion, as the opportunity to forget about one's self and think more about the welfare of others could be a sign of spiritual awakening. Unsuspected healing talents may be detected.

The client may at last be making some sense of his life. No one going through such structural dissolution will emerge without deeper insights into his personality and life. The subtle side of life may also be expressed through the creative arts as in film and dance. This should be encouraged as it can fill the prevailing sense of emptiness.

As this may now represent the close of a cycle, it might be helpful for the client to relinquish all negative emotions connected to people who have hurt him - doing this will help to release any karmic residues that bind him to the past. Only then will he begin to experience a real sense of freedom.

Signposts to Delineation - The Ascendant Ruler

1. The planet ruling the ascending sign represents the client and describes his prevailing attitude and present frame of reference. In order to gain the client's confidence, the first important step of any counsellor - and indeed this is the astrologer's position at this moment in time - is to step into the client's shoes and view the world from his perspective. Therefore, the Ascendant ruler should be examined very carefully.

2. The Ascendant ruler's position by sign and house should be noted. Is it in a sign in which it feels strong and comfortable? For instance, if Mars is in Aries or Scorpio, the signs it rules, the client is most probably feeling confident and able to cope with any difficulties the chart may show. If Mars is in its sign of exaltation (Capricorn) the client may be particularly elated about some matter and the circumstances around him seem favourable to his plans.

If Mars should be in detriment, (opposite the sign it rules either in Libra or Taurus), its usual energy is deflected for some other purpose and the same can be said if Mars is in its fall (opposite its position of exaltation). Mars of course, would be in its fall in Cancer. A planet in its detriment or fall will tend to lower the confidence at this present time (see Fig. 1).

3. When the Ascendant ruler is placed in an angular house (1,4,7,10) the client feels that he is able to influence, and perhaps even control, his

environment, particularly if the ruler is conjunct the relevant angle within 5 degrees. Of course, the Ascendant ruler may be in conjunction to one of the angles (AC, DC, MC, IC) but from a cadent house (3,6,9,12). This suggests that the client's influence over the environment is much more covert. It must be remembered that the extensive research carried out by Michel Gauquelin indicated that planets in cadent houses close to the angles figured quite prominently in the charts of successful people. The research was carried out on natal charts, but it is quite possible that the same applies to consultation charts. It could well be that the planets in cadent houses have to work that much harder to be noticed and this may ultimately bring success.

4. If the Ascendant ruler is retrograde it indicates that the client spends too much time looking back at the past which deters him from moving forward. It is also possible that retrogradation shows an inability to make up his mind. This may suggest that there is little happening in the client's life at present. Check in the ephemeris to see when the planet turns direct for release of the client's potential.

5. If the Ascendant ruler receives aspects mainly of a challenging nature, the client could be very stressed and finds it difficult to cope with his present situation. The square, opposition and quincunx are usually considered aspects of difficulty and challenge.

6. If the Ascendant ruler is in receipt of aspects that are mainly harmonious (sextile and trine), the client may find that he deals with his problems with comparative ease. The conjunction, a very powerful aspect, can show either ease or difficulty, depending upon the planets involved.

7. Planetary besiegement is another indication of stress and difficulty. Besiegement occurs when a planet is placed bodily between two malefics, traditionally Mars and Saturn. Uranus, Neptune and Pluto can also be looked upon as malefic in this instance, since their energies tend to be impersonal, suggesting that the client is caught up in circumstances totally outside his sphere of influence. If all three planets involved in besiegement are placed in the same sign (or house) the difficulty may be more pronounced or intensified than if the besieging planets were a few signs away.

Another form of besiegement is when the relevant planet separates by aspect from one malefic (its last aspect) and applies to another (its next aspect), the kind of aspects involved being irrelevant - however, squares and oppositions are likely to be much more stressful than sextiles and trines. For example: the Moon at 16 degrees Gemini separates from a trine of Mars at 13 degrees Aquarius and applies to a square of Saturn at 17 degrees Virgo.

Ptolemy's Table of Essential Dignities of the Planets

Sign	Ruler	Exalt-ation	Triplicity Day	Triplicity Night	Term					Face			Detri-ment	Fall
♈	♂ D	☉ 19	☉	♃	♃ 6	♀ 14	☿ 21	♂ 26	♄ 30	♂ 10	☉ 20	♀ 30	♀	♄
♉	♀ N	☽ 3	♀	☽	♀ 8	☿ 15	♃ 22	♄ 26	♂ 30	☿ 10	☽ 20	♄ 30	♂	
♊	☿ D	☊ 3	♄	☿	☿ 7	♃ 13	♀ 20	♄ 26	♂ 30	♃ 10	♂ 20	☉ 30	♃	
♋	☽ D/N	♃ 15	♂	♂	♂ 6	♃ 13	☿ 20	♀ 27	♄ 30	♀ 10	☿ 20	☽ 30	♄	♂
♌	☉ D/N		☉	♃	♄ 6	☿ 13	♀ 19	♃ 25	♂ 30	♄ 10	♃ 20	♂ 30	♄	
♍	☿ N	☿ 15	♀	☽	☿ 7	♀ 13	♃ 18	♄ 24	♂ 30	☉ 10	♀ 20	☿ 30	♃	♀
♎	♀ D	♄ 21	♄	☿	♄ 6	♀ 11	♃ 19	☿ 24	♂ 30	☽ 10	♄ 20	♃ 30	♂	☉
♏	♂ N		♂	♂	♂ 6	♃ 14	♀ 21	☿ 27	♄ 30	♂ 10	☉ 20	♀ 30	♀	☽
♐	♃ D	☋ 3	☉	♃	♃ 8	♀ 14	☿ 19	♄ 25	♂ 30	☿ 10	☽ 20	♄ 30	☿	
♑	♄ N	♂ 28	♀	☽	♀ 6	☿ 12	♃ 19	♂ 25	♄ 30	♃ 10	♂ 20	☉ 30	☽	♃
♒	♄ D		♄	☿	♄ 6	☿ 12	♀ 20	♃ 25	♂ 30	♀ 10	☿ 20	☽ 30	☉	
♓	♃ N	♀ 27	♂	♂	♀ 8	♃ 14	☿ 20	♂ 26	♄ 30	♄ 10	♃ 20	♂ 30	☿	☿

Fig 1

> **NOTES**
>
> A planet in its sign of **rulership** is strong and able to express its basic energy without impediment
>
> A planet in its sign of **exaltation** expresses its basic energy with strength and dignity
>
> A planet in its own **triplicity** is said to function with moderate strength
>
> A planet in its own **terms** and **face** functions well
>
> A planet in **detriment** and **fall** is said to be weak or to function with less force
>
> If a planet is neither in its sign of rulership, exaltation, triplicity, term or face it is said to be **peregrine** - that is without energy to function well or influence its surroundings with any force

Fig 2

8. Note the planets from which the Ascendant ruler is separating as these depict people and events the client already knows about. The placement of those planets by sign and house further describes the situation.

9. Note the planets to which the Ascendant ruler applies as these indicate future possibilities; trines and sextiles promise results achieved with ease and squares and oppositions show results achieved with difficulty, if at all.

10. If the Ascendant ruler applies by conjunction to the North Node, the client is heading towards an important time in his life. He will feel that it is a time of growth and that all he does somehow feels fated - the sign and house will give further evidence what this may be.

If the Ascendant ruler applies by conjunction to the South Node, the client may be reliving an old pattern and may have to deal with some unfinished business before he can move on. Other aspects will of course aspect both nodal points and the client could find himself in a position where he has to balance the old with the new.

The Consultation Chart

11. The planets connected to the Ascendant ruler by aspect and mutual reception are of greatest consideration in delineation at this present time. Other planets may not be as important in the present scheme of things, except if they are placed within a few degrees of the angles, that is the Ascendant (ASC), Descendant (DC), Midheaven (MC) and Nadir (IC). The planets, people and qualities they represent suggest a powerful influence on the client's life in the futute and their strength and weakness should be noted. Whatever these planets represent may show issues that the client will be dealing with in the near future, but which may not be affecting his life, whether positively or negatively, at the present time.

12. Note the planet which disposes of the Ascendant ruler as this will give further description of the client's circumstances. A disposing or dispositing planet is the planetary ruler of the sign in which the Ascendant ruler is placed. Naturally, all planets can be disposited or disposed of unless they rule the sign they are placed in.

13. The Ascendant ruler may also be in mutual reception or mixed reception with another planet, which suggests that the affairs of the house containing the other planet are also important to the client at this time. Mutual reception occurs when two planets are placed in each other's sign, for instance: Venus in Capricorn, Saturn in Libra. Mixed reception occurs when one planet is in another's sign of rulership and the other planet is in the first planet's sign of exaltation. For instance, the Moon in Aquarius ruled by Saturn and Saturn in Taurus, the sign of the Moon's exaltation.

14. If a planet is within 5 degrees of the next house cusp, it is usually considered to already be in the next house. It is quite possible that a planet so positioned may influence both houses.

Planets in the First House

Planets in the first house, and the house/s they rule, depict issues that are important to the client at the present time. For instance Neptune in the Ascendant will indicate an urge to transcend personal boundaries which limit self expression. If Neptune co-rules the second house it may indicate that the client has thoughts about using resources in a more charitable way, perhaps in a fund-raising capacity. Alternatively, debts may accrue forcing him to re-evaluate his life. This may only be a wish or desire at present and may have to be put on hold if there is no affirmative contact - i.e. an applying aspect - between the traditional ruler of the Ascendant and Neptune. Nevertheless, since the consultation chart is a tool for guidance and counselling, talking over the client's needs and desires will hopefully clear his mind and help him towards making decisions in the future.

The Turned Chart

If the client asks about members of his family, friends etc., the chart can be turned and read as if the relevant house were the Ascendant of the person under discussion. For instance, if the client asks a question or needs some information about his father, the radix fourth house becomes the father's first house; the radix fifth house becomes the father's second house; the radix sixth house becomes the father's third house and so on.

2

Prognostication: What May Happen

The consultation chart can of course, be used for predicting forthcoming events and it should then be used as a horary chart, which is normally erected for the moment a question is asked. The horary chart has certain observable considerations and strictures but these do not necessarily apply to the consultation chart which describes an event - the meeting between astrologer/therapist and client. Incidentally, the first contact can be over the telephone - it doesn't have to be a physical meeting.

If prognostication becomes part of the consultation (and it often does), it is safer to stay with traditional horary rules when discussing a likely outcome to a question or event. These rules stipulate that only the seven traditional planets are used - Saturn, Jupiter, the Sun, Mars, Venus, Mercury and the Moon - as well as the Ptolemiac aspects of conjunction, opposition, trine, square and sextile. Horary is usually concerned with events and material matters. Other aspects such as the quincunx, half-square, sesquiquadrate and quintile for instance, are probably more concerned with psychological as well as spiritual processes. If the outer planets - Uranus, Neptune and Pluto - seem to have a strong bearing on the matter, it usually indicates that the client's aspirations may be drawn into events beyond his control.

Signification of forthcoming events

Forthcoming events are signified by applying aspects - this is when a swifter moving planet applies to a slower moving planet. The planets in order of swiftness are:

Moon, Mercury, Venus, Sun, Mars, Jupiter, Saturn, Uranus, Neptune, Pluto.

Events and circumstances influencing the client's direction in life will be signified by those planets in applying aspect to the Ascendant ruler or vice versa. The Moon's application by aspect to other planets also represents the client's direction and purpose. If the question or aspiration is to become an actuality, the aspect has to reach perfection, that is it has to become exact. This is also known as a partile aspect. Naturally, this means that it is important to check the movement of the planets in the current/relevant Ephemeris. A positive outcome is likely to occur when the aspect is a conjunction, sextile or trine. Squares and oppositions can bring an affirmative answer in certain circumstances, but with difficulty. In any case, the client (referred to as querent in horary astrology) is not likely to be satisfied by the outcome. However, should the planets be united by an applying square or opposition and also be in either mutual or mixed reception, it may indicate more opportunity to resolve the situation to a favourable outcome.

Another variation of perfection is when a swifter moving planet has already passed a slower moving one, but because of retrogradation it moves back to the degree of the slower moving planet. This also suggests an affirmative answer, particularly with the conjunction, sextile and trine. It often means that one of the parties has had a change of heart and is returning to the original situation, whatever that may be.

Sometimes the planet signifying the client/querent does not apply to the quesited (astrological reference to the matter or person enquired about). However, two planetary motions called *translation* and *collection* can bring about an affirmative answer. Translation occurs when one planet separates from a slower moving planet and applies to another slower moving planet. For instance the Moon at 24 Aquarius separates from Mercury at 22 Scorpio by square and applies to Jupiter at 26 Aries by sextile.

Collection occurs when the querent's planet and the quesited's planet are both applying to another slower moving planet. For example if Venus is at 5 deg Taurus and Mars were at 2 degrees Virgo, it would appear as if the planets concerned no longer had a relationship with each other since Venus has of course, passed the trine with Mars being the swifter planet. However, if we have Jupiter at 6 degrees Capricorn, both Venus and Mars would be applying by trine to Jupiter. Jupiter would therefore act as a collecting point to both Venus and Mars. As with translation, when collection occurs, it usually means that a third factor or third party has helped in bringing the matter about.

Planetary Factors Preventing a Favourable Outcome

Peregrination

Sometimes there may be a benevolent application between the two planets under consideration but both or one may be peregrine. A planet that is peregrine has no strength by virtue of the fact that it is neither in its sign of rulership, exaltation, triplicity, term or face (see Fig 1). This means that there is willingness to carry out the matter but not enough energy to do so.

Combustion

When a planet is within 8 degrees of the Sun, it is said to be combust - the Sun's rays are so strong that they nullify the planet's energy to carry out its plans.

Sunbeams

When a planet is within 17 degrees of the Sun it also causes an impediment. This may not necessarily nullify the question, depending upon how positive and strong the rest of the chart may be, but caution is advised. If the planet in question is applying to within 17 minutes of the Sun, this is termed cazimi and in fact, empowers the planet.

Prohibition

If two planets are applying to one another but another planet intercepts before the original aspect can be completed this usually produces a negative answer. For example, Venus at 5 degrees Libra may be trying to effect a conjunction with Mars at 10 degrees Libra but before he can do so, Mercury at 9 degrees Capricorn completes a square with Mars. This may mean that someone depicted by the intervening planet interferes with the matter at hand.

Frustration

This is similar to prohibition in that a faster moving planet like Mercury at 5 degrees Libra is trying to reach the conjunction of Venus at 10 degrees Libra but before this aspect can be affected, Venus completes a square with Saturn at 11 degrees Capricorn.

Refranation

Two planets may be applying to one another but before they can perfect an aspect, one of them turns retrograde. Alternatively, the planet receiving the aspect from the faster moving planet actually moves into the next sign before perfection of the aspect can take place.

CONSIDERATIONS BEFORE JUDGEMENT

There are some rules specific to horary astrology which may suggest that the chart should not be judged or at least caution should be exercised when judging the chart. Since the consultation chart is an event chart, these rules may not strictly apply, but if prognostication becomes part of the analysis and judgement of the chart, it would probably be a good idea to give some thought to these considerations. If many of these 'considerations' should configure in the chart, it is possible that there are underlying problems which may hamper a favourable outcome. Let's examine these considerations.

Early or Late Degrees Ascending

Some astrologers will not judge a chart if early or late degrees should be rising, that is the first 3 degrees inclusively and after 27 inclusively. It is possible of course, that before the days of modern technology astronomical calculations were not as precise as they are today and if early and late degrees were rising, it was just possible that the real rising sign was the previous or following one. It would have perhaps made it difficult to know if the planet representing the client (or querent) was the correct one. Some astrologers feel that early degrees suggest it is too soon to make any pronouncements on the matter/s under discussion, or with late degrees, that the matter is no longer of importance. This may indeed be the case but it need not preclude judgement with an event or consultation chart. Early degrees suggest the circumstances depicted by the rising sign are just beginning to unfold. If late degrees rise, then the present situation is approaching finality or it is a long, ongoing matter.

The Passage of the Moon

It is considered that when the Moon is Void of Course nothing will happen, even if other planetary factors are favourable. The significance of this in a consultation chart is that for the time being all hopes, fears and objectives in the client's life are held in suspension. There is some disagreement amongst astrologers over the definition of a Void of Course Moon. The usual explanation is that the Moon is Void when it does not perfect an aspect before leaving the sign in which it is placed at the time of the horary question (or consultation chart). However, some astrologers feel that if at the time of the question the Moon is in the moiety (see Fig 3) of the orb of another planet and perfects within a couple of degrees after leaving the sign in which it is placed, this does not constitute a Moon that is Void of Course. Nevertheless, if the Moon does have to cross a sign before it actually perfects an aspect then this should be taken into consideration in the interpretation. Perhaps the matter will only be capable of expression after some barrier has been crossed or obstacles overcome.

It is thought that when the Moon is in the later degrees of a sign its power is waning, especially when in the signs of Gemini, Scorpio or Capricorn. This may not apply when the Moon is in Taurus, Cancer, Sagittarius or Pisces (and neither is it deemed Void of Course when in the latter signs). The Moon is not considered Void of Course if it applies to an aspect of the Part of Fortune.

The Moieties of the Orbs of Planets according to William Lilly

	ORB	☽	☿	♀	♂	♃	♄
☉	17	14.75	12	12.5	12.25	14.5	13.5
☽	12.5	-	9.75	10.25	10	12.25	11.25
☿	7	9.75	-	7.5	7.25	9.5	8.5
♀	8	10.25	7.5	-	7.75	10	9
♂	7.5	10	7.25	7.75	-	9.75	8.75
♃	12	12.25	9.5	10	9.75	-	11
♄	10	11.25	8.5	9	8.75	11	-

Fig 3

The Moon in the Via Combusta - when it is placed between the degrees of 15 Libra to 15 Scorpio - has been deemed weak and that any chart with this configuration is unsafe to judge. If this was the only consideration in an otherwise favourable chart, perhaps judgement could go ahead.

The Seventh House

When the ruler of the seventh house is afflicted, that is either receiving many difficult aspects or is weak by detriment or fall, it is deemed unsafe to judge the chart. It is also thought that when Saturn is in the seventh house the reading will not go well. In a consultation chart this may mean that the client is not going to pay much attention to whatever the astrologer may say.

Malefics in the First House

If the traditional malefics, Mars or Saturn, are in the first house, this certainly does indicate that the client is under a great deal of stress and may really need the astrologer's help. However, it is normally thought that judgement of the chart may be spoilt in some way. Uranus, Neptune and Pluto may also be considered as the modern malefics.

For further reading about horary methods please consult the Bibliography.

3

The Personal Planets

Moonshine ☾

SIGN RULED	Cancer
EXALTATION	Taurus
DETRIMENT	Capricorn
FALL	Scorpio
JOY	Third house
CHALDEAN	Seventh house
QUALITY	Cold and moist
COLOURS	White, silver, pale yellow
MINERALS	Silver, pearl, moonstone
PLACES	Watery damp places, the sea, lakes, breweries, bathing spas, fountains, ports, bogs, docks
BODY	Womb, breasts, female functions, body fluids, the mind, stomach, the eyes (specifically the left eye of man and right of woman), the bladder, the menstrual cycle, the lymphatic system
PERSONIFICATION	Woman, Mother, wife, the Soul, the Anima, public (commoners), traveller, pilgrim, sailor, fishmonger, miller, drunkards, charwoman, midwife, nurse, queen, countess
KEYWORDS	Self-sustenance, domesticity, caring, family, heritage, the past, emotional response, habits, change-ability, mass consciousness, phlegmatic, timidity, tender, fluctuating, traditional, prudent, prejudice, shrewd, pedestrian

The Psyche

Astronomy
The Moon is the Earth's satellite and the distance between them is 239,000 miles (384,000 km). It takes around 27 ½ days to orbit the Earth. There is no atmosphere on the Moon and its craggy face is due to the infinite number of craters on its surface. Comets or asteroids probably made those craters many millions of years ago when they collided with the Moon. The rotation of the Moon is locked to its period of revolution around the Earth which experiences the Moon's four phases. The New Moon speeds towards the first quarter (crescent) then onward to the Full Moon (gibbous); from the Full Moon to the last quarter (gibbous), from the last quarter to the New Moon (crescent). The Moon's gravitational pull on the Earth shapes the landscape considerably as the tidal currents surge back and forth. When the Moon passes between the Sun and the Earth, this is a Solar Eclipse; when the Earth is between the Sun and the Moon, this is a Lunar Eclipse. The Moon appears to be drifting away from the Earth at the rate of 3 centimetres a year. Several hundred million years ago the Earth's day was 20 hours long and the Moon was much closer to the Earth. The effect of the slow Moon drift is to lengthen the day on Earth by two-thousandth of a second each century.

Mythology
The Roman goddess Diana, who presided over the hunt and wildlife, is a principal goddess of the Moon. Her Greek counterpart was Artemis. She was twin sister to Apollo, the Sun god and daughter of Jupiter and Latona (Leto), a descendent of the Titans, an ancient race of giant gods. Fearing the wrath of his wife Juno (Hera), Jupiter deserted Latona when she became pregnant. The unfortunate Latona wandered far and wide before she found sanctuary on the island of Delos in the Aegean sea.

The island may have been wild and desolate, but it was a place of great adventure for the young Diana and her brother Apollo. They enjoyed a free and unrestrained childhood in the forests and hills, mainly in the company of animals. Diana and Apollo are often depicted sporting a bow and arrow suggesting both guardianship and punishment. Apollo guarded young men and Diana protected young women. She became the goddess of childbirth after she helped her mother deliver her brother Apollo. This naturally makes her the older twin and suggests the existence of an earlier matriarchal society. Diana was particularly helpful to young women who died in childbirth, ensuring that they had a quick and painless death. She protected children, wild animals and the defenceless. Diana had little taste for marriage and asked her father Jupiter to give her eternal virginity. This was hardly surprisingly in view of her mother's lack of connubial bliss. Diana's image is therefore, of a rather chaste and cool goddess eschewing the amatory dalliance so popular with the other gods. She is happier in company with her nine hounds and is usually depicted wearing a knee-high hunting tunic armed with her silver bow and quiver of arrows. Sixty ocean nymphs accompany her from whom she demands strict chastity and obedience. She wreaks vengeance on any maiden who dares disobey her.

Astrology
The Moon is a *personal* planet governing specific personality traits. Like the goddess Diana, the Moon governs birth and presides over incarnation into the physical world. Fertility and creativity are the qualities associated with the birthing process. The Moon represents the anima, the Jungian term now commonly personifying the passive, feminine quality in both sexes. The anima governs the subjective world and the unconscious part of the psyche. Hence the Moon's action tends to work through symbolism and imparts acute sensitivity to the subtle world of the unconsciousness. It governs all forms of psychic phenomena.

The Moon reflects the light of the Sun, having none of its own and in the same way, the astrological Moon tends to imitate the qualities of the sign in which it is placed. As it conforms so readily to its surroundings the Moon is very adaptable but also changeable. The source of its fluctuating nature is derived from its four distinctive phases that is from New to Full Moon. Its waxing and waning motion perhaps describes the moodiness and even instability associated with it. Inmates in mental asylums were reported to have become very agitated at the New and Full Moon. Also operations were avoided at the New and Full Moon since it was thought that there was more likelihood of haemorrhage. This might be due to the gravity of the Moon pulling on the liquids of the body a bit like a suction pump. This would of course, slow down the blood's ability to coagulate.

The Moon rules the past and is compelled to follow family tradition and observances. It cannot be objective and is therefore subject to prejudice. The most perilous manifestation of such poor discrimination is the bigotry often depicted by an unruly crowd. The Moon of course, rules crowds as well as the populace, the public and the masses generally. The emotional response governed by the Moon is due to its tie to the past and its reliance on habits and tradition. The Moon rules the pursuance of safety and familiarity.

Along with Mercury, the Moon also governs the mind. It is possible that it emphasises the right brain, the part of the cortex that is involved in fantasy and imagination as opposed to the left brain which governs logic.

Esoteric view
The Moon is a world of silence, a dead planet with no light of its own and no atmosphere. This is of course, in contrast to the Sun upon which all life depends. The Moon therefore, governs the past and that which embodies our emotional and habitual response to people and life. Habits accrue from the past, perpetuating qualities in the psyche that may or may not be beneficial to the present incarnation. The personality is built upon the foundation of the past, whether one believes this to be sustained genetically, through the early family environment or due to the failures and triumphs of past incarnations. The Moon can be described as the first gleam of subjective reality as seen through a child's eyes. The Moon, together with Saturn, suggests 'blockages' in the personality, referring to character traits which interfere with future progress.

A weakly aspected or unaspected Moon can bring problems in nurturing and in the giving and receiving of love. There may be too much receptivity to other people's emotional demands. Sometimes the emotions may seem to be out of place; feelings are aroused over inconsequential matters and conversely there is an indifference to elements of greater importance.

The Moon in the consultation chart is of great significance since it usually points to the client's underlying area of interest. In straightforward horary questions, the Moon is also the querent, so the application of the Moon to other planets will yield an answer to the question asked. The only time it does not represent the client or querent is when it represents the quesited (the person or thing asked about).

The Moon's separating aspects indicate past events and applying aspects suggest future happenings. This of course also applies to the other planets. When Cancer ascends in the consultation chart, the Moon represents the client, and indicates that issues of caring, safety and love may be uppermost in his mind. The home and family might also be of the utmost importance in the client's life at that time.

THE MOON THROUGH THE SIGNS

Moon in Aries

The cold and moist Moon does not always feel comfortable in this hot and dry sign. There is however an ability to solve problems rapidly when there is a danger of tasks remaining half-finished. New ventures are embraced with great vigour and probably terminated just as quickly. The quick instinctual reactions inherent in this position help to initiate action but not always with enough consideration of the consequences upon others. There may be a certain self-centredness and tantrums are not uncommon, but this is a good position for developing leadership skills. Very independent and not easily influenced.

Moon in Taurus

The Moon is strong in its sign of exaltation. A talent to manipulate matter transforms old material into new works of beauty. Also an astute awareness of economic trends suggests money making abilities. Good control of the environment is also apparent. Physical comfort is valued above all else and a liking for good food and drink is often more than evident. It tends to be very tactile and loving with a strongly sensuous nature. There is a likelihood of becoming rich with the possibility of eventually using money for creative and humanitarian purposes. It is steadfast, loyal and dependable though change is not too readily embraced. Projects are seen through to the end.

Moon in Gemini

The Moon's fluctuating quality meets its match in the sign of duality, hence adaptability and versatility are most pronounced. Charm and clever usage of words are qualities that steer the native through difficult situations. There is tremendous resourcefulness in dealing with obstacles and problems and a decided ability to keep abreast of current trends. There is usually a diversity of interests. The mind is so active that it is hard to channel energy entirely in one direction. There may at times be 'too many irons in the fire' and serious commitment may be lacking. There is a strong need for companionship in order to exchange ideas. Vivid self-expression may lead to writing ability.

Moon in Cancer

The Moon in its own sign strongly emphasises maternal, nurturing and caring qualities. This gives a very loving nature and immense compassion. Emotional security is rated above all else with feelings so sensitive that extreme vulnerability is often the result. Apparent timidity can mask an inner strength especially if the protective instincts are invoked - no sacrifice is too great in shielding loved-ones from harm. There is an almost inflexible tie to the past with family culture and traditions still exerting a powerful influence over the present. There may in fact be a tendency to glorify the past, yet there is an ability to reflect current trends ensuring success and popularity through good timing. Clairvoyant ability may also be present.

Moon in Leo

This hot and dry sign warms up the cool Moon and adds a more joyous outlook to its basic timid nature. A charming, childlike quality exists which can be quite disarming though perhaps a little naive at times. This position gives a need to be the centre of attention. It tends to shine in social gatherings and often livens up dull events; it may perhaps be susceptible to flattery though, and this could be a weakness. A tendency to love wholeheartedly may bring initial disappointment after discovering that not everyone has the same depth of feeling and generosity. There is, however, a great inner strength and usually an outward show of confidence. Taking on positions of leadership is not uncommon. Good presentation and excellent taste are hallmarks of this position.

Moon in Virgo

Both the Moon and the Earth signs are somewhat cool suggesting perhaps that instinct gives way to reason with this combination. Here the mind is directed towards analysis and research and the powers of observation can be quite phenomenal. Worry and anxiety and a certain timidity are also present. Doubts arise about personal capabilities spearheading a constant search for perfection. Incessant dissection of facts and negative thinking may induce psychosomatic illness. It tends to feel more comfortable in a subordinate position in life. The Moon rules Virgo esoterically suggesting that there is a strong drive to be of service to others which may be expressed through voluntary works or healing. It feels that the life should be useful.

Moon in Libra

The Moon's nurturing qualities and Libra's strong urge to please create an amiable disposition. Courting popularity by anticipating other people's needs seems to work to advantage. Adroitness at public relations is one result. With the emphasis on togetherness, there is an innate fear of loneliness, however. Great consternation occurs if forced to take sides. Loyalty may be questioned by close associates because of the tendency to 'sit on the fence'. Appeasing disparate and conflicting factions may be a gift but this could be at the cost of personal needs. Direct confrontation often proves difficult for fear of upsetting others. Too much importance is placed on other people's opinions and this may inhibit personal action. A strong sense of harmony is expressed in relationships and in tasteful surroundings.

Moon in Scorpio

The Moon's fall in Scorpio signals an end to many self-centred desires. Circumstances occur where habits and cherished notions need to change and transform. Certainly the anguish over the losses often experienced in this turbulent sign eventually deepens understanding. Much thought is spent pondering the meaning of life. Struggles over power issues may be frequent though. Actions are likely to take an extreme turn. Close relationships can sometimes resemble a battlefield rather than a loving union. At first there might be difficulty in tolerating differences but wisdom gained through loss encourages a more tolerant attitude.

Moon in Sagittarius

The timid Moon seems to become more enterprising in this adventurous sign. A great love of life exists which is expressed through a vibrant and engaging manner. A sparkling sense of humour and even clownish behaviour easily dispel gloomy thoughts. Being able to take a long-term view of matters inclines towards a positive attitude when difficulties arise. Good luck seems to follow suit. Independence is important and commitment may sometimes be difficult. There is an attraction to foreign lands and all things exotic. An insatiable curiosity inclines to deep studies. Sometimes idealistic notions take the Native to abstract and philosophical realms that have little basis in reality.

Moon in Capricorn

The Moon's emotional nature is curtailed in its sign of detriment, yet feelings of inadequacy may actually be a spur to achievement and gaining status in some field of endeavour. Discipline and a serious attitude mark the personality but the existence of a dry sense of humour is not uncommon. Ostentatious behaviour is unlikely. The hard work done behind the scenes often propels the Native to position of power. A self-effacing manner therefore, should not be mistaken for timidity. There is a talent for manipulating the material world and understanding economics. Keeping a cool head in all difficult situations slowly brings leadership ability. It tends to become an expert in chosen field of endeavour. The Moon placed here is very cautious and plans with strategic thoroughness.

Moon in Aquarius

A great capacity for friendship exists in this position of the Moon even if passion is not always evident. A need to relate to many different people encourages a large circle of friends. The caring quality inherent in both planet and sign are expressed in totally different ways. Compassion for world suffering and the ability to organise combative strategies becomes apparent. This may be to the detriment of dealing with personal problems however, which somehow become obscured by humanistic fervour. Putting one's own house in order may present a challenge as there is often difficulty with deep emotions. There is a refusal to make judgements and an effort is made to treat everyone equally. It has a very inventive and intuitive mind and may sometimes appear unconventional.

Moon in Pisces

Both planet and sign have an extremely fluid nature conferring tremendous adaptability, which is both the strength and weakness of this combination. When difficult circumstances arise, an inherent flexibility helps to withstand adversity. Passive resistance is also a worthy trait. However, the possibility of becoming overwhelmed by other people's demands can be a real threat. An ability to empathise gives qualities of compassion and understanding, and a gentleness of manner imparts a healing quality. There may be an affinity with symbols and dreams giving psychic powers. Emphasis on the inner world, a vivid imagination and acute sensitivity bestows artistic prowess. There may however, be a tendency to confuse fantasy and reality.

THE WINGED MESSENGER

SIGNS RULED	Gemini and Virgo
EXALTATION	Virgo
DETRIMENT	Sagittarius and Pisces
FALL	Pisces
JOY	First house
CHALDEAN	Sixth house
QUALITY	Cold and dry
COLOURS	Grey and multi-colours
MINERAL	Quicksilver, topaz
PLACES	Schools, fairs, markets, shops, offices, busy thoroughfares, supermarkets, press, post-office

The Consultation Chart

BODY — The brain, nervous system, memory, speech, the tongue, arms, hands, shoulders(?), the five senses, breathing

PERSONIFICATION — Astrologer, merchant, teacher, young people, siblings, writers, clerks, tradesperson, scholar, secretary, printer, messenger, doormen, poets, sculptor, ambassador, tailor seamstress, office workers, mathematician

KEYWORDS — Self-perception, wit, humour, loquacity, subtlety, cunning, logic, research, tricky, eloquence, gossip, inconstant, mechanical, amoral, youthful, impudent, fluency, common-sense, superficial

The Psyche

Astronomy

Mercury is never more than 28 degrees away from the Sun and because it is so close, astronomers can never see it clearly enough. It orbits the Sun at a distance of 36 million miles (58 million km), once every 88 days. It rotates on its axis once every 59 days. The planet's day therefore, is two-thirds the length of its year. It has no protective atmosphere to shield its surface from the intense heat of the Sun. The temperature soars to about 750 degrees Fahrenheit (400 degrees Celsius) and then plunges to -30 degrees Fahrenheit (-200 degrees Celsius) at night-time. It is twice the size of the furthest plant Pluto and has a rocky surface pitted with craters large and small. It is as dense as our Earth and as cratered as the Moon, having been heavily bombarded by meteorites. One crater is as large as France. Like the Moon, Mercury is a dead world.

Mythology

The Roman Mercury identified with the Greek Hermes places him as the god of thieves, travellers and merchants. Son of Jupiter and Maia, daughter of Atlas, he was born at dawn in a cave on Mount Cyllene in Arcadia. Impatient to know more about the world, he left his cradle at noon the same day. He met a tortoise at the mouth of the cave, killed it and made a lyre. Keen on adventure, he went out into the fields and found some cattle, the property of Apollo. He stole them disguising his actions by making them walk backwards so they could not be traced. Apollo discovered the theft however, and hauled the youngster off to Mount Olympus. Instead of scolding him Jupiter thought Mercury's prank jolly good fun. Mercury gave the lyre to Apollo, who was so enchanted with the instrument he forgave the young godling. He also gave him the rest of his herd. Mercury was worshipped as a god of fertility possibly through the association with cattle. Jupiter, impressed with Mercury's wit, made him his ambassador and the guardian of the roads and the patron of travellers. He became known as the 'Messenger of the Gods'. He helped Jupiter conduct his affair with Io, rescued Mars from imprisonment, arranged for the beauty contest between Juno, Minerva and Venus (later judged by Paris) and helped Odysseus deal with the charms of Circe, the witch.

In his role as messenger he also guided the souls of the departed down to Tartarus, where his uncle Pluto presided over the world of death. He lay his golden staff on the eyes of the dying so that their journey to the underworld was eased through sleep. In this role he is called 'the psychopomp', the guide of souls. He also negotiated with Pluto over the abduction of Kore (Persephone) and conducted Eurydice back to the underworld after Orpheus forfeited the right to keep her.

He is depicted carrying the herald's staff of gold (caduceus or magic wand), given to him by Apollo. In turn Mercury gave Apollo a reed pipe he had made. The caduceus later became crowned with the two snakes whose quarrel had been peacefully resolved by Mercury when he placed the staff between them. (The caduceus has since been adopted as a symbol of healing by the medical profession.) Mercury sports a wide-brimmed hat and winged sandals. His swiftness makes him a likely candidate to be the patron of athletes.

Mercury learnt the art of prophecy from Apollo and devised a game of divination by the way pebbles fell in a basin of water. He also has magical powers over sleep and dreams and is associated with good luck and wealth.

Although Mercury is always depicted as a young god, he did sample parenthood. His sons were Autolycus, the greatest of thieves, Daphnis, a poet, Hermaphroditus of mixed sex and Myrtilus. The qualities represented by his sons are those which Mercury himself seemed to espouse. He was a thief (he stole cattle), a poet (he made the lyre and reed pipe) and his ability to ingratiate himself with everyone indicated that he could take on almost any role. Neither was he always very truthful possibly because he felt that being 'diplomatic' would better help him achieve his aims. He was a very clever god and he is credited in assisting the three Fates in the composition of the alphabet, inventing astronomy, the musical scale and the art of boxing and gymnastics.

Astrology

Mercury is a *personal* planet and attributes various character traits to the personality. As the messenger of the gods, Mercury's main role is to act as the mediator between mortals and the subtle world. He represents the link between the conscious and unconscious mind retrieving information both useful and useless. Similarly he governs the body's system of communication, the central nervous system, which is under conscious control of the mind, and the autonomic nervous system which may be linked to more unconscious processes. Therefore, Mercury's talent for communication represents both the physical and mental aspects of life. Mercury stirs the vocal cords into action and rules the air that vibrates them. He illuminates the mind through his power to mediate between the physical aspect of the individual and the soul, yet he brings inspiration through logic and reason. He bestows the gift in judging the significance of events, relating the old with the new, the past and future through the events of the present. Mercury is unemotional and objective, his energies seem to accord more with the left side of the brain, concerned as it is with facts and physical reality. The right side of the brain governs imagination and fantasy, and is associated more with the Moon. The mental agility ascribed to Mercury means that he can hold many opinions at the same time. He can also argue, quite rationally, on different stratagems, making him quick, clever and extremely changeable. This is just like the mineral Mercury rules, Quicksilver, which changes from a liquid to a solid and back again at different temperatures. His duality is emphasised by the fact that Mercury's behaviour is greatly coloured by the sign in which he finds himself. For instance, when Mercury is in Aries, he thinks he is Mars but instead of brandishing a sword he is likely to wield a pen and have a sharp wit. The closest aspect to Mercury will also influence behaviour. Therefore, if a square from Jupiter was added to that Mercury in Aries, it would give an extremely flexible, knowledgeable mind that was unlikely to have a clear set of boundaries. Mercury's behaviour can also be coloured by his dispositor, e.g., if Mercury is in Capricorn, he takes on grave, Saturnian behaviour.

Mercury's main job is to know and enquire, storing all information without discrimination. From a negative viewpoint, Mercury can be untruthful, given to exaggeration and quibbling over trifles. A cunning fellow though, he tends to diffuse energies through his varied superficial interests. An afflicted Mercury may indicate mental instability with other astrological indicators considered.

Esoteric view
Mercury is said to be the mediator between the individual and God. He is seen as the illuminating and mediating principle using the faculty of the mind. Illumination interprets the significance of events, relating the old with the new, the past and the future through the light and meaning of the present. He releases the thought principle of the mind and directs the way of the individual through life enabling him to become part of the Divine Path. Mercury brings change and is thus, also referred to as the Star of Conflict. Change brings crisis ruled by Saturn with ultimate synthesis governed by Jupiter. The force of conflict leads to eventual harmony.

A weakly aspected or unaspected Mercury may give an enquiring mind and tremendous knowledge but there is likely to be a dissipation of energy and lack of focus in any one direction. Quick thinking is usually evident though depth may be lacking.

If Gemini or Virgo are ascending in the consultation chart, the client will be represented by Mercury. This may indicate a young person or someone who is young at heart and perhaps lacking the necessary experience to handle his affairs without the support of others. There may be focus on studies and travel.

MERCURY THROUGH THE SIGNS

Mercury in Aries

Mercury rules Aries esoterically, suggesting an easy route to universal truths. As Aries is the birthplace of ideas this combination can make the mind extremely acute and resourceful. A razor sharp intellect and an ability to understand symbolism bestows acute perception. A direct, piercing quality to the speech may intimidate others. Certainly there is an ability to pinpoint causative factors to problems very quickly, but there can be impatience with others who are not as mentally agile. Impulsiveness and lack of forethought may be apparent and diplomacy is usually absent. The mind's undeviating quality means that goals are seen clearly and achieved without prevarication.

Mercury in Taurus

The mind may work at a slow pace but this only serves to facilitate a thoroughness of thought and judgement. The thinking process therefore, is purposeful, deliberate and measured. Nothing is hurried and all avenues are explored. There is a great deal of forethought before making decisions. Both planet and sign are cold and dry, indicating that enthusiastic interaction with others grows by slow degrees. Sometimes this may give the impression of disinterest or inertia which is not necessarily the true picture. Ideas are stubbornly adhered to and conflict may ensue through inflexibility. An artistic turn of mind gives good taste and there may be talent in forecasting economic trends.

Mercury in Gemini

In its sign of rulership, Mercury puts strong emphasis on the mind's dual purpose in working with logic and imagination. Its role as mediator between the left and right brain enhances the thinking capacity, suggesting great intellect and easy facility for words. Writing and oration may be a gift and there is certainly a need for self-expression in some field, even if it is only in keeping a journal. There is an ability to understand the different opinions held in areas of competition which gives great mental agility with the capacity to synthesise and integrate opposing ideas. The mind is quick, clever and quite formidable in its presentation of ideas. With so much emphasis on the mind, there can be danger of overload possibility resulting in nervous problems.

Mercury in Cancer

The sign ruled by the Moon, which also represents the mind, introduces a marriage between logic and fantasy. Feelings and intuition play a palpable part in the thought processes producing an extraordinary imagination. This may give a talent for substantial creativity in fields of imaginative writing with an ability to reflect current public needs. A strong intuitive ability also exists which sometimes defies reason and logic. There is an ability to delve deeply into the memory for answers to present dilemmas. The long memory is likely to be very subjective however. There might also be a tendency to live in the past which expressed positively may give an interest in history, genealogy and archaeology.

Mercury in Leo

There is something quite vital about this position since both Mercury, and the Sun the sign ruler, are connected to the Vital or Life Force. This means that the speech and general manner arising from this combination can be quite commanding and magnetic. There is usually power behind the spoken word. An authoritative air quickly attracts adherents and supporters. Organisational powers are likely to be extremely good and the ability to see any situation in its entirety can give powers of leadership. A tendency towards an autocratic manner of speech may alienate others however, and there may be a need to find the middle ground between confidence and boasting.

Mercury in Virgo

In its sign of rulership as well as exaltation, Mercury becomes especially strong with particular emphasis on the mental faculties. Here the abstract and concrete faculty of the human mind unites to produce practical manifestation of ideas. A conscious link exists apparently between the spiritual and physical nature, as if the soul is making its presence felt in the body. This can be expressed through an urge to be of service to others. Here the emphasis is on practical expression of the spirit rather than an abstract one. The mind is likely to be deep, given to logical reasoning and bestows a talent for research. Strong attention to detail gives phenomenal powers of observation. There might however, be a tendency to worry giving rise to digestive disturbance.

The Personal Planets

Mercury in Libra

A position which gives a great appreciation of beauty and the finer things in life. A sense of harmony prevails in thought and action with a determination to see fair play in all things, yet this combination seems to give illusive tendencies, since both planet and sign have a predilection towards prevarication and indecision. There is an amazing appreciation of subtleties but there may only be a mild flirtation with practical reality. However, there is a decided ability to get the very best performance from other people. Certainly grace, poise and impeccable manners opens doors to success. It is sometimes difficult however, for others to determine what lies behind actions and the beautifully spoken words.

Mercury in Scorpio

The ability to probe the mysteries of the mind and the universe can be quite evident. Deep intelligence and a powerful determination leaves no stone unturned in pursuance of the truth. The causes and reasons for any conflict have to be uncovered and dealt with without bias or prejudice. Since there is unlikely to be a fear of confrontation, this placement of Mercury is contentious and challenging. Mercury here deplores inertia and seeks to awaken others to environmental disharmony. The speech is likely to be both provoking and exciting. There is ability in breaking any kind of situation deadlock, or possibly a delight in causing mischief through deliberate antagonism. Certainly a position to effect change in prevailing thought.

Mercury in Sagittarius

Mercury's sign of detriment lessens its power for logic but adds the gift of intuition. No planet has its exaltation or fall in Sagittarius and from a spiritual viewpoint, this brings a point of balance between pairs of opposites. At first Mercury, with its quick butterfly-like mind, feels uncomfortable in this sign as Sagittarius likes to take a rather more extenuated view of most situations, but there is gift of imparting knowledge and a talent in teaching may develop. There could also be a good facility for languages. Conversation tends to be peppered with laughter and quips and there might be an ability to inspire others. Spontaneity and a positive outlook seems to attract good luck. The undeniable honesty inherent in this placement needs a touch of diplomacy at times.

Mercury in Capricorn

The powers of concentration are excellent in this sign. The ability to keep the mind focused in one direction suggests that great achievement can be attained in any field. There is often an economy with words which are usually chosen with care and points are made succinctly and with deliberation. Initially, due to an inner uncertainty, great caution is exercised and a thorough examination is made before undertaking anything new; only then is any kind of commitment undertaken. There is a strong determination to succeed in life. Innovation may not be apparent but an ability to develop existing ideas is very pronounced with a shrewdness in making the right decisions. Thinking is usually conservative and pessimism has to be avoided.

Mercury in Aquarius

Modern astrological thought purports that Mercury is exalted in this sign. Certainly Aquarius has an impartiality that appeals to the planet's flexible and variable nature. This makes the mind open to new experiences bringing a wide understanding and tolerance of other people's ideas. Indeed there is a liking for diversity in opinion promoting an exchange of thought. A scientific turn of mind is often apparent with unusual and even brilliant ideas resulting from time spent in contemplation. Mercury placed here will bring a humanitarian approach to developing labour saving inventions. It makes friends easily since it has the ability to talk on almost any subject, however an inflexibility can be apparent when sticking up for a worthy cause.

Mercury in Pisces

In this sign, Mercury is both in its detriment and in its fall, which traditionally puts the messenger in a very weak position. Logic may be absent and there may be a reluctance to voice opinions, or indeed, sometimes an inability to speak coherently may be in evidence. Shyness may also be apparent. Spiritually however, Mercury in this sign signifies that it no longer acts as a mediator but has a direct line to the source, almost like a hot line to the root of all knowledge. When this power is harnessed, there is indeed a gift of perception unequalled by an other position of Mercury. This may be expressed through clairvoyance or the arts, such as photography, film, music or dance. The imagination will be very impressive but may need grounding.

Mighty Aphrodite ♀

SIGNS RULED	Taurus, Libra
EXALTATION	Pisces
DETRIMENT	Aries, Scorpio
FALL	Virgo
JOY	Fifth house
CHALDEAN	Twelfth house
QUALITY	Cold and Moist
COLOUR	Sky blue, pastel colours
MINERALS	Lapis lazuli, blue sapphire, copper
PLACES	Theatre, beauty salons, hairdressers, art galleries, gardens, fountains, bridal chambers, lodgings, dancing schools
BODY	The womb, navel, kidneys, the hormones, homeostasis, ovaries, venous circulatory system
PERSONIFICATION	Jeweller, musician, draper, artist, dancer, beautician, aromatherapist, hairdresser, actor, perfumer, women, wives, mothers, singers, seamstress, engravers, dress designers
KEYWORDS	Self-gratification, affection, love, money, enjoyment, amusement, hedonism, sensual, lazy, neat, pleasant, gluttony, cheerful

The Psyche

Astronomy

Venus is the brightest planet in the night sky and roughly the same size as Earth, yet the surface of the planet is impossible to see due to the dense covering of clouds of water vapour and sulphuric acid. The clouds are 30 kilometres thick. Temperatures are in the region of 860 degrees Fahrenheit (460 degrees Celsius) - the hottest in the solar system. The temperature is hardly different at night. The atmosphere is made up of carbon dioxide. The volcanic rock found on Venus is similar to that found on Earth and radar probes have revealed that it looks a bit like Earth but drained of all its water. Modern technology reveals that the surface of Venus is a scorched and barren landscape with volcanic rock on coarse-grained dirt. Venus spins very slowly and circles the

Sun in 225 days and very slowly rotates on its axis in 243 days. When Venus is seen in the morning it is referred to as Hesperus, and when it is visible in the evening, is called Phosphorus.

Mythology
The lurid tale linked to the birth of Venus seems quite inappropriate to the beautiful goddess. It is said that she emerged from the sea near the island of Cyprus, into which Saturn (Cronos) had flung his father's genitals after deposing him. The tale is better understood etymologically, through her Greek counterpart Aphrodite. White foam (aphros)gathered around the genitals which Cronos flung into the sea, and from this emerged the goddess Aphrodite. When she came upon the shores of Cyprus flowers grew where she trod. Her spiritual parents were Jupiter (Zeus) and Dione, an ancient sky goddess.

As the goddess of beauty, fertility and love her main task was to bring peace, joy and pleasure to both gods and mortals. She eschewed hard work and enjoyed a hedonistic lifestyle though she diligently applied herself to helping distraught lovers. She aided Hipomenes and Atlanta, Jason and Medea and her own son Aeneas in his love for Dido, yet she was not above punishing those who displeased her; one of these was the sun god Helios who told her husband Vulcan of her affair with Mars. Although Venus presided over love, her marriage to Vulcan was obviously, less than successful - indeed the bonds of marriage were not her domain, but the province of Juno, Queen of heaven. Vulcan, also known as the Greek Hephaestus, was the god of metalwork, and though he was extremely skilled, his unprepossessing looks sent Venus into the arms of others.

Both Mars, the god of war and the handsome shepherd Adonis, were at one time or other the objects of her desire. She bore Mars three children Phobus (fear), Deimos (terror) and Harmonia (concord). According to some accounts, their coupling brought forth a fourth child, Cupid (Eros) the god of heterosexual and homosexual love. When Mars discovered that Venus had fallen in love with Adonis, he apparently sent a wild boar to kill him during the hunt. The soul of Adonis descended into Tartarus where his beauty captivated Kore, the Queen of the Dead. However, Venus still loved him, even in death, and asked Jupiter to let Adonis be her companion during the summer months. Jupiter, also captivated by her beauty, agreed. Nevertheless, her grief was not so overwhelming that she could deny herself an affair with Mercury (Hermes). She bore him a son, Hermaphrodite, who was both male and female.
Venus had a magic girdle that made her irresistible to all, and may have unfairly won her the crown in a beauty contest against Juno and Minerva. Paris judged the contest and was totally captivated when Venus opened her magic girdle. As Paris was a Trojan, Venus was on Troy's side during the wars with Greece,

but her allegiance became even more pronounced when she fell in love with another prince of Troy, Anchises. She bore him a son, Aeneas (who was later involved in the founding of Rome). Venus also became fond of the old man Neptune to whom she bore two sons. Juno was a little peeved by Venus's fertility and cursed one of her sons, Bacchus, with an enormous phallus!

Chastity was certainly not one of her attributes though this seemed to matter little in Corinth where the prostitutes were looked upon as sacred in honour of her cult.

Astrology
Venus is a *personal* planet governing various personality traits. Her aim is to bring unity of purpose and the spirit of co-operation between opposing forces. She endeavours to restore equilibrium in times of stress - she is conciliatory. This can certainly be associated with her rulership of Libra. Perhaps it is not so well known that she also rules over gardens and fields where the link to the earthy Taurus is more apparent. Traditionally, she is a benevolent planet and known as the Lesser Benefic being second only to the Greater Benefic, Jupiter, in bringing good fortune. She is benefic because she is disposed towards conveying happiness. Venus bestows honours, victory, joy and an easy life. She brings rewards for past hard work and gives talents in the arts. Flower arranging, music and the theatre come under her domain. Venus endeavours to be constructive both in attitude as well as in practice. Artistic flair derives from a natural sense of harmony which can be seen in creative works. Venus bestows grace and a genuine regard for others. She imparts charm and qualities which easily win over adversaries. Venus gives a peaceful nature.

Venus is very companionable, as myth and rumour will of course testify. She unites people through brotherhood and love and thereby transmits knowledge and wisdom. Sociable and gregarious, she is naturally very keen on relating, expressing this trait through the bonds of personal love as well as spiritual, unconditional love. Therefore, Venus in astrology represents gentleness, affection, harmony and beauty. She also represents the profligate and promiscuous side of love. Indeed, the less appealing attributes she portrays are lack of taste, dissolute ways, lack of discipline and direction, loving luxury, hedonism, self indulgence, vanity and immorality, enticement, seduction and superficiality. She avoids responsibility and confrontation, disliking friction and unpleasantness.

Esoteric view
Venus does indeed govern the principle of love but through the directing power of the mind. Her function is to fuse the spiritual and physical natures of the individual into a unified whole. The highest aspect of Venus is intelligent love, denuding it from its more gross expression. She governs the embryonic

understanding of causes and conditions and is responsible for the singular consciousness in the individual. This leads to a spiritual love and a desire for a universal wholeness.

An *unaspected* Venus can bring a hedonistic quality into the life where pleasure and self-gratification are all important. Discipline and hard work to achieve goals may be lacking or the client may be easily sidetracked. Popularity may be easy to achieve however, since the client may 'flirt' unconsciously with everyone they meet.

With Taurus or Libra on the Ascendant, the client is represented by Venus in the consultation chart. This suggests that the client may be looking for love. There is also a possibility that the client may be seeking harmony in their lives after having perhaps been involved in some stressful situation or difficult upheaval. Energy is not at a premium at this time. It is perhaps better to deal with life's problems by adopting a diplomatic, conciliatory approach rather than through action and assertion.

Venus through the Signs

Venus in Aries

Venus is in detriment here so the power to harmonise is disturbed and she becomes a little more warlike, a little more aggressive. No doubt the cold and moist Venus feels uncomfortable in the sign of Mars and exaltation of the Sun, both energies of combustion. Venus becomes more selfish and impulsive, contrary to her usual accommodating nature. However, decisions are made much more quickly with less prevarication. There may be a tendency to fall in love quickly and be open about feelings. This can bring an almost childlike trust in others with a refreshing honesty that can be quite disarming. On the highest level, love can be expressed through some pioneering venture in healing/helping others.

Venus in Taurus

Venus in the sign that it rules usually indicates a powerful desire for luxurious possessions. Good taste is apparent as is the collector's eye for works of beauty - only the best is good enough. There is likely to be an excellent understanding of economics and wise use of financial investments as well as a very affectionate and tactile nature, with an expression of love that is usually steady and true. Desires of the flesh are often very strong with a tendency towards over-indulgence resulting in weight problems, yet the spiritual effect of this position is to fuse spirit and matter into an integrated unit. Could it that on a higher level this brings an acute understanding of the material world using that ability to tap resources for more universal and humanitarian goals?

Venus in Gemini

Venus rules Gemini esoterically and emphasises the interplay of opposites. This apparently is the underlying theme of the entire creative and evolutionary process suggesting a strong awareness of the existence of body and soul. This could lead towards the need in finding a partnership that will have a strongly spiritual element within it. Could this be the reason why Venus in Gemini often shows a rather light-hearted approach to love and an unwillingness to commit to anyone too soon? Perhaps more than anyone, they are really looking for their 'soul-mate'. Versatility in all matters suggests many talents or dissipation of energies. There is a great need to exchange ideas and a tendency to become bored easily without adequate mental stimulation.

Venus in Cancer

This position of Venus creates intense feelings and a nature that is extremely vulnerable. Sometimes this might indicate a personality that is very timid and cautious. A dedicated search for emotional security means that romantic involvement is not entered into lightly. The need to nurture is very strong and much love and devotion is showered upon family, children and intimate friends, yet family ties may bind too tightly at times with resultant emotional discord. When the heart is given it is for keeps and there is enormous difficulty in getting over heartbreak. This indicates a great attachment to the past which might bring obstacles in forming future relationships. Positively, there may be an interest in history with particular emphasis on historical buildings and architecture.

Venus in Leo

Venus finds a kindred spirit in Leo since both planet and sign like to be adored. There is a need to feel really special in this position and indeed, there is usually an extraordinary ability to attract others. All gifts and talents seem larger than life and there is little difficulty in gaining a central position in most circumstances. There is usually a tremendous generosity and a wholehearted love of life which rather inspires others. A talent for acting or presentation is often evident and a liking for luxury and pleasure is quite pronounced. However, the nature may be somewhat vain and demanding with a need for constant attention, but with Venus placed here it is hard to resist and easy to forgive.

Venus in Virgo

Venus in its fall may give feelings of discomfort. Both planet and sign have quite opposing natures: Venus likes to flirt and enjoy herself whereas Virgo believes that work must come before pleasure. This may inhibit the expression of love and bring excessive shyness and modesty. Nevertheless, the standards are high but a search for that 'perfect mate' sometimes brings loneliness as there is difficulty in tolerating weakness. This position prefers quality over quantity and there is usually great devotion to a loved one. A marked interest in health, hygiene and nutrition may bring involvement in healing. There is a very rational approach to life, believing only in what is tangible and eschewing the subtle side of life, yet there could be artistic gifts that rely on great precision and accuracy of detail.

Venus in Libra

Venus is naturally in her element in the sign that she rules. There is notable emphasis on harmony that can be expressed through the arts and partnerships. This is a Venus that does not like to be alone and suffers greatly if this should ever be the case. However, contacts are likely to be plentiful. Disliking discord, there may be a tendency to defer to others and reflect their ideas and opinions. A career in diplomatic circles would probably attract or any situation where there is a need to 'pour oil on troubled waters'. The ability to harmonise and bring peace is very strong. This position can indicate the ability to make friends out of enemies. A point of balance may be reached between personal desire and spiritual love.

Venus in Scorpio

Venus here is in detriment as the sense of harmony is lost in this passionate sign. Intense feelings are likely to throw the individual off balance with ensuing difficulties especially in making decisions. This position can therefore tend towards feelings of jealousy and possessiveness as there is likely to be insecurity and a fear of loss. Loyalty and extreme devotion may suffocate the loved one, making the fear of loss a reality. This position of Venus can give a long-lasting love but one which has its fair share of turmoil. There is likely to be a sensuality that is both seductive and challenging. An uncanny intuition gives great perception and an ability to ferret out secrets which would be helpful in any undercover work.

Venus in Sagittarius

There may well be a fun-loving attitude towards relationships and rarely are things taken too much to heart. There is a refreshing frankness about personal feelings with a disarming honesty that intrigues others. Freedom to express one's own individuality is a necessary commodity as there are usually many other interests in the life apart from love. There is often a tremendous zest for life with perhaps a tinge of flamboyance in the nature. Certainly the life and soul of any party, yet a streak of idealism can indicate that physical attraction is not enough to sustain a partnership. There has to be a meeting on a soul level for any relationship to work. Indeed, there could also be an attraction to matters ecclesiastical and that search for 'perfect love' may incline towards a life of religious devotion.

Venus in Capricorn

This is not a Venus who settles for love in a garret and there is indeed a need for material status and wealth before emotional security can be attained. There is great dignity about this position though a cool exterior can sometimes give an impression of aloofness. It is because the heart is not easily engaged that love sometimes finds it hard to find an open door. Partners are chosen with great thoroughness and hardly ever through fiery passion. This can therefore, be a Venus that breaks hearts albeit unwittingly. It is quite possible that choices in love are governed by a sense of duty which shows a sacrificial element in this position of Venus. There is a need to make the 'right' choices as reputation is of greatest importance.

Venus in Aquarius

This is perhaps the friendliest Venus, and one that manages to remain on good terms with everyone. Nevertheless, real intimacy may be hard to attain and only a few close associates are ever permitted into the inner sanctum. Too much emotion suffocates this Venus. No heavy demands are made upon loved-ones, and in fact, they may complain of neglect as they are have so much freedom. Former lovers are never entirely forgotten and usually remain in the background as friends. Attraction is usually to people with similar ideals and such friendships are made at political rallies or protest marches. An ashram might be the happiest abode for Venus in Aquarius where there can be a meeting of many true minds.

Venus in Pisces

Here Venus is in exaltation, indicating that an opportunity exists to express love on its most highest level. This usually suggests unconditional love that is given freely and without resentment. Quite often circumstances arise which demand almost sacrificial devotion; looking after a sick relative for instance. With the emphasis on universal rather than personal love, this may open channels to a healing energy which restores harmony to shattered lives. Spiritually this is seen as an ability to reunite the body with the soul. A strong sensitivity may indeed bring clairvoyant powers. There is also a possibility that a victim mentality may emerge from this position of Venus either through slavish adherence to other people's demands or looking for someone to 'save'. Usually little gratitude is received in return.

A Touch of the Sun ☉

SIGN RULED	Leo
EXALTATION	Aries
DETRIMENT	Aquarius
FALL	Libra
JOY	Ninth house
CHALDEAN	Fourth house
QUALITY	Hot and Dry
COLOURS	Orange, gold, scarlet
MINERALS	Gold, ruby
PLACES	Theatres, palaces, grand houses, halls, dining room
BODY	Heart, eyes more particularly the right eye of a man and the left eye of a woman, Vital Spirits, spine, cells of the body
PERSONIFICATION	The father, husband, male, king, royalty, ruler, magistrate, courtier, mayor, constable, huntsman, goldsmith
KEYWORDS	Self-integration, luxury loving, noble, domineering, extravagant, big-hearted, stately, organising, proud, spendthrift, warm, generous, bold, adventurous,

The Psyche

Astronomy

Our Earth is 93 million miles from the Sun which is of course, the centre of our solar system. It is a revolving sphere of hydrogen and helium gases and huge amounts of energy are released through nuclear fusion. The temperature at its core is 27 million degrees Fahrenheit (15 million degrees Celsius). The surface of the Sun consists of the thin chromosphere which merges into the corona. The corona is as hot as the core, although it extends far into interplanetary space.

Mythology
Apollo is associated with light in Greek and Roman mythology and therefore came to be looked upon as the Sun god. In fact it was Helios who was the original Sun god usually depicted driving his carriage across the sky from east to west. Apollo gradually became identified with Helios. Apollo was the son of Jupiter and Latona, and the twin brother of Diana, the Moon goddess. Diana emerged from the womb before her brother suggesting perhaps the preponderance of the feminine cults in earlier civilisations. Apollo was born on the ninth day of labour, apparently between a date-palm and an olive-tree, and Diana assisted at his birth. As he was fed on nectar and ambrosia, it is no surprise that he came to manhood in four days.

Apollo was an early god of medicine and taught the art of healing to mortals, though he was later superseded in this field by Aesculapius, his son by Coronis, a beautiful maiden of Thessaly. He also presided over music and the Muses - daughters of Jupiter who personified the arts, yet he largely became identified with outdoor life, particularly excelling in archery and was patron of flocks and herds. He is often depicted wearing laurel leaves. His oracular shrine at Delphi was the most venerated of all, a fair testimony to his personal popularity.

Delphi was thought to be the centre of the world and had originally belonged to Terra or Mother Earth (the Greek Gaia). It was guarded by Python, a female serpent with oracular powers. Apollo wanted the oracle for his own and slew the serpent. An alternative version of this story changes the serpent's gender to male and has him attempting to ravish Latona, Apollo's mother. Being a good son, he slew him in defence of his mother's honour. Before Apollo could take up his duties at the famous oracular shrine, he had to atone for killing the sacred serpent. His father Jupiter, sent him to the Vale of Tempe in Thessaly to undergo ritual purification and to learn humility by serving a mortal, King Admetus. Apollo effectively became a bonded servant.

The prophecies at Delphi were pronounced by a priestess in a state of possession; Apollo named his priestess Pythia after the serpent he slew. Contests in music and athletics were held at Delphi and these games also honoured the serpent by being named after him, the Pythian Games. Apollo's favourite instrument was the lyre.

Apollo would sometimes bestow the gift of prophecy upon those he loved, one of whom was the princess Cassandra of Troy, whose predictions fell on deaf ears, however. Apollo had also cursed her because she refused his advances. He seemed destined to be unlucky in love, unfortunately. He was rejected by several maidens: Daphne, Sibyl, Marpessa and Sinope to name a few. He was equally unlucky with the youths he loved - Hyacinthus and Cyparissus - who died young. Nevertheless, Apollo remained the guardian of young men in the same way his sister Diana was the special guardian of young women.

Astrology
The Sun is a *personal* planet governing certain personality traits. In astrology, the Sun is often seen as the personification of the male energy, the Jungian Animus or the outgoing Yang energy, in contrast to that of the more receptive female, Yin energy of the Moon referred to as the Anima.

Astronomically the Sun is the central governing force for its own system of planets. In the same way it is the focal point of integration for the varied forces assigned to the planets in astrology. It creates an alliance between the self and the environment. Traditionally it governs the Life Force sometimes referred to as Vital Spirits or Prana which stimulates the body cells and sustains the form nature. It is vitalising and gives creative expression. It has a thrusting, organising quality, producing the will to live and the urge to rule. It signifies the process of individuation, imparting the impulse to each person to realise themselves and to achieve self-awareness.

Character traits suggest warmth, benevolence, generosity and confidence. The Sun is bold and adventurous when it is allowed to shine unimpeded by difficult aspects. It wants to encounter all the different strands of life. The Sun organises these experiences into a cognitive whole in an effort to gain wisdom and knowledge. Organisation is a trait that is therefore attributed to the Sun.

The Sun's position indicates one's basic sense of purpose and gives the ability to strive for certain objectives. The Sun has a positive, all-embracing quality and lives for action and expansion. Although it gives survival instincts, in Vedic astrology the Sun is viewed as a malefic because it can burn too brightly and burn itself out - or overwhelm others by its brilliance. In the act of combustion, a planet's energies are said to be weakened when it conjoins the Sun within 8 degrees. Paradoxically, a planet which conjoins the Sun within 17 minutes will have its energies strengthened.

Since the Sun rules the male energy it can represent the father in the horoscope, especially in a day-time chart (when the Sun is above the horizon). Sometimes it represents the husband in a female horoscope. Other characteristics depicted are egotism, a thrust for power, boasting and despotic behaviour.

Esoteric view
The Sun's position by sign indicates the basic nature of the present life and gives a key to the particular channel of consciousness that is being vitalised. The sign in which the Sun is placed emphasises the attainment of those qualities which are immediately necessary for further development on all levels: physical, mental and spiritual. The Sun sign indicates the present problems that need to be dealt with. It is related to the temperament and the life tendencies which are seeking expression during the present incarnation. If the Sun and the Moon are in the same sign, this indicates that the Sun can utilise the qualities of the past to best advantage in the present, though it also suggests that the previous life dealt with the same problem (indicated by the sign in which the Lights are placed). The Moon is often referred to as the mind and the Sun as the understanding. The Sun above all sets the pace of the current life.

A weakly aspected or unaspected Sun suggests that difficulty exists in pulling together the various strands of the individual's life. This may result in a difficult transition from one department or area of life to another. Sometimes the different facets of the individual's life remain unconnected. Living a dualistic life could be the outcome.

When the Sun represents the client in the consultation chart it points to someone who seeks to gain a better position in life usually through their own efforts. A need arises to express innate talent rather than follow past expectations whether these be parental or societal. This may be the start of a fulfilling period of creativity.

THE SUN THROUGH THE SIGNS

Sun in Aries

The Sun is exalted in Aries signifying that an opportunity exists for the solar energy or life of the spirit to be expressed in some new form. This often describes an initial idea that swings into activity with force and vigour. There is likely to be skill and daring and an attempt to do the best in all concerns. Courage is a quality bestowed in abundance with a pioneering spirit that puts the person at the forefront of many activities. It is important to be the first in any endeavour. This may sometimes result in periods of isolation as others could find it difficult to keep up. Self-reliance is a quality that develops rapidly. Though not always an easy person to live with he is certainly very exciting. He can be oblivious of other people's needs when in pursuit of own goals.

Sun in Taurus

The solar energy arrives at concrete expression in the first earth sign and the emphasis here is upon consolidation. There is tremendous ability to structure ideas and express ideas practically. An inner illumination heralds practical results. Good taste and discernment in judgement are usually apparent and there is excellent skill in handling resources. There might be a talent in understanding financial trends and professions in banking, accountancy and book-keeping are not uncommon. Good taste and a strong sense of beauty are also evident with an avid interest in the arts. This person will love to own beautiful possessions and there might sometimes be too much emphasis on the material life. There is a great love of comfort with strong physical needs. He is tenacious and persevering with an ability to see things through to the end.

Sun in Gemini

The relationship between body and soul is expressed through the sense of dualism inherent in this sign. This may present a state of conflict wherein the person finds it hard to make decisions. Change is also a trait associated with this sign. Yet this may give tremendous versatility and a natural capacity to hold contrary views simultaneously. In fact the mind can dart from one topic to another with relative ease. The qualities of observation are extremely good and the ability to wield words like a weapon is often apparent. This does confer a restless nature and a low boredom threshold; the need for mental stimulation is extremely important. There is great knowledge on many different subjects and a facility for verbal expression often gives writing ability.

Sun in Cancer

The Sun in the Moon's sign gives the potential for using the best of the past to help with the present. An excellent ability usually exists in building firm foundations to facilitate future goals. Intense love of family, home and tradition are usually a feature of this sign. Great effort is expended in creating sound and practical groundwork for success in life. Qualities of caring, nurturing and protecting are usually evident in the character which are often expressed in caring professions. No doubt there are very deep feelings which sometimes border on extreme vulnerability. He needs a lot of time to become accustomed to new surroundings. Ostensibly timid, he can however call upon great inner strength in times of adversity, especially when security is threatened. Usually has a good eye for antiques and is likely to have a stock-pile of treasures somewhere.

Sun in Leo

The outstanding theme of this sign is a strong awareness of self and the environment which usually results in gaining a central position in society. There is a need to be at the core of excitement and activity. The Sun rules Leo both conventionally and esoterically, and therefore gives possible fulfilment on all three levels of being: physical, psychological and spiritual. This is a character with great magnetism and an ability to radiate happiness and warmth brings popularity. There is usually strong determination to succeed in life and reach the pinnacle of achievement in some area. Although extremely ambitious, he will also need to have fun. Pleasure and work are usually expressed in equal measure. A big heart and generosity attract popularity. There is a susceptibility to flattery with a child-like trust in others that may sometimes be misplaced - however, disappointments can be shrugged off easily.

Sun in Virgo

In this sign, the Sun shines somewhat moderately producing humility and compassion. A refreshing modesty is also evident. There is a strong urge to be of use to others and make a significant difference in the world, preferably in a practical way. This gives a talent for administration and an impressive knowledge of past and present events. There is a tendency to work quietly behind the scenes, which ultimately can lead to great achievement. The attention to detail is quite phenomenal though striving for perfection can cause difficulties. A feeling of dissatisfaction ensues and sometimes a lack of confidence, yet there is often genuine talent and expertise in many areas though these can sometimes remain unconscious. A strong need for service often brings an interest in healing.

Sun in Libra

The Sun is in detriment in this sign because the emphasis here is on the 'not-self'. It is as if a nuclear shift occurs in the solar energy which seeks to create a reflection of itself. The urge therefore, arises to unite with others in order to feel whole and consequently the emphasis of this sign is upon relationship. The motive behind each action is to restore harmony and balance. Sometimes this means that the individual is charming to friend and foe alike. Popularity is gained in an almost effortless way as there is usually great consideration of other people's feelings. Expressing own needs may however, sometimes prove difficult in case this causes a shift in current dynamics. The expression of anger does not come easily, except on the behalf of others. There is a great need to see justice and fair play exercised.

Sun in Scorpio

A battle ensues when the Sun is placed in this sign, often signifying internal turmoil reflected by external friction. A need to rectify environmental defects, real or imaginary, brings an urge to fight and conquer. Life is viewed as a constant need to 'slay the dragon' and whilst this gives great powers of tenacity and resistance, it can sometimes create disharmony in the environment or in personal relationships. There can be extreme loyalty with a genuine interest in others and an immense passion for life. This gives great magnetism and charm. Nothing is done by half measures and the ability to delve deeply into the core of life brings unequalled intensity and depth. No stone is left unturned in the search for answers to whatever the question or enquiry may be. He never gives up and usually returns home victorious. He is usually a good psychologist.

Sun in Sagittarius

The solar forces are well suited to this sign since they have an opportunity to expand to their fullest potential. It is a sign which needs wide scope for self expression. The emphasis is upon freedom and tolerance. Honesty, frankness and a cheerful spirit promote feelings of confidence and optimism. Failure is never an option and opportunities often arise to attain goals with relative ease. A restless spirit and an insatiable curiosity often encourage the search for adventure. The field of education may attract or the travel industry could be an option. Pondering upon the meaning of life may bring an interest in philosophy and religion. There is usually an visionary outlook and buckets of tolerance.

Sun in Capricorn

Though the sun's rays are somewhat depleted in Capricorn this does not detract from the quiet drive inherent in this sign. Tenacity and determination accompany the individual on the road to achievement. There is usually a steady rise to the top of the chosen profession or at least mastery is gained in some field of endeavour. Each situation is studied carefully and once all the facts are to hand, the right decision is usually made. Goals are kept firmly in sight and patience is a virtue often exercised in full measure. The coolness inherent in this sign can sometimes turn to ruthlessness in some individuals. This can however, aid in the ability to withstand hardship and overcome obstacles. There is no shirking of responsibility and a willingness exists to shoulder burdens that would defeat others.

Sun in Aquarius

The Sun is in its detriment in this sign since the emphasis is on co-operation with others rather than upon self-promotion. The light of personal satisfaction is put out replacing selfish drives with an opportunity for spiritual growth. Sharing is the most outstanding quality of this sign, encouraging strong humanitarian concerns and indicating a life lived where it can do most good. Brotherhood and friendship are qualities most evident. There is an excellent ability in co-operation with others and a calmness in the nature which helps restore peace and equilibrium in times of stress. Technical skill is also likely. With so much emphasis on other people's welfare, there might be a tendency to ignore personal matters. A fear of emotional involvement can be evident.

Sun in Pisces

The solar forces are somewhat curtailed in this gentle sign, nevertheless, a spark of inner strength asserts itself in times of adversity. A mask of mildness often hides a strong passive resistance that can be quite formidable. Adaptability, tolerance and compassion are the most prominent qualities of this sign and a strong need to take care of those less fortunate motivates the life generally. Charity work and healing are usually areas that often attract. Kindness can sometimes be mistaken for weakness and victimisation can occur. A need to establish boundaries between self and others may be crucial. There is usually more emphasis on feeling than logic. A rich inner life and strong imagination can give talents in the arts particularly music and dancing.

The Consultation Chart

The Warlord ♂

SIGNS RULED	Aries and Scorpio
EXALTATION	Capricorn
DETRIMENT	Libra and Taurus
FALL	Cancer
JOY	Sixth house
CHALDEAN	Tenth house
QUALITY	Hot and Dry
COLOUR	Red, yellow, orange
MINERALS	Iron, antimony, jasper
PLACES	Smiths shops, furnaces, chimneys, forges, battlefields, deserts, bonfires
BODY	Muscles, haemoglobin, the left ear, gall bladder, adrenal function, blood cells
PERSONIFICATION	Soldier, general, surgeon, butcher, barber, traitor, carpenter, fireman, policeman, tyrant, physician, apothecary, hangman, bailiff, gamekeeper, cutler, engineer, chemist
KEYWORDS	Self-mobilisation, energy, drive, enthusiasm, quarrelsome, strife, anger, courageous, bold, confident, challenging, choleric, contentious, violent, inflammatory, impulsive

The Psyche

Astronomy

Fierce windstorms on icy Mars have slightly eroded its craggy surface. Its irregular appearance bears a suggestion of flowing water in the distant past, some of which is now locked in the thin polar caps. The system of canyons on this planet - up to four 4 miles deep - form an enormous cleft stretching 2,500 miles (4,000 km) across the surface. In its northern hemisphere there are vast lava plains, areas of past landslides and signs of giant outwash channels where billions of tons of water had rushed out in flash floods. Mars can come as close as 35 million miles (56 million km) to the Earth and as far as 250 miles (400 million km) owing to the eccentricity of its orbit. It is half the size of the Earth but also spins once every 24 hours (and 36 minutes) and has similar seasons due to its tilt. It is 25 degrees off vertical whereas the Earth is 23 degrees from the vertical. Thin clouds gather across its mountains except when it reaches its perihelion and then it is subject to dust storms. Mars has two Moons, Phobos and Deimos, which are thought to have been small asteroids captured by Mars's gravitational pull. It circles the Sun in 687 days.

Mythology
This Roman god of war originally ruled over agriculture. As Rome evolved into a more aggressive nation, more warlike qualities were attributed to Mars. He was appointed guardian over the sacred shield (ancile) as the fate of Rome depended upon its safe-keeping.

Ares was his Greek counterpart whose worship originated in Thrace. His adoption by Greece however, was met with little joy as he was not a popular god. Ares or Mars incurred the enmity of all because he loved battle for its own sake, yet his pedigree was impeccable since he was a son of Jupiter and Juno, the chief deities on Mount Olympus who ruled over all other gods. He was of course, greatly revered in Rome and reputedly fathered Romulus, the founder of Rome, on the vestal virgin Rhea Silvia. He ravished her while she slept - or so she said - and she bore him twin sons, Romulus and Remus. The wolf and the woodpecker are sacred to Mars as they helped to look after his twin sons after they had been thrown into the river Tiber by a jealous uncle.

Mars had a stab at domesticity when he married a minor deity called Nerio (meaning strength) yet in his role as the Greek Ares, he remains a bachelor. He tried to court Minerva (Athena) but she rejected his advances. Like Mars she was often engaged in warfare, but added strategy, courage and wisdom to her assaults in war. She occasionally outwitted Mars on the battlefield, much to his displeasure. His association with the Roman goddess of war, Bellona, appeared to have been a closer one as she is variously described as his wife, sister and daughter. However, his most famous liaison was with Venus, goddess of beauty and peace, proving that opposites do attract. Their affair came to an abrupt end when her spouse Vulcan discovered them in a compromising position and exposed their adultery to the other gods. Venus took the humiliation in her stride but Mars was mortified. Nevertheless, the affair must have been fun whilst it lasted because Venus bore him two sons, Deimos (Fear) and Phobos (Rout). It may be deduced from their names that they favoured their father more than their mother and were indeed happy to accompany the warlord onto the battlefield. The daughter of their mating - Harmonia - obviously had a more peaceful nature.

Mars was not a negligent father as the tale of his daughter Alcippe by a mortal woman will testify. When Alcippe was raped by Halirrhothius, a son of

Neptune, Mars killed him without hesitation. He was tried on Mount Olympus for murder but was acquitted. Mars is also known as Ultor (the avenger).

Naturally, Mars was happiest when in battle as it was his duty, in any case, to stir warriors into action. He rarely took sides, yet he did seem to favour the Trojans in their wars against the Greeks. He was always involved in some conflict or other and only occasional imprisonment restrained his thirst for warfare. In his underworld palace, Pluto eagerly awaited the souls of men Mars slew in battle.

Astrology
Mars is a *personal* planet governing certain personality traits. The battlefield where Mars rules supreme brings suffering and death and no doubt this adds to the malefic nature of the warlord's reputation. However it is usually through trial and error, strife and war that new developments, which eventually benefit mankind, seem to arise. This is certainly true of surgery, over which Mars rules, for it was first developed on the battlefield where amputations were commonplace. Scalpels, knives all sharp instruments come under the domain of Mars. On a physical level they cut away all the dross and putrefying matter that would be detrimental to the organism's survival. Psychologically, a quick cut rids the psyche of outmoded thoughts and ideas which no longer serve a purpose. Such drastic action gives Mars a poor reputation, since he brings about the fear of loss. His action can be violent, brutal and cruel, but Mars gives the strength to deal with difficulties and obstacles and may be involved in such things as engineering and chemistry.

Mars is energy and action often making no distinction as to whether the outlet is constructive or destructive. Mars gives the impulse to begin new enterprises, the willpower to persevere in the face of adversity, the determination to succeed, vast resources for survival as well as assertion and great motivation. He also bestows courage, is not afraid of confrontation and delights in taking risks. Mars can also be excitable and coarse which endears him to no-one. Mars is overwhelming and rather intimidating since he tends to invade other people's space both physically and metaphorically. He does not co-operate with others, relies exclusively upon his own opinions and is very argumentative. Mars governs the idealistic drive inherent in an individual and the determination necessary to achieve goals, whether they be physical or spiritual. He gives strength and energy to push action to its ultimate limit, overcoming all obstacles in a relentless dedication to an ideal. Mars governs the passion needed to affect any enterprise.

Mars also governs desire for physical and sensual activities; he is sex without a conscience, the soldier who took his pleasures quickly before the next battle, having little regard for graceful dalliance. He rules the seed from which new forms are made. He is representative of the animus within the individual, the brutish and raw male energy that may at times be repressed through society's need for outward harmony. Mars is anger, self-assertion and passion.

Esoteric view
Mars establishes the awareness and relation of opposites and from a spiritual point of view, is seen as benefic and not malefic. The abrasive effect from the action of Mars upon the individual and the environment often culminates in conflict but which leads eventually to new circumstances and new choices being made. Mars, as well as Saturn, bring liberation from control and the release of a higher consciousness. Mars arouses the entire lower nature and brings about the final rebellion of the personality against the soul, resulting in the death of the personality and form. It is the planet of wilful desire but from gross desire and passion it leads to divine and selfless sacrifice. It experiences life in order to gain wisdom and give life to ideas.

An unaspected or weakly aspected Mars may bring problems with self-assertion, lack of motivation and difficulty in the management of anger. There is likely to be involuntary aggression and over-reaction to seemingly innocuous events. There may also be a self-centred attitude that can be quite unconscious. The person can appear quite strong, even intimidating and may give offence unwittingly.

When Aries or Scorpio ascend in the consultation chart, Mars represents the client. This may describe someone who is poised to take action in order to affect some enterprise or goal. He is prepared to work hard in order to achieve his aims. Assertive, perhaps even aggressive, he is not easily daunted. Certainly an unwavering drive and staunch determination may need to be called upon at the present time.

Mars through the Signs

Mars in Aries
Strong in his own sign, Mars becomes even more wilful, self-motivated and extremely focused. He projects his sights upon some new, pioneering project. Energy is at a premium suggesting a great force that tends to overwhelm and intimidate others. He needs no encouragement from anyone to get on with the business at hand - like the original boy scout, he springs into action at a moment's notice. Though he may become impatient if other people do not

share his energy, drive and enthusiasm. Mental and physical challenges appeal to his sense of adventure and boredom sets in if life becomes too harmonious. Usually he has a great deal of courage, fears no-one and does not rest until goals are achieved. May have to be aware of a tendency to 'burnout', since he does not know when to stop. Mars plays to win and is very single-minded.

Mars in Taurus

Mars is in detriment in this sign indicating that the earthy Taurus tends to slow down Martian energy. A leisurely commencement to all activities promotes an image of indolence until inertia becomes a force to be reckoned with! However, enjoyment of life underpins all activity and he feels there is little sense in rushing around accomplishing nothing. Energy is contained and applied constructively without overdoing things - there is a strong belief that 'slow and steady wins the race'. This usually proves true since there is often great tenacity with an ability to overcome all obstacles. Not always self-motivated and needs encouragement from others to get involved in new activities. However, before involvement in any task commences, there is usually good preparation so as to build upon a solid foundation. Slow to anger, but can become a raging bull when driven too far. Very sensual.

Mars in Gemini

A quick mind with strong powers of thought. Ideas are put into action immediately. This position bestows tremendous versatility and there is an ability to keep track of many different concepts simultaneously. Will probably like working under pressure and able to 'think on his feet'. A powerful intellect is normally in evidence. Topical concerns are of greater interest than historical ones functioning extremely well in the 'here and now'. May be excellent in putting a team together to work towards a common purpose. So many ideas can overload the nervous system and it may be difficult sometimes to finish what is begun. Overall, Mars needs constant stimulation otherwise bores easily. A ready wit enchants others.

Mars in Cancer

Mars in its fall signifies that the courage and daring normally associated with the fiery planet is somewhat diminished. Securing personal wealth, health and happiness are held to be of great importance. Risks involving unfamiliar territory are shunned. External discord may be avoided but internal conflict is quite common. This is a very sensitive position for Mars and fluctuating moods may be frequent sometimes truncating communication. Powerful inner tensions and deep emotions characterise relationships. A strongly caring nature can sometimes become a controlling one, although there is a natural caution and avoidance of speedy involvement. Fidelity is of great importance and slights, real or imagined, are not easily forgotten. The imagination can reach great heights which can be positively used in artistic fields.

Mars in Leo

The dynamic drive of Mars finds a natural outlet in this sign. Special skills of organisation develop through a structured management of energy. The action is swift but steady. No venture is entered into without extensive research into the creative and pleasurable benefits. Tasks may be undertaken that seem to defeat others. Powers of leadership become apparent due to an ability to survey the whole and pull disparate strands together. There is great determination to succeed and gain the respect of others. This may however lead to a susceptibility to flattery. Image and presentation are important and there could be real talent in the promotion of self and others. Entrepreneurial skills may be in evidence. Usually found in the centre of activity and rarely on the sidelines.

Mars in Virgo

The direct action of Mars pauses in this sign in order to take stock of prevailing circumstances. No commitment is made to anyone or anything until everything is thoroughly examined and put to the test. This gives phenomenal attention to detail and possibly great authority in chosen subjects. Such great precision bestows skills in crafts, writing and surgery. Extremely high standards, imposed upon self and others, can sometimes prove burdensome. A willingness to work harder than anyone else can lead to periods of exhaustion and weakness. Worrying over trifles may also be a more negative symptom of the intense drive towards perfection. Despite obvious talents, innate modesty and self-effacement may hinder personal recognition.

Mars in Libra

The power of Mars is lessened in Libra, the sign of its detriment. Mars is said to be temporarily quiescent in the sign of the balance. Much time is spent looking at both sides of any question tending to inhibit action, albeit temporarily. Long deliberation however, may mean that opportunities may be missed. Yet there is little likelihood of 'acting in haste and repenting at leisure'. Once decisions are made, they are usually the right ones. Weighing up opposing factions gives excellent powers of strategy which can prove useful in competitive situations. Predicting the opponents next move comes easily. Prefers teamwork and usually needs a great deal of encouragement to start anything new. Finds decision making an awesome task.

Mars in Scorpio

Mars in its own sign gives great reserves of strength. Action is taken without causing a ripple or a stir accomplishing mammoth tasks without fuss. The capacity for hard work is very impressive as is the ability to battle against opposing forces. Mars also rules Scorpio esoterically where the soul's pilgrimage around the zodiac is brought to a point of climax. A need to face challenges great and small ensues and battles are constantly having to be fought and won. An inner strength develops that seems to overcome all obstacles. There is determination to achieve goals which may defeat others. But this is also a position of extremes and can produce either the saint or sinner. Power and strength obviously exists but the greatest challenge maybe to tolerate weakness in others.

Mars in Sagittarius

Mars feels comfortable in this position as its fiery nature finds encouragement in a sign that tends to be as forthright as the planet. A positive outlook ensures much time will be spent dreaming about future possibilities. There is often tremendous vision of how things ought to be, although reality doesn't always come up to the ideals. An exuberant manner and broad outlook tend to inspire others and talent in oratory is not uncommon - words seem to shoot straight from the heart. The search for honesty and truth guides all decisions, however, diplomacy may need to be cultivated. The sense of adventure is very keen and contact with foreign countries a distinct possibility. There may be a talent for prophecy.

Mars in Capricorn

Mars in its sign of exaltation tends towards controlled and structured activity. The tumultuous energy of Mars is steadied and directed towards some specific design. Goals are executed with precision and action is carefully planned. Full concentration is given to the matter at hand so little time is wasted on extraneous pursuits. Every effort counts. Reserving energy for only what is important means that little action is taken if future objectives appear vague. Excellent organisational powers are likely with this position bestowing the kind of discipline and control that achieves results. This Mars is not effusive in praise for others and tends to expect none in return. An outward shyness masks great determination.

Mars in Aquarius

Current and future trends are more important with this position than the events of the past. This may bring interest in new technological developments with great understanding of mechanical and electronic devices. Scientific pursuits tend to attract and there is a need to delve deeply into prevailing ideas and how they can benefit others. The depth of knowledge and innovative talent is impressive. Some misunderstandings may occur however, with people who may not be as far-seeing. Friends are made from all walks of life, with emphasis being placed on mutual interests rather than status. There is a great emphasis on freedom of expression and an abhorrence of commitment. Nevertheless, champions the spirit of co-operation between people of different ideological persuasions.

Mars in Pisces

The energy of Mars can be somewhat dissipated in this position and there may be a tendency towards prevarication and confusion. Indecision occurs because of the lack of strong focus and direction, but since the intuitive faculties are so strong in this sign, action is usually based upon acute perception. Trust in one's inner knowledge needs to be developed, which will ultimately lead to success. Depletion of energy may occur through brooding over past mistakes that really need to be chalked up to experience. Periods of quiet and seclusion are crucial in order to restore resources and regain strength. This position of Mars can deal with isolation better than most using the time for creative inspiration.

4

The Social Planets

Thunderbolt is One ♃

SIGNS RULED	Sagittarius and Pisces
EXALTATION	Cancer
DETRIMENT	Gemini and Virgo
FALL	Capricorn
JOY	Eleventh house
CHALDEAN	Ninth house
QUALITY	Hot and Moist
COLOURS	Navy blue, indigo, purple
MINERALS	Tin, amethyst, topaz, emerald, marble
PLACES	Courts, altar, town hall, churches, travel agency, racetracks heaven, the Elysian Fields
BODY	The liver, the lungs, the arterial circulation
PERSONIFICATION	Masculine, judge, senator, lawyer, cleric, foreigner, travel agent, councillor, priest, bishop, student, draper
KEYWORDS	Self regard, lucky, protective, content, temperate, faithful, magnanimous, honest, charitable, excess, plenty, sanguine, just, honourable, religious, horse-play

The Psyche

Astronomy

Jupiter is the largest planet in the solar system, more than two and a half times bigger than all the planets put together. Despite its size, it rotates very quickly - once in 10 hours. Like the outer planets, Jupiter tends to be more gaseous than rocky though it has a rocky core. Its prevailing clouds comprise hydrogen, helium, methane and ammonia. The clouds seem to band around the planet with belts of bright, variable zones. It has an extraordinary red spot. Jupiter's magnetic field stretches far out into space - although the clouds are cool measuring minus 150 degrees centigrade, the energy radiating from Jupiter's magnetic field is far hotter than the Sun's surface and produces more than 500 times the fatal dose of radiation for a human being. Jupiter has four moons and the closest, Io, is greatly affected by Jupiter's gravitational pull with its surface subject to sulphurous volcanic eruptions. Europa has an icy surface, being some distance from Jupiter and the other moons, Ganymede and Callisto are crated as well as icy. It takes 11.9 years to revolve around the Sun.

Mythology

Jupiter was allied to the Greek Zeus and the myths that accompanied him. Jupiter was particularly venerated in Rome along with Juno (Hera) and Minerva (Athena). He was a weather god rather than a creator god. He did not create the mortal world - that task was left to Prometheus. However, human beings as well as the godly pantheon came under Jupiter's special protection. Jupiter ruled from Mount Olympus, the highest peak in Greece overlooking the Vale of Tempe. He was worshipped as the god of the sky and king of heaven and ruled over the rain, thunder and lightning. He was the guardian of the law, the defender of truth and protector of justice and virtue.

Jupiter was the youngest son of the Titans, Saturn and Ops, and the brother of Neptune (Poseidon) and Pluto (Hades). Saturn, fearing that his children would usurp him, swallowed them whole as they were born. Upon the birth of Jupiter, however, Ops duped her husband by making him think that the stone she had wrapped in swaddling clothes which he swallowed, was his youngest son. When Jupiter grew to manhood, he confronted his father in battle and forced him to disgorge his siblings. Together with his brothers, he divided his father's kingdom by shaking lots in a helmet; Neptune was to rule over the sea and Pluto became the god of the underworld whilst Jupiter inherited the sky. Each brother received a gift from the Cyclopes, the giants with a single eye, whom Jupiter released from bondage. Jupiter received the thunderbolt, a weapon of punishment; Neptune, a trident and Pluto a helmet to make him invisible.

Though Jupiter was the protector of the human race, including strangers and travellers, his punishments were swift and terrible against those who broke his laws. This he did by sending down a thunderbolt and striking the offender dead or transforming him into some hideous beast. He was also a god of divination and tested the fates of mortals by holding up a pair of scales. He was not above jealousy and would quickly dispense with a rival in love. Neither was he faithful to his wife Juno and in fact, his behaviour was subject to intemperance and prodigality. He was prone to excesses of every kind particularly in matters of love and there are many stories of his conquests and subsequent paternity suits. No mortal woman, or divine goddess, was safe when Jupiter cast his lecherous eyes in her direction. Unable to vent her anger on her spouse, Juno was relentless in her persecution of his various paramours. Jupiter's legitimate children with Juno were Mars, Juventas and Ilithyia.

Two revolts against his kingship nearly succeeded. Both were masterminded by his grandmother Terra (Gaia or Mother Earth)) since she felt Jupiter had become too arrogant and overbearing. With the help of Hercules (Heracles) he defeated his adversaries and retained his position of supremacy.

Astrology
Jupiter is the first *social* planet in so much as emphasis is now on social obligations and social integration. Jupiter bestows a positive outlook and is known as the Greater Benefic. He brings optimism, joy and rewards for past good behaviour, or benefits accrued from good karma. He brings the feeling that the world is a good place to live in and gives an urge to expand and grow. This may be in both a spiritual, religious and material sense, so he is associated with the divine and the profane.

Jupiter looks to the future with a positive mind and has little time to dwell over past mistakes, which should be integrated within the psyche and used as the stuff of growth and wisdom. Jupiter gives the ability to philosophise and utilise everything for future resources. Jupiter is the freedom to express innate creativity and has his eye fixed firmly on distant horizons. He is not afraid to take a gamble on future possibilities since traditional ideas have little attraction for him. He finds the new and exotic much more captivating. Staying with the safe, tried and tested inhibits growth and Jupiter's main thrust is towards expansion. Looking towards the future brings qualities of prophecy and an uncanny sense of making the right decisions. He therefore deserves his other appellation as the Lord of Luck. Jupiter is the planet of hope and faith. The benevolence he bestows is for mankind generally and for the betterment of society. Jupiter rules the protective side of the law. He needs freedom to experiment and does not like to be tied down to one train of thought or perhaps even one relationship, like the mythological Jupiter. Also like the deity, the astrological Jupiter, can be profligate, greedy, antisocial and quarrelsome. He does not know how to steer the middle path and is prone to great excess in every direction. He has grandiose ideas but sometimes lacks the necessary discipline to carry them out. He likes to accumulate and is hardly ever satisfied and his gambling instincts can make him a frequenter of racetracks. Sometimes he prefers to rely on luck than hard work.

Esoteric view
Jupiter represents an all embracing love and comprehensive wisdom that serves to unite the whole of creation. He brings together soul and form, head and heart, as well as will and wisdom into a synthetic interplay. The fusion of heart and mind is apparently the subjective purpose of manifestation. Jupiter gives an inherent tendency towards fusion, as he represents the ultimate synthesis after Mercurial change and Saturnian crisis. After Venus has awakened the individual consciousness, Jupiter endeavours to connect the individual with the rest of existence. This brings greater understanding of the true nature of Reality leading to an expansion in thought and understanding eventually creating synthesis between heart and mind. This encourages love on a universal and less personal level and gradually awakens the soul's need for god.

An unaspected Jupiter suggests difficulty with boundaries causing a tendency towards profligacy and excess. Problems with reality may exist with goals sought beyond the scope of current expertise. Positive thinking may however, be quite pronounced since the individual may eschew limitations.

When Sagittarius or Pisces ascends in the consultation chart, Jupiter will represent the client. This may describe someone who is trying to expand their lives beyond their present circumstances. The individual may be seeking to develop their knowledge and wisdom through studies or travel. A sense of adventure is present as well as a need to accumulate wealth.

JUPITER THROUGH THE SIGNS

Jupiter in Aries

There is a refreshing and almost childlike faith in life that encourages a positive attitude which sometimes makes dreams come true. Consideration of failure is rarely entertained and there is faith in one's ability to overcome all obstacles. Life is lived with an eye on future possibilities without much reference to past experience. More reliance is put on present inspiration. There is an attraction to all new ideas and this may indicate a pioneering and adventurous spirit that thrives on challenging situations. A philosophy of 'nothing ventured, nothing gained' seems to describe this position of Jupiter. The mind is focused and steady and there is no lack of enthusiasm, however, there might be a need to make better preparation for unforeseen difficulties.

Jupiter in Taurus

A strong kinship with the earth may bring an interest in environmental issues. No armchair philosopher here. When sufficiently aroused, there is an ability to attend to the practical things in life and create a secure base for living for self and for others. There might be an interest in the produce of the earth such as food, nutrition and gardening as well as an interest in minerals. Financial resources and attracting wealth are usually in evidence since both planet and sign are interested in the good things in life. There is a possibility of becoming too acquisitive and interested only in physical comfort and sensual enjoyment. If things come too easily there is a possibility that inertia may result and a difficulty arises in starting new enterprises.

Jupiter in Gemini

Jupiter in its sign of detriment finds its normal visionary outlook concerned more with trifles and everyday occurrences which inhibit progress in other fields. Gemini is a sign of fragmentation and there may be a tendency to dissipate energies in too many different directions, although this may bring great knowledge, versatility and flexibility of mind. This is probably a good position for a teacher or journalist as communication skills are usually excellent. There is a need to broadcast the written or spoken word - this also describes someone who likes to spread gossip. Good luck comes from having many contacts and knowing people in the right places. An ability to find a point of contact with a variety of different people makes for an interesting life.

Jupiter in Cancer

Jupiter in its sign of exaltation brings an inner alignment with the greater whole and an acute ability to reflect collective needs. This can bring popularity and success with the public as there is an uncanny ability to judge and supply current requirements. Intuition is working at its peak in this sign. Benefits may accrue from the family - an inheritance may come just when it is needed most. It is possible that the family proves supportive generally and a feeling of belonging pervades the life. A comfortable home can be made easily in strange places and foreign lands. There is often great generosity and kindness to others. A deep faith in traditional values encourages the caring and nurturing of others.

Jupiter in Leo

Both Jupiter and Leo have an immense appetite for life and this combination tends to favour good luck and prosperity. There is usually a need to have the best of everything. A total faith in one's own abilities, as well as insisting on seeing the best in others, gives an appealing personality. Indeed, it would be hard to ignore such energy, enthusiasm and dynamism rolled into one person. Exhibitionist tendencies are in evidence however, and there is an excellent ability for self promotion. There might be a strong need for attention thus occasionally alienating those one seeks to impress. Though good taste is likely to show in decor and dress, there is a tendency towards excess in pursuing the good life.

Jupiter in Virgo

Jupiter in its sign of detriment indicates that it is hard work rather than just good luck which will bring success. This position suggests that the individual may at times be placed in disagreeable circumstances and feel that life is full of drudgery. There could be a constant feeling that there is an easier way of attaining one's goals in life. Soon enough the pains taken to accomplish tasks will bring greater fulfilment - more so than if things had been handed down on a plate. This may bring a change in personal desires making the individual become more conscious of other people's needs. Ultimately a strong drive to be of service develops and even powers of healing may become evident. Job satisfaction is paramount with this position.

Jupiter in Libra

The spirit of fair play is greatly emphasised when this planet and sign unite. An interest arises in encouraging the co-operation between people and countries and a search for harmony in all things is the guiding force. Great generosity and the consideration and wishes of others bestows a talent for making beneficial contacts. It is knowing people in the right places that brings success. There is a great need for relationship on all levels and careers in diplomacy and personnel may attract. There is indication of exquisite taste and interest in objects of art, home decor and beauty generally. The manners are usually charming and there is a pronounced dislike of coarse behaviour.

Jupiter in Scorpio

Life may not be a simple affair with this combination but there is usually great strength in dealing with adversity. The philosophy in life is to study the competition based on the assumption that everything has to be fought for. Living a superficial life does not appeal and there is often an interest in delving into the human psyche which could lead to the study of psychology. An insatiable urge to know what lies behind human existence could also bring an interest in occult subjects. Mundanely, much time may be spent in sorting out other people's problems and finances. This could show involvement in corporate finances, taxes, insurance and real estate. Money may accrue from legacies or from grateful clients. On the physical side, an activity like deep sea diving may be appealing.

Jupiter in Sagittarius

Jupiter in the sign that it rules emphasises intuition and an expanding consciousness through time spent in contemplation of the meaning of life. There is a natural orientation towards higher goals and the life may be spent in study or travel. Understanding the meaning behind symbolism encourages growth in wisdom. It often appears as if the mind is engaged elsewhere however. Mundane matters are sometimes ignored and there may be difficulties in dealing with the physical world. This position often describes the inspired teacher, writer or scholar. There may indeed be a talent for languages as well as understanding the significance of dreams. A religious or philosophical attitude is often evident.

Jupiter in Capricorn

Jupiter in its fall is said to reach the lowest point of material expression suggesting a strong desire for money and possessions. Whilst this may indeed produce a flair for business there may be an overly strong attachment to the material world. According to esoteric principles 'love is fallen and blinded' when such desire is rampant. This may indicate an individual whose main goal is the satisfaction of material needs perhaps even through ruthless means without due consideration of others. It is possible, however, that there comes a turning point when money and possessions no longer seem to satisfy. The highest aspect of this position may indicate using and wielding resources for the good of the whole. There is usually good business acumen and an ability to recognise quality.

Jupiter in Aquarius

This is the sign of Jupiter's esoteric rulership suggesting that wisdom and wealth might be used for the benefit of others. There may be a tendency towards righting the wrongs of the world which could suggest involvement in politics or welfare, although a tremendous need for freedom of expression may breed an illusive manner and lack of personal commitment. There is a likelihood of involvement in world events and a disinterest in the affairs of one's family and close neighbours. Emotional situations make this individual feel uncomfortable. This is a position which indicates an extremely gregarious nature. Social interaction is often preferred when it has an academic or impersonal setting. There is usually an understanding and appreciation of cultural differences.

Jupiter in Pisces

Jupiter in the sign that it rules is one of the best positions for attuning to current fashions and trends. This may be expressed through film, books, photography and the arts as well as in fashion and beauty. On a more psychological level great reservoirs of compassion bring empathy for the less fortunate. The individual comes into contact with people who champion all the important causes of the time. There is usually a relaxed attitude towards life and having faith in the fact that in time, everything will be justly resolved. There is an ability to withstand hardship because of the flexible nature. Periods of isolation are not uncommon and the devotional, religious life may appeal.

THE RINGMASTER ♄

SIGNS RULED	Capricorn & Aquarius
EXALTATION	Libra
DETRIMENT	Cancer & Leo
FALL	Aries
JOY	Twelfth house
CHALDEAN	First house
QUALITY	Cold & Dry
COLOURS	Black, ashen
MINERALS	Lead
PLACES	Deserts, woods, valleys, churchyards, wells, caves, ruins, graves, dark places, holes, mountains, coal mines, dirty places
BODY	Skeletal system, bones, blood clotting mechanism, teeth, the ears (specifically right ear), the skin, hair, spleen
PERSONIFICATION	Old people, miner, plumber, labourer, farmer, father in night-time chart, monk, beggar, politician, grandfather, chimney sweep, shepherd, scavenger
KEYWORDS	Structure, decay, obstacles, delay, depression, hard work, solitary, severity, discontent, reserved, severe, patient, austerity, chronic, atrophy, deformity

The Psyche

Astronomy
Saturn is easily recognisable by its three lovely rings which are composed of billions of icy fragments ranging from fine dust to enormous chunks. Starting from the far side the rings are lettered A, B and C. Although Jupiter, Uranus and Neptune also have rings, none are as spectacular as those possessed by Saturn. There are 18 moons close by, of which Titan is the largest and the only satellite to have an atmosphere, consisting of nitrogen and methane. Saturn takes around 29.5 years to orbit the Sun.

Mythology
Saturn in Roman mythology was the ancient god of agriculture who taught mortals how to till the fields. He was identified with the Greek god Cronos whose name was similar to 'chronos' meaning time and Saturn became identified with the passage of time. He was the youngest son of Uranus and Terra (Gaia) who represented heaven and earth respectively. Uranus, lacking paternal feeling and afraid of being usurped, imprisoned his early brood in a secret place. The strongly maternal Terra, seeking to rescue them, appealed to the younger Saturn for help. Saturn demanded that his father release his siblings, and when the old man refused, Saturn castrated him. Saturn in his turn became master of the universe. Who dared oppose him after such a dastardly act?

He was the husband of Ops (the Greek Rhea) goddess of plenty. His rather impressive elder children were Juno, goddess of marriage, Neptune, god of the sea, Pluto, god of the dead, Ceres, goddess of the grain and Vesta, goddess of the hearth. He is usually depicted bearded carrying a sickle (a harvesting tool) and an ear of corn (signifying agriculture and sowing).

A prophecy spoke of Saturn's own dethronement by one of his children and he wasted no time in swallowing the first five when they were born. Upon the birth of his sixth child, Jupiter (Zeus), his wife Ops wrapped a large stone in swaddling clothes and gave it to Saturn to swallow instead of her youngest son. Later Jupiter waged war on his father and dethroned him. Saturn was forced to disgorge the elder children and the stone was placed at Dephi to mark the navel or the centre of the earth. It seems that father and son were eventually reconciled since Jupiter allowed Saturn to rule Italy during the Golden Age of the universe, a time of perfect peace and happiness. His festival was began on 17th December each year and became known as the Saturnalia, during which time the Golden Age was restored for seven days. Everyone was invited to eat, drink and be merry; a period of goodwill ensued, devoted to festive banquets with the exchange of visits and gifts. A special characteristic of this time was that slaves were given their freedom - they were served by their masters at table and treated like equals. Trade and executions were halted and military manoeuvres were postponed. These celebrations later became part of the traditional Christmas activities after the pagan era came to an end.

Strange, then, that Saturn is hardly known for his joy and mirth. It is possible that the Saturnalia is more identified with the Roman myth rather than the Greek one. An alternative myth tells of Saturn confined to Tartarus, a cave in the deepest part of the underworld, after the brawl with his sons. Certainly some of the painful associations with the astrological Saturn are analogous with the feeling of having descended into the tortuous depths of Tartarus or hell.

Astrology
Saturn is a *social* planet, its energies suggesting interaction with society usually through obstacles and difficulties. Jung said, 'there is no coming to consciousness without pain' and in the same way the suffering and difficulties which Saturn imposes are said to act as a bridge to higher consciousness and understanding. These difficulties are usually expressed through some limitation imposed upon the life either temporarily or permanently, which can manifest in heavy burdens, great responsibility, sacrifice or ill health. Difficulties are said to provide choice and an opportunity to progress.

Saturn's role as the god of agriculture infers that he is the 'sower and the reaper', figuratively and metaphorically speaking. In this way he is seen as lord of karma which represents the law of cause and effect (as you sow so shall ye reap). In Sanskrit karma stands for 'action' and in Vedic (Jyotish) astrology, Saturn is seen as the planet of action. Not in the sense of energy or swiftness but through being forced to act upon or confront some situation arising from the past. It appears that with each new incarnation, all the thoughts and actions of past lives are attached to the soul as it transmigrates to each new body. Saturn represents the crystallisation of past events which need to be confronted and dealt with in order to prepare for the future.

Saturn's role as Father Time implies that everything is accomplished in time and the delays and obstacles he imposes are created in order to yield an opportunity to reflect and make more informed decisions, yet the feelings often associated with the difficulties and obstructions are likely to be despondency, depression, loneliness, fear and pessimism. In his most negative expression, Saturn induces feelings of mistrust, suspicion and discontent.

Traditionally, Saturn is referred to as the Greater Malefic since his actions can sometimes be inimical to life and certainly the obstacles he presents in the way of progress can often create despair. Saturn's nature is one of contraction, creating feelings of inhibition, oppression and inadequacy. At the same time he forces the individual to face the less pleasant aspects of his nature and smash crystallised, entrenched attitudes. These may be in the form of rigid defence patterns in thought and attitude. As the body is a necessary vehicle for the expression of spirit, Saturn's action often induces physical as well as mental stress, which can be the foundation of illness. Saturn's depiction with the sickle also earns him the title 'the grim reaper' or the one who brings death of the physical body.

The Saturnalia represents the paradoxical part of his nature since its emphasis is on freedom from labour and punishment, albeit temporarily. Could it be that after paying off karmic dues, through toil and suffering, the reward is liberation from constraints and limitations? Could it be that through dedication and application to duty, the qualities and gifts gained develop the kind of discipline which helps to achieve both material and spiritual success? Without Saturn's gift of discipline much of life would lack structure. He bestows the gift of concentration and practical application. He is the builder and the architect. He looks seriously upon life so that experience can be assimilated and knowledge increased. This can incorporate the things we need to learn in order to find the balance between spirit and matter. Saturn is associated with matter and the necessity to deal with and confront the difficulties of physical life. Eventually there is contact with the spirit through wisdom and understanding.

Saturn can sometimes represent the father in the horoscope, especially in a night-time chart (when the Sun is below the horizon).

Esoteric view
Saturn represents the outermost bounds of the soul's journey into matter and teaches how to bring order out of chaos, beauty out of ugliness and peace out of strife. Saturn disturbs and breaks up existing conditions enabling the influence of Mercury (change) to be more fully expressed. In other words, Saturn destroys that which holds back free expression of the soul making visions more intuitively perceived when obstructions have been removed. Saturn brings crises into the individual's life so that spiritual growth can be effected through confronting difficulties and taking responsibility for one's own actions. Saturn is experienced as a hard taskmaster since the obstacles he appears to put in the way of progress often cause suffering and discomfort. But Saturn's role as the Lord of Karma is apparently to present opportunities for correcting past mistakes and pay off old debts in order to make great leaps in spiritual and material evolution.

A weakly aspected or unaspected Saturn may indicate that the client sets inappropriate boundaries or limitations within particular areas of life. Great effort may be expended upon trivialities whilst important issues are ignored. There may be a need to weigh up the pros and cons of each particular situation in a more structured and practical way.

If Capricorn or Aquarius are ascending in the consultation chart, Saturn will represent the client. It is possible that the client may have a very serious and responsible outlook on life at this moment or be thoroughly depressed. Life may not be moving fast enough for him and he is likely to be facing delays and disappointments. It is also possible that he sees little reward for all his hard work though with time his efforts should bear fruit. Restrictions imposed by others will ultimately restore order and discipline into his life. He is likely to develop qualities of prudence and common sense.

Saturn through the Signs

Saturn in Aries

The fall of Saturn in Aries may be symbolic of the fall of mortals into generation and their subsequent struggle with the material world. This placement may indicate the use of creativity purely for physical and material ends as the individual grapples with issues of survival. Births and beginnings may be especially difficult. However, a more esoteric view describes a conflict between spiritual and material values. This position of Saturn suggests that it is important not to rush into any situation without examining all the relevant facts. Steps towards eventual goals should be planned with care. Impatience has to be curbed and obstacles should be looked upon as being instructive rather than as stumbling blocks. An authoritarian attitude could upset others and may need to be tempered with tolerance.

Saturn in Taurus

It is always possible that inertia may result from this combination since neither sign nor planet have a reputation for swift action. Yet this gives a very steady approach to life always thinking things out carefully before making any kind of move. Resultant decisions tend to be correct and there could be special talent in banking or making a killing on the stock exchange. The ability to handle money develops through experiencing some initial financial hardship. A high price is put on security and safety. The slow and steady nature of this combination assures a talent with making things grow, indicating horticultural abilities. Other areas of expertise might be in carpentry or the building trade. A strong artistic streak could be expressed through singing, sculpture and painting.

Saturn in Gemini

Saturn in this position creates a very logical turn of mind and inculcates a practical disposition. A rational approach to life's problems suggests structured thinking and a sound intellect. Initial problems may come in communication, there may even be a speech impairment, but this provides an opportunity towards development of the mental and communicative faculties. Nothing is taken at face value and everything has to be worked out step by step before decisions are made. There is always a demand for fact - not fiction. It is just possible that there could be a pedantic quality to this combination. Nevertheless, a thorough approach to problem solving assures eventual success. Life is often taken very seriously and negative thinking may have to be watched.

Saturn in Cancer

This is the sign of Saturn's detriment and the spiritual meaning of this position is indicative of the conflict of the soul within the environment. This may be expressed through difficulties within the family and domestic sphere. Early childhood struggles may lay the foundation of acute sensitivity and vulnerability that may hamper full emotional expression. An emphasis on self-consciousness and the fear of being hurt leads to the development of strong protective defences. This also suggests a symbolic imprisonment and it may be important for the individual to learn to trust and become more open. Ultimately, the protective instincts may work towards caring for those who are less fortunate and building a new foundation upon which others may prosper. Inner emotional conflicts may lead to finally creating outer harmony.

Saturn in Leo

Saturn is also in detriment here, indicating that his power is lessened, whether that be for good or ill is hard to tell. Traditionally of course, it is a weak placement for Saturn and this may indicate low self esteem and difficulty in expressing creativity. There may be lack of confidence where personal talents are concerned. Self promotion becomes difficult and obstacles in achieving success seem to arise with some frequency. An initial fear of challenge and being usurped may cause inhibition, but struggling with such issues leads to developing humility. Better control of the environment is gained and dealing with power and authority becomes much easier when the self is put to one side. The ability to handle both success and failure in equal measure eventually creates a powerful persona.

Saturn in Virgo

Both planet and sign are seriously disposed towards hard work, efficiency and thorough attention to detail. Excellent qualities of precision steer the individual towards intricate art forms as in fine lace making and jewellery design. Other outlets for such an expression of exactitude are architecture and engineering. The ability to concentrate for long periods will aid application in difficult tasks ensuring eventual success. However, the drive for perfection may hamper progress at times as there could be a feeling that nothing is quite good enough. Excessive discernment could lead to crippling modesty and inhibition, and a tendency towards negative thinking is likely especially if subjected to criticism. However, the superb powers of discrimination inherent in this combination should develop the capacity to correctly judge each situation.

Saturn in Libra

As the Lord of karma, Saturn's exaltation in the sign of the balance represents perfect alignment between body and soul. The Law of karma stipulates that every thought and action has a reaction and Saturn is the instrument of cause and effect creating opportunities for the individual in making the right choices. These may at times be difficult since the correct balance has to be sought between personal gain and benefit to others. Ethical judgements become extremely important to the individual and this is usually a matter of personal conscience rather than external praise or blame. Doing the right thing sometimes hampers action because any commitment is taken very seriously. A cool head and correct judgement can be useful qualities in the legal profession.

Saturn in Scorpio

Saturn's position in the sign of change and transformation suggests that there is enormous ability to deal with crisis situations. Entanglement with other people's problems seems to be a common feature but there is usually excellent ability in sorting them. This is usually in the area of taxes, insurance and wills. Accountancy or the legal profession may attract. There are times when the journey through life may seem especially hard. However, there is usually formidable strength present which aids in overcoming prevailing difficulties. No stone is left unturned when seeking solutions. It may be that losses feature occasionally with this combination. However, the lesson of this alliance of planet and sign is to let go of past hurts and learn how to share and forgive.

Saturn in Sagittarius

This placement indicates that the individual tends to live by certain philosophical or spiritual beliefs. A strong moral code may be the guiding principle behind all actions. Doing what conscience dictates becomes extremely important. A search for truth may open up opportunities in the field of education, law and publishing. Certainly here is someone who knows their own mind. Sometimes however, there may be intolerance of other people's weakness which may produce an autocratic manner. This stems from disappointment when others are unable to live up to their commitments. There seems to be an inability to tolerate failure. There may be a need to recognise and understand that other people may be much more vulnerable and uncertain about their path in life. There is a dedication and seriousness with this combination that helps create success.

Saturn in Capricorn

Saturn in the sign of its conventional as well as esoteric rulership promises material as well as spiritual success. Career issues are often prominent though the way to the top can be a long and arduous one. It may often appear as if the path in life is a solitary one without much support from others. Initial hardship is often the spur towards success. It might be that the process towards achievement rather than the final accolades becomes more important. The individual tends to be calm and yet quietly assertive. Working for oneself rather than for others seems to attract. However, this eventually bestows much strength through having to rely on one's own judgement. Taking on responsibility becomes second nature. Passion for work may sometimes interfere with family commitments.

Saturn in Aquarius

Saturn is strong in its own sign. Effort is made to achieve individual responsibility within a group setting where some humanitarian cause is the spur to motivation and achievement. This placement strengthens the ability to rise above the mundane aspects of physical life. Clarity of thought is often present because of a detachment from illusion. Since logic governs decisions, it is possible that outward behaviour may appear impersonal at times. A structured and calm thinking process brings the individual into the realm of science, physics and engineering. There may also be mathematical ability. Sometimes there may be difficulty in confronting personal emotions and the challenge may be to make the leap from a cool scientific approach to one of more humility and kindness.

Saturn in Pisces

The planet of structure is not always very comfortable in the sign which often has problems with boundaries. Much time may be spent in trying to untangle personal and other people's emotions. The circumstances in which the conflict occurs may be within the sphere of work where a feeling of exploitation prevails, or having to face restricting conditions in a marriage where sacrifices may also have to be made. It is possible that dealing with an over-demanding family could inhibit opportunities for pursuing personal interests. There may be a great yearning for freedom since both planet and sign create a situation of bondage. Dealing with such restricting circumstances will however, lead to developing great reservoirs of knowledge and resources.

5

ALL CHANGE: THE OUTER PLANETS

URANUS, THE INTRUDER ♅

ASSOCIATED SIGN	Aquarius
EXALTATION	Scorpio
DETRIMENT	Leo
FALL	Taurus
QUALITY	Electric
COLOURS	Deep rich blue
MINERALS	Uranium, amber, radium, zinc
PLACES	Airfields, technological plants, sky, air, ether, earthquakes
BODY	Pituitary gland, the eyes, brain (dura mater), breathing, etheric body, nerve fluids, heart valves, motor nerves of speech, membranes of body, the rhythmic processes of the body
PERSONIFICATION	Eccentric people, scientists, revolutionists, grandparents, bohemians
KEYWORDS	Self-discovery, spasmodic, psychic, foresight, genius, eccentricity, altruistic, humane, restless, unexpected, sudden, abrupt, original, intuitive, rebellious, freedom, telepathic, shock, electric, accidents, abnormality, cramp, ruptures, spasmodic, perverse, awakening, occult

The Psyche

Astronomy
Discovered in 1781, the planet was originally referred to as Herschel in honour of its discoverer Sir William Herschel. Appearing as an aquamarine disc, its axis has an extreme inclination to the plane of the ecliptic. Since Uranus lies on its side, each of its poles experiences a day that lasts 42 years when facing the Sun. The atmosphere comprises of hydrogen, helium, methane and ammonia. Uranus experiences extremes of temperatures around -330 degrees Fahrenheit (-200 degrees Celsius) in its upper clouds. It has five major satellites, all of which rotate in a contrary direction to other planets, the largest of which

is named Titania. The others are Ariel, Umbriel, Oberon and Miranda - all Shakespearean characters apart from Umbriel. Uranus also has nine feint narrow rings. It takes 84 years to orbit the Sun.

Mythology
Terra, or the Greek Gaia (Mother Earth), was born out of Chaos and then produced Uranus (the Greek Ouranus) without the aid of a male, becoming the world's first single parent. In both Greek and Roman mythology Uranus was the original sky ruler long before this title was conferred upon his grandson Jupiter. The eventual marriage between Uranus and Terra personified the unity between heaven and earth. The rain Uranus poured upon Terra made her fertile and she became fruitful. Their offspring however, were quite unappealing. From the couple's first mating sprang the Titans, unprepossessing giants, who in early legends, were looked upon as the Elder Gods. Later came the Cyclops the one-eyes giants who were even less attractive, and the Hecatonchires, the 100-handed, 50-headed monsters who were quite grotesque. Uranus and Terra had one last terrifying offspring and that was Typhon, a 100-headed monster serpent.

Quite understandably, Uranus found fatherhood rather unpleasant and utterly abhorred his children. Fearing dethronement for lack of paternal warmth, he banished his progeny to a remote and forbidding dwelling in the depths of the earth called Tartarus. Or, as otherwise graphically described, he tried to push his children back into Terra's body.

The long-suffering Terra appealed to Saturn - a younger son - to rescue her elder children. Saturn being the soul of acquiesence and duty confronted his father, became deaf to the older man's protestations and sliced off his manhood. Terra had armed him with a flint sickle to accomplish this task. Saturn flung his father's genitals into the sea at a place said to be by Cape Drepanuum. From the few spots of blood that fell to earth sprang the three Erinyes or Furies, pitiless avengers of crimes of patricide and perjury. Another fable suggests that Venus, the goddess of beauty, emerged from the sea in which the god's genitals had been flung. After his terrible end, Uranus no longer appears in the early myths.

Astrology
Uranus is the first of the outer planets sometimes referred to as the trans-Saturnians or spiritual planets. The outer planets seek to raise mortal consciousness through bringing an awareness of universal or global issues. World events at the time of their discovery are usually seen as representative of the planets' energies and suggest the area of rulership. When Uranus was discovered in 1781, events on earth took a great leap forward particularly within the technological arena. The Industrial Revolution brought mechanised factories

into existence resulting in the division of labour and increased productivity. Two major revolutions at that time paved the way towards replacing entrenched aristocratic forms of government with more open, elective systems. The American War of Independence 1776-1783 (the American Revolution), cut ties with imperialistic Britain and her new constitution declared that 'all men were created equal'. This sentiment was echoed during the French Revolution in 1789-1799 with the cry of 'Liberty, Equality and Fraternity'. Certainly the western world was ripe for reform.

Until 1800 the principle fuel was wood, its energy derived from solar energy stored in plants during their lifetime. Electricity was the new revolutionary fuel. Experiments in electricity began a few years after the discovery of Uranus. The early pioneers in electromagnetic induction were born around this time; Michael Faraday (1791-1861) and George Ohm (1787-1854) were such two. Uranium, a chemically reactive radioactive element, the main fuel used in nuclear reactors, was discovered in 1789 which eventually led to the discovery of radium. Radium is now used in the treatment of a few kinds of cancer, as cancer cells are more sensitive to radiation than normal cells.

Around 1750, literary taste began to change from the classical conventions towards the Romantic movement in literature. This was characterised by reliance on the imagination with freedom of thought and expression. Freedom being associated with Uranus of course. As the Romantic movement grew however, it seemed to have developed Neptunian nuances as the imagination was praised over reason, emotion over logic and intuition over science. The Romantic movement ended in 1870. Neptune was discovered in 1846. Until the 18th century, Saturn marked the last reaches of the universe and was looked upon as the boundary between humanity and the gods. The action of the astrological Uranus is sudden, swift and shocking and breaks up the crystallisation of Saturn. Though unpredictable and disruptive, the action of Uranus can be catalytic. Earthquakes, revolutions as well as electricity come under his domain.

The astrological Uranus represents reform as a result of departure from the old way of doing things. There is a rejection of mass dogma and a rebuttal of outmoded traditions that are no longer useful. The action of Uranus is to deviate from the norm and go beyond set boundaries, thus it becomes the planet of deviation and divorce. Uranus needs freedom to act and this usually creates an indomitable will. His actions are firstly seen as disruptive, which may be on a personal level or global scale, causing instability, tension and stress. Uranus does not like restrictions resulting in characteristics of perversity and eccentricity. Though Uranus is linked to genius, he can also distort the thought processes, leading to mental imbalance under certain circumstances.

Due to his position in the godly pantheon - being the granddaddy of them all - he can often represent the grandparents in the chart.

Esoteric view
Uranus came before Saturn in the early godly pantheon suggesting that the spiritual ideals (Uranus) are due to be concretised in matter (Saturn). Uranus was unconditioned time whereas Saturn became finite and conditioning time. Uranus brings manifestation onto the physical plane, initiating a new order of life and conditions.

All physical phenomena has an electrical origin which is transmitted through the Ether of space the field in and through which energies travel. Uranus rules Ether and transmits the rays of light to Earth. The marriage of Uranus and Terra was symbolic of the union between air and earth; ideas initiating form. Uranus as the carrier of light has connection with physical eyesight as well as etheric vision, that which sees beyond physical manifestation.

Its cosmic pull creates an irritating energy that links to occult (seeking scientific knowledge) rather than mystical (pure faith) expression. Uranus endeavours to unite the lower and higher self through intelligent use of the mind. It stimulates the knowledge of universal interdependence on a conscious level leading to expression of brotherhood and service in physical life. Uranus, as well as Neptune and Pluto, are said to affect the soul life rather than the personality life. The soul will follow its own path regardless of custom and convention, as does Uranus. Libra is designated the sign of Uranus's esoteric rulership perhaps signifying spiritual unity.

At the time of their discovery, all three outer planets brought humanity to a new level of consciousness and therefore, have a more universal and generational effect with regard to their sign placement.

A weakly aspected or unaspected Uranus can cause sudden disruptions in the client's life perhaps precipitating action before adequate groundwork has been carried out. There is also a likelihood of eccentric behaviour which the client may find hard to control. He may find the management of new age ideas that he so readily champions, difficult to put into practice. He tends never to take advice.

When Aquarius ascends in the consultation chart, Saturn should of course be taken to represent the client. As Uranus is also associated with Aquarius, it should also be considered as representing the client, though in a secondary capacity. The planetary strength should then be compared. If Saturn is strongly dignified then perhaps the client may still be content to continue with his life in the old traditional way, at least for the time being. He may want change but circumstances may not be conducive to his desires. If Uranus is stronger, perhaps by being placed in Aquarius, on an angle or receiving benevolent aspects from the Fortunes, then the client's restlessness and need for change is becoming more apparent. In some cases, the client may be motivated by humanitarian concerns.

NEPTUNE, EARTH SHAKER ♆

ASSOCIATED SIGN	Pisces
EXALTATION	Cancer?
DETRIMENT	Virgo
FALL	Capricorn?
QUALITY	Nebulous
COLOURS	Lavender, purple
MINERALS	Oils, gasses, ambergris
PLACES	Misty places, fogs, moors, the sea, rivers, streams, damp places, oil rigs
BODY	Connections to auto-immunity, pineal gland, solar plexus?, fungi, coma, lymphatic system, eyesight
PERSONFICATION	Seaman, fisherman, healer, medium, singer, mystic, psychic, shaman, prisoner, repressed races
KEYWORDS	Self-idealisation, dissolution, nebulous, vague, fraud, scandal, poison, dissolution, weakening, ecstasy, confusion, hypersensitivity, parasite, lethargy, hallucination, mystery, aesthetic, mysterious, seductive, treacherous, emotional, chaos, obsession, romantic, peak experiences

The Psyche

Astronomy
Discovered in 1846 at 25 Aquarius, Neptune takes about 165 years to orbit the Sun and an average of 14 years to pass through one sign. It is blue in colour though telescope pictures have shown it to have different zones and a dark spot due to snow storms. There are methane ice crystals floating in the atmosphere. It also has a feint ring system. The two biggest satellites, Triton and Nereid, move around Neptune in a retrograde motion. Six further moons have been discovered since 1989 of which Naiad is the largest.

The Outer Planets

Mythology

The image of Neptune holding his trident is immediately recognisable in artistic depiction. Familiar as god of the sea he was like other gods, initially connected to fertility. In Roman mythology he was allied with the Greek Poseidon who also ruled over streams and rivers. In earlier myths, as Poseidon, he was known as the 'holder of the earth' and 'earth shaker'. The Romans invested Neptune with much of the mythology associated with Poseidon.

Neptune was brother to Jupiter, god of the sky and to Pluto god of the underworld. He is depicted as a bearded and imposing figure accompanied by a dolphin (as well as his trident of course). He received the trident from the Cyclopes when he and his brothers released them from Tartarus, the underworld prison of Pluto. Jupiter had received the thunderbolt and Pluto a magic helmet from the grateful one-eyed monsters. Neptune was allegedly swallowed by his father Saturn along with many of his other brothers and sisters but one story suggests that his mother Ops substituted a foal in his place.

Neptune, like his brother Pluto was less than happy with his allotted domain. He coveted dry land and tried to grab Athens but the city was awarded to Minerva (Athena) instead. Yet he did manage to claim a time-share in Troezen; Minerva was the other part owner. His other bids for land, and there were many of them, failed.

His sumptuous underwater palace, off Aegze in Euboea, had spacious stables where he kept white horses and a golden chariot. Storms and gales ceased when Neptune approached driving his mighty steeds. The sport of horse-racing is attributed to him. One tale goes that Ceres (Demeter), weary of the search for her daughter, transformed herself into a mare so that she would be safe from unwelcome suitors. However, the wily Neptune transformed himself into a stallion and immediately mated with her. From their union sprang the nymph Despoena and the wild horse Arion. The association with horses refers to an early myth depicting the horse as a symbol of fertility.

In his role as the Greek Poseidon he married Amphitrite, one of the Nereids, although she initially refused his proposal. He sent a messenger after her, a youth named Delphinus who pleaded his case so well that Amphitrite consented to marry the sea lord. They had three legitimate children: Triton, Rhode and Benthesicyme. Neptune was as lustful as his brother Jupiter and had many love affairs favouring nymphs belonging to springs and fountains. He fathered several wild and cruel children, among them were the giant Orion and the Cyclops Polyphemus. He also mated with the Gorgon Medusa (presumably when she was still young and beautiful) and became the proud parent of Pegasus, the famous winged horse. Yet Neptune was of a quarrelsome nature. Reputedly bad-tempered, vindictive and violent, furious tremors and earthquakes erupted when Neptune was aggrieved. The battles in which he fought were so ferocious that the shaking ground made Pluto fear the earth would cave in upon his underground palace.

Besides horses, bulls are also associated with Neptune. Minos, king of Crete asked Neptune to send him a bull for sacrifice. The one he sent was such a magnificent specimen that Minos decided to keep it rather than sacrifice it incurring Neptune's wrath. Neptune made the king's wife Pasiphae fall in love with the beast and mate with him.

Neptune was also merciful and saved the inhabitants of Thessaly from floods by activating an earthquake. He saved Ino and her son Melicertes when they flung themselves into the sea. He appointed Castor and Polydeuces the protectors of sailors and gave them the power to lull storms. People prayed to him to protect them from earthquakes.

He favoured the Greeks during the Trojan War and sent a terrifying sea monster to desecrate the land where Troy stood. Before king Priam defended Troy in the famous wars, his father king Laomedon, had asked Neptune and Apollo to build the walls around the city of Troy. When their task was accomplished, the king refused to pay for their services and Neptune vowed to avenge himself on the Trojans.

Astrology
Neptune is referred to as an outer or spiritual planet having more influence on global events than personal matters. He raises the consciousness through dissolving boundaries which tie the individual to the limiting force of matter. Like the mythological Neptune, the astrological counterpart has little use for walls or boundaries as he is the idealist who sees beyond the material form. He dissolves structures in order to link up with the invisible realm of inspiration and vision. This may lead to spiritual yearnings, religious leanings and mediumship.

Neptune is tremendously impressionable but seeks to define himself through creative ways in music, poetry and dancing. If the creative muse is difficult to express, then the proclivity towards escapism becomes aroused resulting in the abuse of drugs and alcohol. He instills the individual with a great yearning to become part of the whole, to link with something greater than earthly life has to offer. This can create an empty void. The search to fill the emptiness can be a harrowing one as the way of Neptune is through sacrifice and selflessness. Neptune can, therefore, also represent victimisation. But ultimately, through suffering compassion for others begins to develop. The sensitivity of Neptune gives both aesthetic appreciation and an ability to achieve understanding of the unseen world. It can also bring fantasy and illusion, and dissatisfaction with daily life as it fails to measure up to the ideal. There is great susceptibility to glamour and romance though when positively expressed may find an outlet in creative writing, meditation, prayer and healing. Negative expressions of Neptune may bring escape through mental dissociation or chasing an easy life through fraudulent schemes.

The planet Neptune was discovered in 1846, a time when clairvoyance and mediumship seemed to have ignited the public's imagination. Neptunian mysticism gave rise to 19th century Spiritualism which is based on the belief that messages can be received from the dead, usually through a sensitive medium. Modern New Age practices apparently have their roots in 19th century Spiritualism with the emphasis on a holistic approach towards understanding life and its problems and the inter-relatedness of mind and body. Again this echoes the Neptunian idea of becoming part of the whole.

Mesmerism or hypnotism as it later became known, was a popular healing method during the time of Neptune's discovery. Hypnosis works by creating an altered state of consciousness and apparently produces deeper contact with the emotional life resulting in the exposition and releasing of repressed feelings and anxieties. Hypnotism was practised by French neurologist Jean Martin Charcot in Paris under whom Sigmund Freud later studied. Freud (1856-1939) initially used hypnosis in treating his patience and he is of course, known as the 'father of psychology'. It is interesting that the glyph for psychology (ψ) is quite similar to the one used for Neptune (Ψ).

Modern forms of anaesthestics became recognised and used during the middle era of the 19th century. Alcohol and opiates had always been used during operations throughout the centuries but these were entirely unreliable. Either the patient was stupefied for several days after the operation or failed to recover.

Neptune is often seen as the higher octave of Venus, though some say Mercury, because Neptune seems to strongly influence the nervous system, which is ruled by Mercury.

Esoteric view
Neptune stands for the soul's imprisonment in matter and hence its link to Pisces, the sign of bondage, and the twelfth house which rules all places of confinement such as prisons, asylums, hospitals and perhaps even monasteries. Neptune dissolves all physical distinctions in order to create unity. It breaks down the barriers of the material plane. Neptune stimulates spiritual and psychic illumination, as distinguished from the cognitive processes of the mind ruled by Mercury. Neptune is the mystic whose consciousness underpins the forces of idealism which leads towards spiritual understanding and a higher vision.

Yet illusion also beckons because Neptune is sensitive to the lower psychic plane and to the astral plane which is thought to be linked to mankind's emotional nature.

Symbolically, the water element is usually thought to represent the emotions and of course, water was the domain of the mythological Neptune. Neptune endeavours to illuminate and expand individual consciousness to the extent that it becomes capable of understanding true reality and becomes aware of the Universal soul and the finer world existing within and beyond the solid earth. Cancer is the sign of Neptune's esoteric rulership.

A weakly aspected or unaspected Neptune in the chart suggests that the client is extremely impressionable and may have difficulty in distinguishing fact from fiction, in some areas of his life. However, there is likely to be great sensitivity which may be expressed through clairvoyance or healing. Any talents are likely to be expressed sporadically and discipline may be hard to maintain.

When Pisces ascends in the consultation chart, Jupiter as the traditional ruler should be examined and judged before the consideration of Neptune is undertaken. A comparison should then be made of the two planets, judging which is stronger by aspect, sign and angularity. Should Neptune's influence dominate over that of Jupiter, it could be that the client is reaching for much higher and more spiritual understanding and meaning to his life. This may initially be expressed through sacrifice and loss but eventually leading to the gift of healing and compassion.

PLUTO, THE RICH ONE ♇

ASSOCIATED SIGN	Scorpio
EXALTATION	Leo ?
DETRIMENT	Taurus
FALL	Aquarius ?
QUALITY	Cathartic
COLOURS	Maroon, dark red
MINERALS	Plutonium
PLACES	Undergrowth, subterranean caves, wasteland, undergrowth, graveyards, 'hell', Tartarus, the unconscious
BODY	Genitalia, reproductive system, bladder, colon, prostate gland, enzymes, sacral vertebrae, solar plexus, defecation, pus
PERSONFICATION	The masses, powerful people, healers, sexton, boatman, undertaker, miner, detective, psychologist, therapist, dictator

KEYWORDS	Self-purification, ejection, revelation, plutocracy, power, force, fanaticism, strength, willpower, zeal, the unconscious, unscrupulousness, largesse, influence, death, regeneration, fate, magic, elimination

The Psyche

Astronomy
The planet Pluto - smaller even than the Earth's Moon - was discovered in 1930 at 17 degrees Cancer conjunct the malefic fixed star Wasat. Its diameter is only 1,430 miles (2,300 km) and is made up of rock and ice. During its summer, the frozen nitrogen evaporates creating a temporary atmosphere. Pluto has one moon suitably named Charon after the boatman who carried the souls of the dead to the underworld. It has a very thin atmosphere and a frosty surface. It takes 249 years to revolve around the Sun in a very eccentric orbit, which is more elliptical and tilted, relative to the orbits of the other planets. At times this brings it within the orbit of Neptune and thus closer to the Sun.

Mythology
Pluto was associated with the Greek Hades, god of the underworld and lord of the dead. He was the son of Saturn and Ops and brother to Jupiter and Neptune. After overthrowing their father, the three brothers divided the world between them by casting lots in a helmet. Jupiter won the sky, Neptune acquired the sea and Pluto became god of the underworld, though this prize was not quite to his satisfaction it seems. His chagrin was understandable as his palace beneath the sea was a grim and dark place surrounded by sombre cypress trees. He was an unpopular god, feared by all because he granted no favours. Nothing could move him. He ignored prayers and was unappeased by sacrifices. People's pleas usually fell on deaf ears.

    The dark and murky river Styx separated the world above from the world below so Pluto enlisted the help of Mercury in guiding the souls of the dead to the underworld. Mercury would lay his golden staff on the eyes of the dying easing their transition to the underworld through a peaceful sleep. The aged boatman Charon demanded a coin from the dead souls before he ferried them across the river to the fearful Tartarus. If they refused to pay up they were left stranded on the bank for a 100 years. The first grim stop was Eerebus, then the hapless souls entered the Asphodel Fields, an even more shadowy and cheerless place guarded by Cerberus, the three-headed, dragon-tailed dog. The dead, lacking consciousness and bodies, surrendered to a shadowy existence in grinding continuance of their former lives.

    Rarely did Pluto visit the world above except on some nefarious affair. He made sure he wore the helmet that made him invisible before embarking on his journey. It had been a gift bestowed upon him by the Cyclopes after he released them from Tartarus on Jupiter's order. On one of these excursions he came upon the lovely maiden Kore (Persephone) playing with her friends in a cornfield. Just for once the hardhearted Pluto felt a tug at his heart strings and fell in love. Not one to hesitate, he seized the distraught maiden and carried her off to the underworld. His chariot was a splendid one drawn by dark-blue steeds, though Kore of course, was much too distraught to notice. Her aggrieved mother Ceres (Demeter) abandoned her duties at once, and began the long search for her daughter. Jupiter decided to intervene since Ceres was goddess of the harvest and in her absence the earth lay fallow. Although Kore was now Pluto's bride and Queen of the Underworld, she was allowed to spend a few months on earth with her mother each year. Hence the descent of cold winters upon the earth when Kore goes back to be with her husband in the forbidding underworld.

Somewhat grudgingly Kore began to tolerate her new spouse though the union was never blessed with offspring. Indeed, Pluto endeared himself to no-one except Mars since the warlord was kind enough to send him so many souls slain in battle. Naturally, theirs was an uneasy alliance.

Pluto's underworld contained a spark of hope in later legends. Although it was still regarded as a place of retribution, the souls of the 'good' could expect to be fairly treated. There were three judges in Tartarus - Minos, Rhadamanthus and Aeacus - who adjudicated over the dead where three roads met. Those who were neither virtuous nor evil returned to the Asphodel Fields and those who were considered evil were sent to the punishment-field of Tartarus. The fortunate few who were virtuous in life, went to Elysium or the Islands of the Blest where they enjoyed great happiness and tranquillity. They could also choose the time of their rebirth.

Pluto also has a connection with wealth since it was believed that precious metals came from his kingdom. He was referred to as Dis or Orcus, the giver of wealth. Manilius refers to the second house as the Gate of Hades and the Portal of Pluto and the second rules resources and finances.

Astrology
At the time of Pluto's discovery in 1930, the basic structure of society was undergoing tremendous upheaval. A ban on the consumption of alcohol had been in force in the United States since 1920 and only ended in 1933. It was known as the era of Prohibition. Many people believed that intoxicating liquor was responsible for the rising incidence of poverty, violence and crime. Paradoxically, people drank more during Prohibition than before. The era that saw the rise of the 'speakeasy' (an illegal saloon) and the bootlegger (illegal seller of alcohol) also witnessed escalating criminal activity.

The Outer Planets

In the late 1920's and early 30's, the democratic governments of the world failed to control the economic hardship and mass unemployment caused by the Great Depression. This fuelled the Fascist Movement world-wide, particularly in Germany under Adolf Hitler, Italy under Benito Mussolini and Spain under Francisco Franco. Fascism, which emphasises nationalism, decrees total subordination to the state with unquestioning loyalty to a leader. This totalitarian regime exhorted its adherents to "Believe, Obey and Fight!" Fascist countries saw the role of women as passive home-makers and mothers for future fodder for the armed forces.

The cataclysmic nature of Pluto was verified with overwhelming force by the bomb dropped on Hiroshima on 6th August 1946 killing around 130,000 people. This occurred a month after an eclipse of the Sun at 17 Cancer, the degree of Pluto's discovery. The atom bomb was created by manufacturing Plutonium in a nuclear reactor. This immense energy was set free when bombarded with the atom Uranium.

Traditional astrology has always associated Saturn with death but obviously his domain is enthusiastically shared by Pluto. Pluto is often responsible for mass destruction. The planet does represent physical death although its action is usually associated with transformation indicating a renewal of phenomena in either a physical or psychological way. This means the end of one way of life and the beginning of another. Pluto's action is quiet and deadly with upheavals that highlight the storehouse of past experiences. These need to be faced, dealt with and forgotten. Pluto's action suggests a purging of the unconscious, forcing confrontation with either personal, family or racial taboos. This is normally an exceedingly painful eruption as all the repressed dragons and goblins spring out on the world stage after years of forceful repression. Pluto represents what Ebertin calls Force Majeure suggesting that the individual may be caught up in circumstances beyond his subjective field of operation, like war for instance. He then becomes part of a group destiny complying with Pluto's connection to the masses.

As with the myth, the astrological Pluto invites one to descend into the underworld, or the deep unconscious, before experiencing rebirth. The reward for accepting the invitation is freedom from psychological complexes or physical obstacles and the emergence of new concepts. Pluto is responsible for spiritual and psychological surgery. Its very name implies birth and transformation since Pluto (the Greek Plouton) stems from the Sumerian Buro-tun signifying 'deliverer of the womb' and 'teems with, be full, burst forth'. Pluto is therefore, connected to physical birth, the womb or genitals, as well as the reproductive system.

Esoteric view
The purpose of Pluto is to cause transformation in order to destroy those factors that hinder synthesis. In action Pluto tends to act invisibly or unconsciously. His business is to bring about destruction, physically or psychologically in order to build anew. Pluto drags to the surface all that inhibits the personality from true expression and produces death of those hindering factors which prevent synthesis. Pluto governs the lesser burning ground in order that he may live in truth in the higher land of light. Pluto's transformative action brings one from the depths of hell to the light of heaven by working through the destructive and urging powers of spiritual Will. By destroying the bonds of Matter, liberation of spirit occurs. The death of the physical body is through conscious choice as the goal is to be reborn in spirit. Pluto is connected to Pisces esoterically, suggesting dissolution, transformation and rebirth.

When Pluto is weakly aspected or unaspected in the consultation chart, it may indicate unwilling subjugation to the will of others in a specific area of life. There is a possibility that complete annihilation of one phase of life occurs before a totally new one begins. An example of this would be in taking on a new identity or name and relocation to another country and cutting all ties with the past.

When Scorpio rises in the consultation chart, Mars should naturally be looked upon as the traditional ruler. However, as Pluto is also associated with this sign, it would be helpful to examine the planet's position and strength in the chart. If Pluto is making his presence felt strongly in the chart, it is possible that the client needs to synthesise the enormous changes taking place in his life and be ruthless in severing ties with the past.

6

THE MAGIC DRAGON AND THE WOUNDED HEALER

The Magic Dragon

Astronomy
The North Node (Dragon's Head) and South Node (Dragon's Tail) are points in the sky where the path of the Moon crosses the path of the Sun. The point where the Moon rises from the southern hemisphere to the northern hemisphere, via the ecliptic, is referred to as the North Node. Exactly opposite in the zodiac lies the South Node. The imaginary connecting line between both points is the Moon/Node line or nodal axis. The Nodes' motion is always retrograde so that they move backwards through the zodiac signs. A complete retrograde cycle of the Nodes takes 19 years.

Mythology
Traditionally the Nodes of the Moon have been referred to as The Dragon's Head and Dragon's Tail (Latin Caput Draconis and Cauda Draconis respectively). The names derive from the fact that eclipses occur at the Nodes obscuring the light of the Sun. In the same way, the Moon's light is dimmed when the Earth passes between the Sun and Moon. It was thought, predominantly in Indian culture, that a great dragon had consumed the Lights.

The dragon is a powerful symbol in the folklore of many cultures. It often has a terrifying visage with great flapping wings, huge claws, a serpent's tail and fiery breath. The dragon is often seen as evil and pernicious, and its destruction is requisite in attaining peace and harmony. An Egyptian myth for example, relates how the Apophus dragon of darkness, was conquered every morning by Ra, the Sun (light) god. The legend of St George and the dragon also describes the tale of victory over evil. In Hindu mythology, Indra, god of the sky and giver of rain, slays Vitra, Dragon of the waters, to deliver rainfall. In Oriental mythology, however, the dragon symbolises celestial and terrestrial power, wisdom and strength. In classical mythology, the dragon represents guardianship. It is the dragon of Ladon that guards the golden apples in the garden of the Hesperides. Juno (Hera) received the golden apples from Mother

Earth on her wedding day. The Greeks and Romans believed that dragons were able to convey the secrets of the earth to mortals.

Astrology
The North Node is evidently exalted in Gemini and falls in Sagittarius. Traditionally, the North Node has a better reputation than the South as it has a benefic action. It brings advantages and is fortunate for life and health particularly when conjoined to the Ascendant and in good aspect to other planets. Its action is likened to that of Jupiter. It is seen as the contact point whereas the South Node is viewed as the separation point. The North Node aims towards the future and a new cycle of experience, yet there is need for courage to experience the new circumstances that greet us at the North node. The path becomes open for greater fulfilment.

The South Node is apparently exalted in Sagittarius and has its fall in Gemini. Traditionally it is malefic. Its action is to obstruct, crystallise and hinder, somewhat like Saturn. It is seen as the separation point in contrast to the North Node which is the contact point. It tends to describe past habits, well-trodden experiences and established behaviour patterns that may be detrimental to present life growth. The South Node therefore, pulls the individual back to old habits and the North Node offers new opportunities for growth. The South Node drains the organism and is harmful for health.

From a more spiritual viewpoint, the Nodes represent the major key towards understanding life as part of a continuing thread through the many lifetimes of incarnation. The Nodal line shows the soul's path in the current life (whilst the rest of the chart adds information as to how the life-journey is made). The Nodes also point to alliances, relationships, associations and organisations. Strong nodal contacts between charts in synastary point to fateful relationships. Vedic astrology sees the North Node (Rahu) and the South Node (Ketu) as dealing with the concept of death and rebirth, transformation and regeneration and the unfolding of individual consciousness. This is because of the Nodes' role in the eclipse of the Sun (consciousness) and Moon (mind) and the obscuration of their light. Evidently, after the eclipse, when the Luminaries are free to shine again, there is greater energy and power.

The planets ruling the North and South Nodes should further describe the circumstances which need to be experienced in the unfolding consciousness of the soul and personality. If the Nodal line configures with specific planets in the consultation chart, the issues represented by the planets may be fated in some way. The situation is likely to indicate issues that need to be addressed most urgently, to avoid future repetition. Naturally if the North Node is involved, a new and ultimately positive situation occurs which could have future important ramifications.

Chiron

Astronomy
The asteroid Chiron was discovered in 1977 in an eccentric orbit between the planets Saturn and Uranus. Astronomer Charles T. Kowal of the Hale Observatories in California discovered Chiron at 3 degrees 8 minutes of Taurus on 1st November. Around 320 km (200 miles) in diameter, Chiron has a dark surface and a comet-like orbit but is much larger than any known comet. Chiron was the first asteroid seen in the outer solar system - most of the asteroids are much closer to the Sun usually somewhere between Mars and Jupiter. Chiron was listed as minor planet 2060. In 1988 Chiron seemed to double in brightness.

Mythology
Chiron was a centaur - half man, half horse - and various myths exist describing his birth, life and death. Although most of the centaurs were savage, Chiron was wise, civilised and kindly. His wide-ranging knowledge assured him rulership over the Centaurs. His particular interests were archery, music, prophecy and above all healing. A son of Apollo, Aesculapius, who became the god of healing, learnt his arts from Chiron. Chiron's knowledge of healing derived from his own unhappy and unfortunate birth. His father was the stern god Saturn and his mother was Philyra, a sea nymph. Saturn's dalliance with Philyra was an adulterous one and to evade the watchful eye of his wife Ops, he coupled with the sea nymph disguised as a horse.

Chiron was born half man, half horse and disgusted his mother. She rejected him at birth and asked the gods to 'make her other than she was' and was turned into a Linden tree. The orphan Chiron had to fend for himself. Since he had an immortal father, the part of his divine self had great wisdom. He became the teacher of both mortals and gods and among his pupils were Jason and Achilles. Though his mother despised him, a nymph called Chariclo did not object to his looks and married him. A daughter, Endeis, was the fruit of their union.

His death was accidental, brought about by Hercules who wounded Chiron in the knee with a poisoned arrow. Unfortunately he could not be healed, but neither could he die because he was immortal. His fate, it seemed, was to suffer eternal pain. Ultimately, Chiron was able to evade his torturous fate by relinquishing his immortality to Prometheus. Prometheus, one of the Titans, was known as a benefactor of humanity. He stole fire from the gods and gave it to the mortals, for which naturally, he was cruelly punished. Jupiter had him chained to a rock in the Caucasus, where he was preyed upon by an eagle who pecked at his liver. After exchanging places with Prometheus, Chiron died. He was set up in the heavens by Jupiter as the constellation Centaurus.

The Consultation Chart

Astrology
Chiron in astrology has many enthusiastic adherents and equally as many who feel that his place in the chart is superfluous. In the same way some astrologers feel that the chart can be easily delineated or judged by using only the seven traditional planets. There is undoubtedly a great deal of truth in this. Certainly I feel that the easiest route into delineation is initially from a traditional viewpoint and then perhaps moving on to look at other factors, like the outer planets and Chiron. If an outer planet or Chiron are in prominent positions in the chart, it would probably be unwise to ignore the message inherent in the placement.

The chart or map of the heavens is only a cosmological signpost to the psyche and the individual astrologer chooses his personal instruments to elucidate understanding. However, staying with traditional rules is advisable if prognostication is part of the judgement or delineation, particularly employing the traditional rulers of the signs. A more psychological view of the consultation (or natal) chart opens the door to whatever the astrologer feels better equips him or her in delineation.

Chiron in psychological astrology signifies the part of the psyche that is deeply wounded but where healing can also take place. It is interesting that Chiron was discovered at the degree of the Moon's exaltation (3 deg Taurus), signifying the emotions, the mother, and the wound of rejection perhaps?

The mythological Chiron was wounded twice in fact: once at his birth and then physically by an arrow. In the same way, the chart may show by Chiron's placement where we are wounded physically or psychologically. We are then given the choice to either feel overwhelmed by our wounds or to learn from them and use the new-found wisdom in some positive way. Like Chiron, as indeed with many therapists and healers, childhood wounds serve to help in the development of understanding and compassion. The intensity of this wound depends upon the placement of Chiron in the chart. Should it be configured with another planet for instance, perhaps in a hard aspect such as a conjunction, square or opposition, the wound is likely to be deeper and more painful. In a consultation chart, it is tempting to say that Chiron's placement describes a transient wound, but this is not necessarily the case. If Chiron is particularly prominent in the consultation chart, it may indicate that the time has now come for dealing with the individual's inherent difficulty and wounding. An opportunity arises for the client to face whatever may be troubling them.

7

ALL AROUND THE HOUSES

Activities relating to particular houses are generally looked upon as being of a transient nature where the consultation chart is concerned. Emphasis on a house or houses suggests that the client is dealing with the issues connected to that house/s, at this point in time. However, it is possible that present psychological issues and events may also highlight life-long problems. Descriptions of the houses can therefore, at times, be considered to include the more permanent qualities of the birth chart. These descriptions are divided into three sections: Physical, Psychological and Spiritual.

The *Physical* section refers mainly to the body parts ruled by the house in question and briefly, their function. After relationships and money, clients (at least in my own experience) seem to be eager to discuss their ailments - or maybe it is my own interest in pathology that attracts issues dealing with health! Nevertheless, clients do hope that the astrologer will discover the cause of their ailments and when they are likely to get rid of them. Health matters should of course be treated with caution.

The *Psychological* section can pinpoint the issues faced by the client at the present time and conflicts in those areas may become the psychological underlay to the disease or ailment suffered by the client. It would therefore be helpful to look at the ailment and the issues of the house/s in question and offer help and guidance in this regard. The Psychological section generally, will probably be the most useful guide in understanding the client's present dilemma.

The *Spiritual* section may to some extent expand the meaning of the houses and this may be of interest to some clients. Many people however, are polarised in personality needs, they are concerned with more earthbound, practical matters, and are not unduly bothered with the meaning of their problems and suffering. Yet there are those who do consult an astrologer at times of their greatest anguish and pain because they no longer understand the point to their trials and struggles. The Spiritual section serves as a guide in helping the astrologer to unravel some of the client's conflicts in a deeper way. Ultimately, each client's perspective of life should be accommodated without the astrologer forcing their particular viewpoint on the client.

Some houses are traditionally viewed as more fortunate than others. This derives from the ability of the house to support life, so survival is the name of the game. For instance, the first house is designated the most important house of all because it governs the constitution and naturally, a good and healthy constitution armed with a positive and happy outlook suggests vitality and the strength to combat the vicissitudes of life. The fifth and ninth houses are deemed fortunate because the qualities assigned to them support life - joy and faith respectively - but also because they are in trine to the Ascendant which is of course, an aspect of ease. Following the fortunes of the latter are the third and eleventh houses, as they create a sextile to the first house, also an aspect of ease.

The fourth and tenth begin to create difficulties because they form challenging squares to the first and of course, the seventh opposes the Ascendant and planets therein can affect the health especially if they closely aspect the ascending degree.

The energies of the sixth and eighth houses are quite detrimental to health since they rule ill-health and death respectively, creating the inconjunct (also known as the quincunx) aspect of 150 degrees, often termed one of ill-health. This aspect can also be seen as one of vision as well, therefore suggesting that the difficulties of the sixth and eighth can generate insight, awareness and ultimately change.

The second and twelfth houses are obviously a semi-sextile (30 degrees) away from the first, and ostensibly have nothing in common with each other. The twelfth offers dissolution whereas the second rules the amount of prana (vitality or energy) the constitution can draw upon, so a weak second house may be detrimental to health - in a consultation chart, this may only be a temporary condition.

Descriptions of planets in houses are naturally given to stimulate thought and facilitate interpretation and cannot be taken literally in every respect.

THE FIRST HOUSE

Physical

The first house governs the physical body and its degree of receptivity to disease. It describes the constitution as a whole and gives an indication of vitality or lack of it at the present time. The rising sign may determine or predispose the part of body affected by physical ailments, i.e. Sagittarius rising emphasises the hips and thighs. The face as well as the eyes, ears, nose, tongue and teeth also come under the rulership of the first house. It particularly governs the head as well as the brain. The pituitary gland is ruled by this house. Known as the master gland because it regulates the output of other glands by producing stimulating hormones. Also the pineal gland is ruled by this house and though apparently not functional, it releases the hormone melatonin, thought to be connected with establishing the body's daylight cycle. Esoteric thought suggests it governs the Third Eye and spiritual perception.

Psychological

The first house is of supreme importance because it governs the client's manner of expression and present attitude towards his surroundings and the circumstances he finds himself in at this moment. It is the lens by which he perceives his existence at this time. By observing the ascending sign, aspects to the ascending degree as well as noting the position of the Ascendant ruler, it is possible to develop a sense of empathy with the client and identify his frame of reference. A correct summation of the client's emotional and mental attitude at this moment in time will help to develop trust between astrologer and client.

If the rising sign also governs the twelfth house, this suggests that self assertion and optimism are at a low ebb. The client may feel unsupported, isolated and trapped by his life circumstances. The ease or difficulty in handling the present life circumstances will of course depend on the aspects to the ascending degree and the planetary ruler. It may be helpful to suggest to the client that this may be a period where he is probably learning more about self-reliance and developing inner qualities of strength by having to fall back on his own resources.

If the rising sign also governs the second house, this indicates that the client's chief concern at this moment is with his finances. Judgement should be made as to the ease or difficulty he experiences in his financial affairs. It may also indicate that he has to be especially resourceful at this time to create the kind of life he may wish for himself. If his values change in the process, then his basic outlook and attitude to life will also be subject to transformation.

Spiritual

If one believes that life is part of a series of incarnations, then it might become apparent that the physical body is a storehouse of subtle vibrations abundant with past-life memories. Besides the physical body, which grapples with the material problems of day to day living, the human being possesses three other bodies. These are the etheric body which transmits the vital energy or life force; the astral body which relates to the person's emotional state and thought patterns and the causal or spiritual body which influences Soul purpose. All these bodies are part of the Aura, the field of energy surrounding the physical body.

The first house therefore rules spiritual as well as physical action and the emergence of the Soul purpose. Some clients may be concerned more about finding their path in life, what they have to learn in this incarnation and what the lessons may be at this present time. If such a client is concerned with the deeper meaning behind his present life circumstances, he will probably want to know how best he can handle the situation and possibly how he can contribute to society. In the consultation chart, the rising sign and planets placed in the first house will determine a more transient image of the energies that the client has to face than those determined by the natal chart.

Planets in first house

Moon
The client may be in a fluctuating state of mind at this moment and decisions should be put off until he can see the larger picture. His views tend to be very subjective and coloured by his emotions which may seem overwhelming. He becomes overburdened by environmental pressures. He may be too quick to react to what is happening around him seeing insults where there are none, yet he has an instinctive awareness of the subtle nuances in his surroundings. This gives him an acute understanding of other people's needs. He will gradually allow other people to rely upon him for emotional support and thereby he will become more aware of his own strength.

Mercury
This is the house of Mercury's Joy where mutual emphasis on the mind suggests intelligence and deep thought. This enables the client to deal rationally with any prevailing difficulties, reason rather than emotion being master. Oratorical ability may be apparent and this should give the client greater confidence in self expression. Too much emphasis on the mind however can show mental strain. In Hindu astrology, the first house rules the senses, as does Mercury, so afflictions here might emphasise problems with hearing or speech.

Venus
A charming and pleasing attitude seems to attract the benevolence of others. The consideration of others' needs might bring good fortune and success in life. There may be a feeling of peace with the environment and any problems

and pressures are dealt with in a positive manner. A sense that happiness may be just around the corner makes it easy for the client to see the good in others which in turn helps foster amicable relationships. There may be a tendency however, to expect good fortune without making too much effort.

Sun
This position shows that the client may be learning more about himself and his real needs. Opportunities occur to influence others, since power and authority may be thrust upon him. He may well have a stimulating effect upon others and be able to inspire and enthuse others to grow into their full potential. The client's sense of identity becomes stronger and he gains a sense of self importance. The main pitfall is that he may become too full of himself which may alienate where at first he attracted. There may also be a need to do everything with gusto possibly leading to exhaustion.

Mars
Associated with the first house through rulership of Aries, the first sign, Mars here indicates the development of strength and courage through struggling with opposing forces. An urge to take action without forethought might be evident, but the client fully realises that only he can help himself now. With the mind set on personal needs, other people's sensitivities may be overlooked, albeit unconsciously. Extra energy becomes available with fresh input into new and existing projects. Assertion and willpower may be in abundance. Dealing with anger is a possibility and making decisions on impulse may have to be watched.

Jupiter
When placed in the first house Jupiter promises a period of prosperity and expansion coming into the client's life. This should be an extremely lucky period when the right decisions are likely to come easily. Faith and trust in the good will of others seems to attract the kind of opportunities that may have future benefits. There is no dwelling on the past and all thought is for the future. There may be an abhorrence of restrictions and any plans made will more than likely be on a big scale. The kind of optimistic attitude present now indicates that the client is not likely to take heed or caution and may overextend his credit and finances. An idealistic attitude may need grounding in reality.

Saturn
A close association with the first house through the Chaldean order of planets suggests strengthening of the positive aspects of Saturn. A serious approach to life is likely to be adopted. The planet's basic nature of course, is to bring obstacles and delays and no doubt these may be quite evident just at the

moment, however, these may well be surmounted with ease. This is likely to be a challenging time and health issues may be on the client's mind, though there should be a strong determination to overcome any illness. Projects begun now are likely to be of a lasting kind since the proper preparation has usually been made.

Uranus
At this time the client may feel that he is not in total control of his life and whatever he wants to do seems to go wrong - whatever he says might be misunderstood. Outer circumstances do not seem to accord with what is happening inside. Some changes of a profound nature are taking place and the client may want to dispense with the past and the old way of doing things. He needs to take a new direction in life. There may be a sudden departure from the normal scheme of things. Courage is needed to face new people and new circumstances and though this means uncertainty there is also much more excitement. New activities in science and technology may come to his notice. Partners and friends may think him obstructive just for the sake of it. The emphasis is on personal freedom.

Neptune
This is a favourable time for pursuing interests of a spiritual nature. Indeed clairvoyant qualities may be in evidence. There could be a greater sensitivity towards people and human suffering. The subtleties of life and inner meaning become more important than outer trappings. There could be a growing faith in the goodness of humanity and the possibility that one can be redeemed through love. The client may aspire to such highly refined goals but it may be through the process of sacrifice and selflessness. For a time the client may feel that he has no voice, that he is exploited and a feeling of impotence may inhibit action. This experience may be his path towards renouncing the ego where personal ambitions merge with those of a higher will.

Pluto
A situation is presenting itself to the client which may temporarily halt his more personal plans. He has to deal with very important matters that may even alter the course of his life in ways he had not foreseen. He may be tempted to go from one extreme to another before he can find a true balance in his life again. It is possible that circumstances will arise which will give him a taste of power. He may be put into a situation where he has to take control. He may be lifted above the normal scheme of things and could be involved in some selfless and charitable project. Personal concerns may not be of such importance. How he deals with this situation may increase his inner strength.

The Second House

Physical

The throat and neck are principally governed by this house as well as the thyroid gland. The thyroid glands helps to regulate metabolism, the process of life by which tissue cells are renewed from chemical substances carried in the blood and derived from digested foods. The thyroid gland also participates in the development of the embryo and therefore has a direct influence on the reproductive system. The parathyroids, situated behind the thyroid gland are also ruled by this house and their function is to control the uptake of calcium from the blood. The larynx, or vocal organs are also ruled by this house.

Psychological

This is the house of psychological and material resources. It can indicate the client's present ability to function in the material world through shrewd manipulation of his finances. It can show the manner by which he attains wealth, the value he puts on his personal goods and how he develops his income. What indications there are of his chances of profit and gain.

Emotional security also comes under the domain of this house, whether he feels secure in his present circumstances or not as the case may be. To some extent, this house also governs the client's intrinsic values. Is he avaricious and possessive refusing to share his goods and himself with others or does he use his resources, both physical and psychological, in order to help others. Emotional possessiveness may be a feature of this house especially if survival issues are in question. Since food is a substance also governed by this house, food-related illness can be considered here.

Spiritual

This house is indicative of the amount of Prana or energy the client has at his disposal at this time. Prana is the Hindu name for Vital Force or Life Force. Prana is the impact of solar forces emanating from the Sun and absorbed by the Earth before it enters the etheric body and passes to the physical body via the Vital Fluid ruled by the Sun. An abundance of Vital Force or Prana signified by beneficial planets and aspects at this time show the client to be strong and vitalised, able to withstand whatever obstacles he has to confront. In other words, how much confidence and drive is at his disposal. Malefics here can disturb the health.

This can also be the house of illumination - or not - as the case may be. Is the client's vision of reality limited to material values? Does he view money as the passport to all his dreams? Perhaps he manipulates others for his own ends? Or does he slowly begin to acquire spiritual values, his priorities becoming more concerned with the welfare of others. He may become involved with raising money for charities. Ultimately he may either be driven by desire for his own satisfaction or alternatively find a purposeful direction to his life.

Planets in the second house

Moon
Emotional security is sought not only through an exchange of feelings but also through a financial settlement. Money becomes an important issue and needs to be dealt with before any commitment to a relationship is made. A fluctuating situation may exist right now since there may be indecision with regard to intrinsic values. Time is needed to make proper judgements and in the meantime, the life may be subject to a see-saw of emotions. Security and emotional well-being rests upon having a comfortable home, good food to eat and attaining quality possessions. Some possessiveness may be apparent because of the fear of losing loved-ones.

Mercury
Finances gain greater importance in the client's life just now and there may be development of financial expertise. The mind seems concerned with different ways of making money with talents in this field becoming more evident. If one source of revenue dries up, he will soon find himself thinking about other possibilities. It is important to assimilate the facts of each new project before moving on to new ventures. The practicalities of all money-making schemes should be carefully considered and there is a chance of putting ideas into a concrete form. Correspondence will feature greatly and money could be earned through writing.

Venus
A strong connection with this house derives from the planet's rulership of Taurus, the second sign of the zodiac. This may put the emphasis on seeking and hopefully, attracting the luxuries of life. Certainly there is a need to surround oneself with love, beauty and pleasures of various kinds and every possibility of money becoming available to afford such items of comfort. There is an ever-present desire to have the best that money can buy. Self-indulgence may have to be watched however, as the appetites are particularly strong at this time especially for food, which could lead to weight problems. Sensual appetites are also rife and there may not be much evidence of self discipline.

Sun
Much vitality seems to bless the client just now and he may feel confident in obtaining all the resources he needs. A well aspected Sun can bestow

tremendous energy and the client may feel that he is able to accomplish all his goals. He may have to make sure that he is not driven by a sense of greed. It is possible that the growth of financial success will foster a strong sense of security. A sense of power and self worth may be gained through acquiring money and possessions. There may be much thought spent on what really constitutes security and power.

Mars
Great potential for amassing finances and developing projects which will bring worthwhile remuneration. The right motivation and strategic prowess is likely to be part of the client's armoury just now. Resources gained however, may be subject to easy dispersion. Easy come, easy go as the saying goes. What is more likely to happen is that money gained will soon go out through the arrival of a bill at the same time. Nevertheless, the wherewithal to pay off debts is likely to be at hand. Working hard for the necessities of life might encourage entrepreneurial skills. The client may develop the right instincts about stocks and shares.

Jupiter
A close association exists between Jupiter and the second house through the Chaldean order of planets. As Jupiter is considered to be the planet of wealth this combination may indeed bring good fortune into the client's life. Indeed, there could be an over abundance of resources though the client may feel that he never has enough. A drive for the good things of life may lead to dissipation and self-indulgence. Greed, avarice and acquisitiveness may be issues for the client to deal with, yet conversely, there could also be impulses of great generosity. Food and drink may be taken to excess at this time.

Saturn
Difficulties may arise in resources and this is a time of hard work in order to acquire sustenance and wealth. It is not possible to rely upon the benevolence of others at this time. Everything depends upon the client's ability to plan and structure his working life in order to keep the wolf from the door - yet every opportunity exists however, to acquire great wealth. Each and every penny will be treasured because nothing has come easily. A serious approach to life and money may suggest miserly behaviour and this combination of planet and house may teach important lessons about sharing.

Uranus
Finances are likely to be subject to fluctuation since the management of resources may be erratic just now. The need for discipline may go unheeded, but there is a possibility of sudden wealth becoming a feature of life just now,

which might come through winning prize money, games of chance or through a legacy. This will bring great excitement but also disruption to the normal everyday routine. New conditions may be beneficial if a new lifestyle is readily adopted. The client could develop a talent for new ways of making money.

Neptune
This is a very good time to develop fund-raising activities on behalf of some good cause, and if this is the client's aim just now, help and support is likely to arrive from unexpected quarters. A common bond, towards some idealistic aim, is likely to bring a feeling of comradeship and spiritual union. It may not be the best time to seek personal wealth, in fact, finances may be at their lowest ebb. Resourcefulness is likely to be the most positive outcome during this time of insolvency, making way for the attainment of new spiritual values. Some deceit or embezzlement may be experienced through others and caution is advised in all money matters.

Pluto
As Pluto is a planet of extremes, financial matters attributed to this house may be subject to great fluctuation. It is possible that a great monetary loss afflicts the client or conversely and much more happily, he may be in receipt of a huge amount of money. Pluto likes to clear away debris and all loose ends and this will also apply to financial matters. It is time to sort out insurance, taxes and legacies. The client may have to release some possession dear to him, maybe as a symbol of letting go of a possessive streak which has created problems in the past. Pluto in the second can also bring changes in general health as it can affect energy levels. The client may have to examine his diet.

The Third House

Physical

The shoulders, chest, arms, hands and fingers are ruled by this house. Some say it also rules the breath and the lungs but traditionally the lungs belong to the fourth house. The third house may well rule the thymus gland which atrophies in adulthood but is thought to have some connection with immunity in childhood.

The third house governs the lower, practical mind. It rules expression in speech and mode of gesticulation. The nervous system which is a dual system comes under the domain of the third and reflects the duality associated with this house since it divides into the Central Nervous System and the Peripheral Nervous System. Each system has both sensory and motor nerves but has different functions. The Central Nervous System includes the brain and spinal cord. The brain is responsible for cognitive and many other processes governing communication. The PNS, which connects the nerves and spinal cord with the outlying regions of the body, further divides into the somatic system that chiefly controls the skeletal muscles and the autonomic system controlling heart muscles, glands and digestion. This surely confirms that thought influences physiological function. Temporary disturbance of the mind may also manifest under planetary affliction.

Psychological

Self expression and mode of communication come under the domain of this house. How is the client making himself heard at this time? Is he finding the right words by which to express himself? He may be feeling somewhat restless and begins to look for new challenges to stretch his mind. This may involve studies either for pleasure or to enhance his professional standing. He may decide to study languages. His restlessness may involve undertaking many short journeys at this time. Since communication is the key to this house there may be emphasis on speech making and debates. Other areas of communication that are particularly emphasised just now include reports, letters, the postal service, written deeds and contracts. Also, rumours abound at this time perhaps not to the client's liking.

This house also governs brothers and sisters, who once upon a time were more important to existence and survival than in prevailing times. Psychological issues with siblings may still need sorting, however. Do his siblings act in a friendly and supportive way, standing beside him against adversity, or does the client feel betrayed by the very people he thought he could count on? How far do these issues extend into the past? It may now be time to deal with this, especially if resentment is part of the equation.

This house also rules neighbours who again in times past may have been more important to survival than today. Good neighbours can give a sense of belonging in the community whereas difficult ones can be a source of terror. How is the client dealing with such issues at the moment?

Spiritual

This is a house of duality, principally suggested by the division of body and soul. The lower mind is connected to the body or the physical aspect of manifestation. It deals with practical issues emphasising the use of logic to satisfy curiosity. This house refers to the beginning of awareness of the more subtle issues governing life. It is the house describing the initial steps taken on the path towards spiritual understanding. Outer planets placed here particularly suggest a correlation with a search for higher knowledge.

It is the house of Manas, or the mind substance and planetary emphasis here at this time may show a gradual awakening of the mind to more subtle forms of communication. This may include an interest in telepathy or mediumship. Perhaps the client is now appraising his external situation in terms of memories of past-life experiences. It is often the attitudes developed in former incarnations that form the pattern of present thinking which may be either favourable or detrimental to present life circumstances. Our siblings, as well as parents, are the people who initially activate past life memories and if these are traumatic, the memories may become locked within rigid and perhaps destructive thought patterns. Subsequent relationships can reactivate those thoughts and emotions. If the third house is emphasised at this time it may be helpful to look at the client's relationship with his siblings in order that he may exorcise the unhappy emotions connected to those first early relationships.

Planets in the third house

Moon
The fluctuating Moon experiences its Joy in this house of duality producing a mind that is flexible, adaptable and imaginative. An instinctive ability to communicate with people at all levels bestows popularity. The client may at this time be concerned with writing, either in a professional capacity, or having to deal with more correspondence than usual. Studies are undertaken which may be connected with caring/healing, literature or travel. There is much movement and more frequent journeys may occur on behalf of the family. Relationships with siblings and neighbours may fluctuate perhaps due to misunderstandings.

Mercury
An association with this house comes through Mercury's rulership of Gemini, the third zodiacal sign. This indicates a present quality of mind that is quite volatile and preoccupied by a variety of topics. There may be too many irons in the fire perhaps making it difficult to focus in one direction. A thirst for knowledge however, may indicate important studies of some kind. A changeable state of mind makes the client unpredictable. There is likely to be a great deal of communication from many different sources. Emphasis on the nervous system may induce tension and anxiety.

Venus
An ability to get on with all types of people helps the client achieve his aims and objectives. People in the immediate environment respond co-operatively and communications may well flow with ease leading to greater understanding. Knowing instinctively which attitude to adopt can accomplish much in

prevailing negotiations. New and influential acquaintances may appear on the scene. A tendency to weigh things up fairly brings opportunities to settle outstanding quarrels with siblings and neighbours. There may however, be a tendency at this time to sit on the fence and avoid commitment.

Sun
The client begins to gain more influence in his immediate environment through improved methods of communication, which may just mean he becomes more sociable and looks up old friends, family and neighbours. Perhaps he has bought himself a computer and is now busy making contacts through the Internet. He begins to understand and appreciate people of different backgrounds and endeavours to value different opinions expanding his consciousness in the process. He begins to stretch his mental powers through some form of study. He may have to watch a tendency to be too opinionated.

Mars
The warlord is associated with the third through the Chaldean order of planets which suggests that a razor sharp mind may be at the client's disposal. He finds that he always has the right words at his command. This may give tremendous powers of self-expression and repartee. Verbal debates turn in his favour as he argues his case well. Arguments may however, incur the enmity of those around him as they begin to resent his need to always have the last word. Arguments may occur with close associates. Studies where active research is required may arise. Sporting activities may be a way of burning up surplus energies at this time.

Jupiter
Knowledge of many subjects may find the native involved in an advisory capacity as well as in some areas of education. He becomes a good speaker, knowing instinctively how to put ideas across, and an excellent disseminator of knowledge. An insatiable curiosity may give a love of learning for its own sake. Reading more philosophical literature may start to attract. He hardly has time to spare to co-ordinate the different strands of his life effectively as he is so busy. Everything seems to expand more than he anticipates and work is doubled. There is greater emphasis on contacts with siblings and neighbours.

Saturn
People in the close environment, including siblings and neighbours, start to create problems. Misunderstandings may occur which need great effort to resolve. Extra patience is needed when people prove to be uncooperative. Confidence in self-expression may be somewhat low at the present time tending to inhibit social interchange. Harder work is needed to acquire knowledge and

expertise. Knowledge will create greater confidence. Deeper fields of interest seem to attract though there may be a tendency towards depression or negative thinking.

Uranus
Unexpected events occur within communications. Thinking becomes less linear and more comprehensive. This may indicate superior intellect or being misunderstood by the people closest to him. Ideas may be a little ahead of his time and he could appear a little odd or eccentric. This may however, be a tremendous period of creativity just needing a correct channel for expression. There may be a feeling of restlessness and decision making could become difficult. Sleep may be disturbed since the nervous system could be over-activated. A disruption to the mental processes may create irrational fears. People seem to pop in and out of his life making this period an exciting though erratic one.

Neptune
The imagination is now at a premium since Neptune dissolves all barriers, both mental and physical. A time of great inspiration and creativity with forays into writing, literature and travel. It is possible that recent creative blocks will now easily be dissolved. However, difficulties may arise in dealing with the practicalities of life. There could be danger of mental stress. Misunderstandings may occur with close relationships, siblings as well as neighbours. It's probably best not to believe all one hears at the present time. Gossip and scandal may prevail.

Pluto
Circumstances arise in the client's life that threaten to unsettle his mental equilibrium. He is torn in two different directions finding it hard to make the right decisions as he rightly feels that decisions made now will be important for the future. Circumstances arise forcing him to think more deeply about life and death issues. He may be attracted to studies that give him more insight into human nature, such as psychology and anthropology. People he has lost contact with reappear in his life. Past issues of sibling rivalry may have to be settled. Conversely, he may now lose contact with people he has been close to. New neighbours may threaten his tranquil life as they turn out not to be a patch on the old.

The Fourth House

Physical

This house rules the stomach, the digestion of food being its function. It churns the food mixing it with acid and enzymes that help to break up the food. Under stress the stomach may become extra acidic, giving rise to indigestion and other gastric ailments. High up in the abdominal cavity, close to the stomach, is a network of nerves comprising the Solar Plexus, the seat of emotions. Under stress these nerves tighten and the breath becomes much more shallow inhibiting the flow of oxygen. Traditionally, the lungs are also ruled by this house, perhaps because the breath inaugurates birth and life. The fourth house is concerned with the cycle of birth, life and death.

The breasts are also under the dominion of this house, which in females are involved in milk secretion or lactation. As milk/food is essential to survival, issues of security may underlie any physical problems arising in this area.

The adrenal glands also seem to be associated with this house. There are two of them situated above each kidney. Each gland is divided into an inner Adrenal Medulla and Adrenal Cortex. The former produces the hormone adrenaline preparing the body for physical activity, often described as the hormone of 'flight or fight'. The Adrenal Cortex produces two steroid hormones which play an important part in the metabolisation of fats, carbohydrates and proteins as well as playing a part in sexual development.

Psychological

As part of the Terminal Triangle (along with the eighth and twelfth) this house rules the end of life and decay. As such, it is quite possible that the client is at this moment reassessing the foundation of his life, looking back, perhaps, at his past relationship with his parents and family and maybe thinking of making changes. Habit patterns of the past and the parent's expectations may now be subject to reappraisal. The client may begin to re-organise his inner boundaries and becomes more aware of how he really needs to bring happiness into his life. The identification with his familial background and race, often in an undifferentiated way, is now an issue subject to reconsideration.

This house traditionally rules the father and issues concerning him. The psychological influence of the parents is described by this house particularly with regard to the client's ability to love and capacity for nurturing. If the fourth contains malefics, the client's relationship with his parents reveals a possible difficulty in emotional matters.

There may of course, be involvement with property, which may entail buying up real estate, moving house or perhaps becoming an estate agent. The treasures of the earth are featured in this house; mines and minerals for instance as well as orchards and gardens. There may be a strong love of the land resulting in nationalistic fervour. Interests could develop in archaeology, genealogy as well as family psychology.

Spiritual

The fourth house serves as an anchor for the Soul and describes the initial surroundings it has to deal with. It is the attitudes accumulated in past incarnations that attract the Soul to conditions that reflect them in the current physical manifestation. It rules the last thoughts of the previous incarnation bringing joy or perhaps perpetuating past conflicts into the present incarnation. Past-life conditions are initially enacted within the family environment. The early family structure will then set the tone for future relationships. The ties with the family are of karmic origin and any negative feelings should perhaps be faced then forgotten so that they do not encroach upon the future.

Since the conditions showing the end of life are also featured by this house, it suggests that our last thoughts and experiences of the current incarnation form the basis of our next incarnation. This house may also show the experiences of the Soul within the mother's womb, therefore, giving rise to our deepest, though often unconscious, feelings and emotions. It is also the house of mass consciousness and giving rise to telepathic gifts that tune into the public mood. The spiritual family or ashram is indicated by this house reflecting love of home, land, patriotic fervour and ultimately the love of humanity as a whole.

Planets in the fourth house

Moon

The Moon is associated with this house through its rulership of Cancer, the fourth sign. Family relationships and domestic issues tend to confront the client. Contact with family members may be subject to fluctuation and change. Problems from the past may surface causing tensions to rise. It is a time to confront and settle ancient misunderstandings, yet great effort is needed to change old habits and attitudes. Issues involving caring may arise. Perhaps there is a need to look after a sick relative or discussions about residential care may ensue. There may be thoughts about moving home and creating a new base, or perhaps there is a desire to enter a retreat or sanctuary. Matters involving real estate may need to be sorted out.

Mercury

A need arises to understand the self and personal environment probably through family concerns. Heated discussions may ensue causing difficulty in objective decision making. Thoughts may dwell too much on the past which could inhibit present and future plans, yet there could be an increasing interest in history and genealogy which may bring feuding families closer together. There could be much paperwork to sort through in connection with the home and family. Home studies could be featured just now.

Venus
A search for peace in the home may bring a desire to settle differences with family members. The client may be called upon to act as a mediator between warring parties though there is a basic inclination in fact, to avoid such strife and discord just now. Peace at any price may only serve to obscure rather than deal with outstanding family problems. There may be a renewed interest in the home at this time. Money may now become more available giving the client the opportunity to decorate the home to individual taste with no regard for the cost. An interest in gardening may bring a deeper interest in horticulture.

Sun
An association exists between the Sun and the fourth house through the Chaldean order of planets. This may be a crucial position for the Sun since the past may interfere with anchorage to present conditions. It is possible that the family and home make such enormous demands that other issues have to be suspended. Added responsibilities are thrust upon the client without warning. There might also be illness within the family because the 'vital powers' are weak when the Sun is placed in the fourth, apparently. Yet this may be a time for inner spiritual development through an interest in reincarnation, ancestry, genealogy, etc. Rather than dwelling on the past it would be more useful to learn from it and build new foundations. Buying or selling property now may be symbolic of the client's urge to actually change the foundations upon which his life is built.

Mars
Disputes and arguments are likely to arise within the family home. Harmony may be a rare commodity just now. Anger long suppressed, may come to the surface, which may ultimately turn out to be quite positive, as ensuing discussions could release long held resentments. Parents may be particularly demanding at this time and may try to interfere. Unexpressed feelings may lead to stomach problems. There may be much activity in laying the foundations of an enterprise or making practical home alterations. Occasional struggles, may however, be a feature of family life for the time being.

Jupiter
The client has the wherewithal to build a better and more prosperous life foundation. This could be done on a spiritual level by eschewing past habits

and going forth with new philosophies and ideas or on a material level whereby a spanking new home reflects acquired wealth. Certainly there should be a feeling of security and optimism. It is possible however, that there may be a feeling of restlessness and a move may be imminent. A likelihood of buying one's dream home perhaps. Expansion in the home is likely through a new addition; perhaps this signals the birth of a child. The home may be physically extended through the addition of a loft or patio.

Saturn
Circumstances at home may be difficult and somewhat restricted at this moment, giving little elbow room. Family concerns seem to intrude on the individual's life calling upon the kind of sacrifices which leave little time for personal pursuits and objectives. Looking after an elderly relative could be a burden or perhaps a labour of love. There may also be a need to restructure foundations after the departure of a family member. This might mean leaving an old home for a new one or learning to live without a loved one. It is possible that the end of an old way of life is imminent. Throwing out old treasures may be a hard task but it could reflect the acceptance of a new beginning. Security needs to be found within oneself as it is almost impossible to rely upon anyone else just now.

Uranus
Upheavals in the home seem certain to take place with maximum disruption. This may create a feeling of alienation making the individual feel almost 'rootless' at this time. Estrangement from family members could exacerbate difficulties all round causing widespread breakdown in communication. It is possible that the break-up of the old is really paving the way for the new. The introduction of more modern ideas may interrupt the tranquillity of family relations. This may entail a simple house renovation or the introduction of new technology, like a computer. Traditional values seem to have little importance within the family circle just now. This may eventually be to the good.

Neptune
The foundations of the home or family become less secure. Building works may be suspect and do not go to plan. Misunderstandings occur within the family, which appear to be no-one's fault though some family members may not be contributing an equal share to home expenses. All this may indicate that its time to view one's own place in the family structure and perhaps time to sever one's roots. A time to leave the nest also means that it is no longer possible to rely upon the family for emotional sustenance. Perhaps the time

has also come to build a more spiritual foundation to life by starting afresh in a place more conducive to one's ideals rather than relying on family tradition.

Pluto
Some family members may at the present time be difficult to get along with and the household may be dominated by a person who seems bent on causing the greatest friction. Power struggles may occur between parents and children. The upheavals occurring at this time may be hard and difficult to bear but they may be instrumental in booting skeletons out of the closet giving the family a chance to settle ancient arguments and rifts. It might be tempting to settle old scores in a deleterious way which will however, only serve to perpetuate bad feeling and exacerbate family feuds. Forgiving and forgetting past family hurts creates better understanding for the future.

THE FIFTH HOUSE

Physical

The fifth house rules the back as a whole, back of the shoulders (scapula region) and the sides. Rulership is also given to the spinal cord and the vertebral column which support the back. The vertebrae, consisting of 33 bones, divide into the cervical, thoracic, lumber, sacral and coccyx regions of the spine. The fifth house probably relates more specifically to the thoracic area - the middle back.

The heart, the muscular organ that pumps blood through a system of blood vessels to all parts of the body, is ruled by this house. The blood proteins, which are important in maintaining the correct balance of the blood plasma, are manufactured in the liver which also comes under the dominion of this house. Plasma is the watery substance in which the blood vessels and nutrients are transported. The liver also produces blood clotting agents and of course, has many other functions amongst which are the storage of glycogen and iron which are taken from the food we eat. Rulership is also therefore, given to the stomach (as well as the fourth), which helps to break up the food.

Children and parturition are also connected to the fifth. Tradition has it that the bearing of children is promised if 'fruitful' signs are on the fifth house cusp (Taurus, Cancer, Scorpio and Pisces). The Moon, Venus and Jupiter placed therein also promise progeny. The 'barren' signs, (Aries, Gemini, Leo and Virgo) deny children or give a small family. Mars, Saturn as well as the Sun also tend to deny children when placed in this house or tend to bring difficulties in conception.

Psychological

This is a joyful house oriented towards pleasure. Quite possibly the client needs to have fun at this moment of his life, perhaps because he has been dealing with family responsibility (echoes of the fourth) or working hard (thoughts of the sixth). His pleasures tend to be found in the theatre and the arts as in painting, music and dancing. Sports or visiting 'taverns' may also attract! These days such watering holes are equated with pubs, clubs and other places of entertainment. The leisure industry also comes under the rulership of the fifth house. Hobbies enjoyed for recreational purposes are described by this house. Whatever gives the client pleasure is found here and emphasis on the fifth house might indicate that the client either spends his time in idle fun or is very enthusiastic about some particular interest. It is possible that he may be thinking of turning a hobby into a career. This could involve some hazard as this is the house of risk and uncertainty. Perhaps he is thinking of giving up a mundane job to pursue his interests? Or does he eschew hard work and hope to gain his riches by games of chance? Is he involved with gambling and does he have gambling debts?

The appetites are likely to be quite strong at this time and he may want to surround himself with good food, plenty to drink and generally indulge himself with luxury, beautiful clothes and expensive furniture. Indulgence may also take the form of love affairs, joyful they may be but perhaps not have the blessing of marriage. This house is more likely to describe 'affairs' rather than committed relationships, although courtship does belong to this house which of course, may be a prelude to marriage. Sexual pleasures are more likely to be emphasised at this time which no doubt is the reason why children also come under the rulership of the fifth house! The client may find himself in the parent-role or he becomes more involved with problems or aspirations of an existing child. Alternatively there may be problems with a child if malefic planets are found here. Scandals also seem to feature in this house.

Spiritual

This is thought to be the house of the Soul and referred to as the Mansion of the Soul. If the Soul is taken to be the part of the individual which somehow portrays the purpose for the present incarnation, then perhaps the fifth house can give a clue to the Soul's present point on the earth's compass. A desire to create individualistic works may be an unconscious urge to uncover the meaning of the present incarnation. The person becomes more conscious of himself, his attitudes and how his thoughts and actions affect people around him.

Emphasis on this house indicates how far the personality with its egotistical aims has fused with the more impersonal drives of the Soul. This is found within the energy of Love. Does he pursue self-centred interests being entirely focused on his pleasures or does his expression of love aid others? The joy he experiences now is based on the freedom and release he feels in finding his purpose in life. This gives him tremendous vision and the willpower to achieve his creative goals. He develops the kind of strength and magnetism that attracts others and bestow leadership. He may be specially gifted and talented in whatever he chooses to do.

Perhaps his interest in children now is not only for creating progeny, but he becomes concerned for their welfare on a more humanitarian level as in some rehabilitation programme. Helping children with special needs may attract.

Planets in the fifth house

Moon
A yearning to externalise inner needs and find new creative outlets may be of importance just now. This may take the form of a renewed interest in hobbies and pastimes for which he has special talent. At this moment he needs to establish himself as an individual. It is possible that some special expertise may lead to professional status. No longer content to be part of the crowd, he now wants appreciation for his unique gifts and talents, yet he hesitates before stepping outside familiar territory being somewhat apprehensive knowing there are risks involved. He is naturally creative. This may of course, also involve some new and challenging situation with children.

Mercury
Not content to hide his light under a bushel, the client now needs to externalise his talents in different fields of creativity and he becomes absorbed in his own interests. In fact, he could be multi-talented with his fingers dipped in several pies possibly featuring writing, painting and music. There may be a call to perform in public, delivering speeches or perhaps becoming involved in the dramatic arts. Teaching children could be a prominent feature. Involvement in a project that puts him at the head of creative teamwork may reveal leadership abilities.

Venus
With the Joy that Venus experiences in this house the pleasure principle becomes greatly emphasised. The client definitely wants to follow his heart and indulge in interests that inspire and offer fulfilment rather than those which are carried out purely for duty's sake. This might be a particularly happy time in the client's life without too many cares to cause him grief. There is now time for recreation bringing renewed interests and an added zest for life. Skill and success in the theatrical arts or indeed in any creative pursuit may

bring honours. This could also be a highly romantic period where relationships bring joy but perhaps lack commitment. This may not be a problem if both parties are happy with the situation. Too much ease may bring a hedonistic attitude however, and perhaps responsibilities are ignored. Children could be a real source of pleasure just now.

Sun
As ruler of Leo, the fifth sign, the Sun feels comfortable in this house. This may be a time to relax and follow the dictates of one's own heart. At this point in his life, the client may become dissatisfied with the image he presents to the world and wants to explore other avenues of expression. He puts on different masks to see how they fit. Ultimately he just wants to become himself whatever that may be. Therefore, recreation and hobbies become important and at first, he just seems to want to play. This is his way of finding out what suits him best. He may take up creative pursuits for the first time. He may of course, seek to be the centre of attention just for the sake of it.

Mars
Most things the client does right now bring him to other people's notice. He may try to extend his talents further and achieve the kind of goals he did not at one time think were possible. Energies need to be directed wisely however, otherwise exhaustion may follow such intense activity. He becomes highly competitive and goes in pursuit of adventure. Romance may be a little rocky but exciting though commitment could be lacking. Children will be fun but also quite tiring. There is a need to take risks, gamble and forge ahead with matters that prove him to be alive and kicking.

Jupiter
A tremendous need for exploration and adventure sees the client in pursuance of his dreams. He may travel widely across the physical terrain or through the mental planes of the mind. He is not content with staying with the familiar - he now wants something new in his life. He dips his finger in many varied pies as if seeking something special. He wants to be an individual. Not content in going along with the crowd - he wants to stand out. He also wants fun and not to be constrained by duty. An increasing sense of adventure puts the emphasis on freedom. This could be a particularly happy period which brings blessings in love, romance and money.

Saturn
Pleasures may have to be sacrificed for the sake of duty. All creative acts are painstakingly executed with little initial reward. The client feels thwarted in pursuance of his own needs. There is a tendency at this moment to devalue

oneself through lack of appreciation. He feels reluctant to make spontaneous gestures in case of criticism. A serious attitude may lead to pessimism and negativity. He has to take heart because all the hard work and perseverance are likely to pay off eventually. Creative projects or pregnancy may lead to exhaustion, in fact, there may be some difficulties with children. Delays may be experienced in conception.

Uranus
There may be a feeling of boredom at this time and perhaps a tendency to take more risks than usual. Restlessness may be best expressed through a new interest. There is a need to stretch talents to the limit and not worry about what people may say. Perhaps it is time to be more innovative and break away from the mainstream of current thought. Certainly the client's non-conformist attitude makes him stand out in a crowd. Children may prove difficult right now since they too want to assert their individuality. They are not likely to conform to traditional family values. Love affairs may be electrifying but possibly brief.

Neptune
In this position Neptune can urge the client towards creative works that will benefit humanity. This might be expressed through drama or music therapy or any other therapy which involves using the creative imagination. The client may be in a position to inspire others by his kindness and compassion. Ego trips are likely to lead nowhere as the emphasis is on selflessness. Creative performances in the theatre/film world may be much admired. Romance now takes on an almost surrealistic quality. It can be a very uplifting time but reality may bring a few surprises. Perhaps some sacrifices may have to be made in relationships. Children may become difficult to understand at this time, and possibly talk more about imaginary playmates.

Pluto
It is possible that the client has something quite unique to present to the world. It may be time to take a chance and turn his life around. He is likely to make a powerful impact on others through his creative acts. There is a tendency to become totally absorbed with certain projects perhaps to the exclusion of other activities in his life. He may indeed have to adopt a single-minded approach as all tasks are likely to be hugely challenging. Whatever he does now may create dramatic changes in his life. Big adjustments may have to be made due to the arrival of a new addition to the family, such as a child. There may be a feeling of resentment if talents are not recognised.

The Sixth House

Physical

This is the house of sickness, as opposed to the first house which is the house of health. Indications in this house reveal how the vital force is disrupted. The sign on the sixth house cusp tends to reveal the part of the body afflicted at this time:

Aries - head, brain
Taurus - throat
Gemini - chest
Cancer - breasts and stomach
Leo - back, heart
Virgo - intestines

Libra - lower back, kidneys
Scorpio - genitals
Sagittarius - thighs, hips
Capricorn - knees, bones
Aquarius - calves, ankles, circulation
Pisces - feet, immunity

Generally speaking, if the sixth house planetary ruler is stronger than that of the first house ruler, the disease has a strong hold on the individual at this time. Planetary strength of course, is mainly judged by its supremacy in Essential and Accidental Dignity.

The small and large intestines, are principally under the rulership of the sixth house. The small intestine absorbs nutrients and enzymes here complete the digestive process. The duodenum, the first part of the intestine, receives food from the stomach and then passes it to the jejunum and ileum which absorb the end products of digestion. The large intestine, or colon, is where most of the water is absorbed from the food residue, so by the time the residue reaches the rectum it consists of solid faeces where it has no nutritional value. Therefore, food is also ruled by this house, as well as by the second.

The sixth house shares rulership over the liver with the fifth house, linking into the digestive system through its storage of bile responsible for emulsifying fats, as well as the storage of vitamins. To some extent the kidneys are also ruled by this house. Their main function is to take unwanted substances from the blood and to pass them on to the bladder to be excreted in the form of urine.

Psychological

This is one of the more difficult houses since it is indicative of a breakdown in the client's general welfare. It is possible that emphasis on this house points to the client's concern over health issues, his own or that of close friends or family. A decline in his own health may be due to the stress of coping with everyday life particularly with matters appertaining to work. The client's basic dissatisfaction or unhappiness may even be unconscious, and the sign on the house cusp, besides pointing to the part of the body afflicted, may be indicative of the psychological underlay to his illness. It may in any case be much safer for the astrologer without medical knowledge to discuss the client's illness from an emotional/psychological viewpoint. Here is a brief list of possibilities describing the psychological conflict underlying the physical illness.

Aries The client may be dealing with issues of anger that he finds hard to express. Frustration of objectives comes through his own inability to assert himself and face problems with courage. He needs to lead rather than follow.

Taurus Money problems beset him or he is facing a conflict of values. He may find it hard to express his creativity. The words seem to stick in his throat. He should try to find where the blocks to progress lie.

Gemini He cannot make up his mind on important issues and may have a problem communicating his needs. He needs to focus with positive intent in one direction rather than dissipate his energies. Issues with siblings may need to be addressed.

Cancer Family issues may be effecting him on a deep emotional level. Possibly past emotional hurts have not been addressed and still effect present relationships. It may be necessary to re-establish contact with family members and work on difficult issues.

Leo May find it difficult to follow his own creative urges perhaps because his talents remain unrecognised. May have problems with children. Should perhaps identify where his personality may have dis-empowered others as this may indicate why he lacks their support now.

Virgo Resentment that he is always in the background whilst others get the credit. He is always playing second fiddle. He may also be the subject of unfair criticism. He should start believing in himself and be more positive.

Libra	Relationship problems and fear of loneliness make the client more dependent. This may suffocate the partner. Now is the time to learn to stand more securely on one's own two feet.
Scorpio	Difficulty in getting over losses whether financial or emotional. Big upheavals occur and it's time to move on and let go of negative emotions.
Sagittarius	Freedom curtailed in some way. There is a need to expand and discover new horizons, but there may be obstacles in the way of progress. Need to backtrack and sort out problems.
Capricorn	Humiliation is suffered, probably at work. He may not get the promised promotion and goals sought may not be forthcoming. Disappointment suffered makes the future appear bleak. Needs encouragement.
Aquarius	Finding it hard to fit in with his peer groups. Feels lonely and misunderstood. He might be very clever and ahead of his time, but others think him an odd-ball. Needs to find people who share his views.
Pisces	May be dealing with issues of exploitation and victimisation. Wants to run away and hide. Needs to learn how to confront problems rather than escape through negative forms of expression as in drugs and alcohol.

It is also important to look at the ruler of the sign on the sixth house cusp, since its sign and house placement may be indicative of the client's present problems.

Of course, the sixth house also relates to healing and it is possible that the client now finds his true vocation within this area. Nutrition could be of interest, with the sixth house connection to food, as well as all matters relating to the health, hygiene and food industry. This might include surgery, general medical practice, dentistry, nursing and complementary therapies. Small animals are also ruled by this house, so veterinary surgery can be included.

Matters to do with the client's work environment may be on his mind particularly his role as an employee. Servants and slaves were traditionally ruled by this house attesting to its restrictive nature and generating feelings of victimisation.

Spiritual

This is the house where the first steps are taken towards spiritual living rather than vocalising some vague ideologies. Practical application of spirituality may result in service to others often expressed in charitable works, caring for the sick or infirm members of the family or dedicating the life towards healing. Sacrifice of personal needs and desires may lead to a period of solitude and celibacy.

Hindu astrology suggests that the sixth house bears the residue of difficult past karma that may manifest itself in the form of illness. This may in turn forge an interest in various methods of purification in order to create a body that is a worthy vehicle for the Soul. Such methods may include physical exercise, breathing exercises, interest in nutrition and adopting a more wholesome way of living. This may lead to taking an interest in environmental issues as well as working for the benefit of the animal kingdom. Further drives for purification of the body may extend to clearing emotional residues from the astral/emotional body which could take the form of self-healing, counselling, past-life regression therapy or dream analysis. The goal is to develop a realistic perspective and a sense of discrimination when engaged in purification practices in daily living. Anything taken to extremes can of course, be prejudicial to health and welfare.

Planets in the sixth house

Moon
Some anxiety and vulnerability may be experienced through environmental changes that effect health and work. This could involve scrutinising past habit patterns to make sure that they do not interfere with the functioning of the body and/or everyday life. Diet may need to be changed and perhaps improved. It may be time to look into the emotional underlay of any physical illness that arise through past emotional conflicts. The daily work routine may need to be reviewed to make sure that health issues do not arise through lack of employer care and duty. Also the client may need to ask himself whether he is in the right job and if it is time to move on. A strong sense of service may involve the client in a caring profession or voluntary work.

Mercury
This is a strong position for Mercury since it is associated with the sixth house through the Chaldean order of planets as well as through its rulership of Virgo, the sixth sign. The mind is busy acquiring detailed knowledge with particular

interest in research and finding solutions to problems. Too much mental activity may cause anxiety through setting extremely high standards and then failing to live up to them. The strength of the mind in this position may either induce psychosomatic illness or give it the ability to heal the body. Matters to do with health may occupy the mind encouraging an interest in nutrition and perhaps writing on health matters.

Venus
Selfless love develops and is probably expressed through a new interest in service and healing. The joy of helping others to find happiness and achieve freedom from poverty and illness will give great satisfaction. Even if work is hard it is carried out with a serene heart. Sacrifice for a loved one is done willingly. Care needs to be taken to ensure that sacrifices do not lead to exploitation. There may be greater ease in getting along with colleagues in the work environment and improved working conditions gradually make work a joy. An interest in beauty and complementary therapies may develop.

Sun
The client begins to curb individualistic desires in order to help others achieve a sense of their own importance. He becomes organised, accepting boundaries whether self-imposed or imposed by others. He adheres to routine tasks without complaint and begins to acquire the kind of discipline that will help him achieve success in the future. He may even become a specialist in his field of work. However, the vitality is said to be lowered when the Sun is placed in this house possibly because the client labours under conditions not conducive to his welfare. He becomes a workaholic and never rests, or is in a job with no prospects. Perhaps by identifying where the problem lies, and correcting it, vitality may be restored.

Mars
The fiery planet is associated with the sixth through the Chaldean order of planets. This is best expressed through healing for Lilly tells us that Mars, especially with Venus in this house is 'argument of a good physician'. Mars of course, rules surgeons. Psychologically, this implies that Mars cuts out that which has outlived its usefulness, its incisive nature quickly discerning the root of any problem. Otherwise, this powerful energy may feel a little constricted in a house that is basically about service to others. Nevertheless, if these energies are diverted to the service of others, great achievement in healing and service is possible. Finding the right niche in the work area can lead to great achievement since a lot of energy may be made available to help in executing difficult tasks.

Jupiter

A promise of improvement in the working environment seems to promote a more positive attitude which in turn has a beneficial effect upon the health. Employment may become more congenial making the mundane execution of the work load more pleasurable. The employer/employee relationship improves and future prospects look promising. Though there is a feeling of expansion, ideas have to be contained within the bounds of plausibility. These constraints may be very helpful however, since it will help the client focus on what he really wants out of life. Could have a real vocation to serve and may be attracted to spiritual or religious observances or rituals.

Saturn

Courage is needed to get through this particular period since life may seem more like drudgery than fun just now. The emphasis is on work rather than play and this can be very dull indeed. Nothing seems to happen to make the pulse race with excitement. There might be a feeling that no matter how hard the client works there is very little appreciation or pay. An appraisal should be made of the prevailing life routine. The client should ask himself if things have been going on for longer than necessary. The obstacles to change may appear immovable and help should be enlisted to get through this difficult time. A negative outlook may lower the immune system.

Uranus

It is possible that there is no longer much joy in a routine that has sustained the client until now. This is probably in the field of work where restlessness and boredom may set in and there is a need to change methods of working. New technology may be introduced which may unsettle the client initially though this could ultimately bring a new level of awareness and improved working methods. The old pattern of life and work needs to change and resistance may bring possible illness. Disorders affecting the nervous system may result perhaps of a spasmodic nature. Some possibility of accidents occurring at work which may really be an outward symbol of basic dissatisfaction and the need for change.

Neptune

This position of Neptune may be indicative of the client's need to be of service to humanity. Working without reward may mean simply giving time voluntarily, perhaps as a Samaritan, working in a charity shop, or becoming a hospital or prison visitor. The client wants to be of use to others in a tangible way. Or he may decide to take up work within the caring and healing professions. Financial remuneration may not be forthcoming at first and there may be a struggle initially to establish oneself. It is possible that health at this time may be undermined and the immune system may need building up. The client has to ask himself if he is happy in his station in life. A respite from work may help to put things into better perspective.

Pluto

Pluto's quality of elimination tends to act drastically in the area of health. An extreme case could indicate replacement or removal of an organ or the client suffers from a disease that is difficult to diagnose. From a spiritual point of view however, an eliminative disease indicates wiping the slate clean of negative past karma. This obviously can only be of consolation to someone whose consciousness is so evolved that he can receive such information. Otherwise Pluto's position here can indicate sweeping changes within the work environment or trouble with subordinates, tenants and employees. Possibility of unselfish service to others on a large scale.

The Seventh House

Physical

The area between the navel and the top of the legs is ruled by the seventh house. The infant receives sustenance from the mother via the umbilical cord and once this is cut, independent life begins, as represented by the first house. The connection between the seventh and its opposite house becomes clear since the first house governs Life and the seventh the umbilicus. It seems natural therefore, that the uterus, the organ that holds the developing child, should also come under the dominion of this house. The reproductive organs generally are ruled by the seventh though there seems to be shared rulership with the eighth. Planets in this house, especially the so-called malefics, can affect the health since they oppose the first house. There is also shared rulership over the kidneys, bladder and intestines with the sixth house.

In horary, decumbiture and consultation charts, the seventh house also refers to the physician. Planets in the seventh and particularly the planetary ruler of this house will reveal whether or not the physician will heal the patient. This will primarily depend upon planetary dignity or debility as well as aspects between the first and seventh house planetary rulers. Tradition has it that should the seventh house ruler be afflicted, the client is not likely to pay much heed to the astrologer's advice!

Psychological

Binding partnerships come under the rulership of this house. Romance is secondary since the focus is primarily on contractual marriage; 'affairs of the heart', without legal commitment, are primarily ruled by the fifth house. This stems from the days when marriages were arranged for political and financial reasons rather than the fulfilment of romantic bliss. Emphasis on the seventh house indicates that the client is ready to enter into a lasting relationship and all the responsibilities that may entail. He finds that life has little meaning if he stands alone and now prepares to walk his path through life with someone by his side. How smooth that path may be depends upon the planetary picture.

Contractual alliances signified by this house may also indicate that the client is thinking of going into business at this time. Therefore, the seventh rules serious partnerships of all kinds. The spirit of co-operation is highly noticeable in his search for harmony and peace.

When this house is strongly emphasised, there is also the possibility that there may be too much reliance placed on the opinion of others. Other people's views may unduly influence the client and he may find himself in circumstances not of his choosing. Yet the search for harmony and peace may need to be fought for since paradoxically, this house also rules open enemies. These may be found within the marriage and business contracts, through an opponent in a law suit or in international warfare. In contest charts, this house rules the opponent. Ultimately this house seems to represent both harmony and warfare!

Spiritual

The seventh house from a spiritual viewpoint describes how the individual treads the middle path between the opposites represented by the body and soul, or spirit and matter. Total immersion in the spirit brings an imbalance as surely as the unqualified adherence to the material life. The emphasis is therefore on choice and decision-making. Love that brings two people together in partnership can be of a selfish, divisive nature whereby the couple involved become oblivious to the world around them and the needs of others. They become too absorbed in one another and this creates an imbalance. Love where the heart chakra is awakened brings a more unconditional love and with it right human relations. Then the balance between the spiritual and material life occurs naturally and people participate in a relationship as equals. This leads to achieving an inner balance and a deep recognition of one's needs and those of others. This may lead to employment in humanitarian organisations typically Amnesty International, Greenpeace etc. The battle with 'open enemies' now becomes a fight for truth and right human relations for all. The satisfaction of personal needs becomes of secondary importance.

Planets in the seventh house

Moon
Associated with this house through the Chaldean order of planets, the Moon urges unity with others and promotes shared experiences. Success in relationships comes through easy adaptation to the other's needs. However, there is a possibility of losing one's individuality by living in constant reflection of other peoples' opinions. Commitment to a permanent relationship is of importance now rather than casual romance. A need to care for someone and be cared for becomes necessary for emotional security. The client may have to ask himself if he is not holding on to a relationship out of a sense of security rather than true love.

Mercury
The client finds himself mingling with a great many people where he can exercise his talent in communicating with others. His ability to understand different viewpoints brings popularity and establishes good contacts. Even if plans do not work out at the moment, having the right connections will be of importance later on. He may find himself becoming easily bored if the opportunity to exchange ideas does not arise. However, a need to be with others may tempt him into alliances he may regret. Or he could find himself saying what other people want to hear. He might be accused of being superficial. It becomes necessary to guard against being unduly swayed by other people's ideas.

Venus
Associated with this house through its rulership of Libra, the seventh sign, a great emphasis is put on relating to others. Popularity and meeting with many people who are willing to help the client progress in life. Interaction with others seems more harmonious than usual. Relationships entered into are not undertaken lightly and commitment is the keynote. Loyalty is sought within relationships and even 'enemies' now become more amenable since differences are worked out more easily. With so much emphasis on relationships, there may be a tendency to rely too much upon others for physical and financial sustenance. No longer keen to stand alone, he sacrifices all for the sake of companionship.

Sun
The urge to unite with others is very strong so much so that there is a threat of losing one's own individuality. Living alone is no longer part of the equation and much energy is spent in relating to others. Marriage is seriously considered whether there is a likely partner on the horizon or not. The need for

companionship seems to outweigh almost all other considerations. A time when a more dependent attitude arises and a positive search for harmony is sought. It is likely that the social life improves since the search to associate with others is so pronounced. There is a need however, to curb the intensity by which relationships are sought otherwise prospective partners may feel overwhelmed.

Mars
'Marry in haste, repent at leisure' is the phrase that comes to mind with Mars in this house. There is an urgency to unite with someone in a committed relationship mainly because passions have been aroused. This may be fine if there are other factors in the relationship that are both stimulating and interesting, once passion has died down. Otherwise lovers may become enemies. This is not the easiest position for committed relationships as harmonious agreement is usually lacking. The client may find it hard to compromise. He does not like depending upon others yet circumstances may arise where he is forced to take a back seat at times. Uncomfortable though it may be, it may teach him a sense of balance.

Jupiter
Emphasis on relationships brings with it a need to find fulfilment on every level. A commitment can occur at this time but not for long if there is a feeling of constraint. A need to understand oneself is crucial as the urge for freedom may outweigh the need for togetherness. Security becomes unimportant and the emphasis rests on the realisation of inner needs. A search for partners that are fun, light-hearted and yet interesting ensues. This might be a time when infidelity threatens a hitherto stable relationship through the need to explore new partnerships. There may be an attraction to people of a different culture.

Saturn
This placement often indicates a serious approach to relationships. There is no fooling about and laughter and fun may be in short supply. The client may feel that it is time to 'settle down'. A search ensues for someone who fulfils the client's more practical needs. Relationships may not be very exciting but that seems of little importance compared to the security they offer. Duty rather than love may be more apparent in relationships just now. Saturn is a malefic planet and in the house of 'open enemies' may show that there are deep and somewhat difficult issues to work out with a loved one or with a business partnership.

Uranus
A measure of unpredictability enters the client's life since he begins to espouse new ideas about relationships. Or he may enter liaisons with partners who

demand more independence than he has encountered before. There is a need therefore, to deal with one's own sense of insecurity. Existing personal relationships may also be faced with disruptions. They may crack under the strain unless they are revitalised in some way. Partners' needs become difficult to comprehend. New relationships made at this time are likely to be transitory unless the commitment to one another also includes outside interests.

Neptune
This may be a time when the client feels he has found his ideal partner and refuses to listen to opinions to the contrary. Well meaning members of the family or friends introduce reality at their peril. It is possible that the client finally discovers a flaw in his present relationship which casts him into the depths of depression. Tolerance and forgiveness may need to be exercised. This planetary placement may bring mutual dependency rather than true love - his partner may lean heavily on him and a feeling of obligation arises which can be quite draining. There is a possibility of finding one's true soul-mate at this time.

Pluto
There is something quite compulsive about relationships at this time, and they are also likely to be somewhat turbulent. Power struggles are conceivable and these can be of an intensity that threaten to obliterate all traces of love. Indeed, love and hate seem to alternate in mutual expression of feeling. This could be the classic syndrome of 'can't live with them, can't live without them'. It is quite possible that what was once love will turn into a situation where the couple concerned become mortal enemies. As each tries to gain power over the other, it is important to find out why this may be so. It may be a case of projection, each person seeing their failings represented in the other.

THE EIGHTH HOUSE

Physical

This is considered to be a difficult house since along with the fourth and twelfth house, it forms part of the Terminal Triangle. Therefore it rules dissolution of energy and physical death in contrast to the hardy second house opposite. The groin area comes under the rulership of the eighth house including the genitalia and organs of reproduction indicating perhaps that within the seed of death there is a promise of new life. The bladder which connects to the kidneys through the ureter tubes is also governed by this house. The organs of elimination, the bowels for instance find a place here too. Poisons are associated with the eighth, since they corrode or destroy the whole or part of the organism and this house is of course, about decomposition. Not surprisingly, this house is often associated with ill-health.

Psychological

Outwardly the house of decay, death and loss seems to have very few redeeming features. It governs all that has outlived its usefulness and is now ready for the scrap-heap. When this house is emphasised in the natal or consultation chart, there is likely to be 'fear and anguish of the mind' as Lilly puts it. It brings obstacles and inhibiting factors that stand in the way of progress, or so it seems; experiences that really do feel like a descent into Tartarus. It reveals that 'flawed' part of ourselves which we try to disown by projecting it upon others. Yet we meet that flaw again and again as a character trait in other people. It is the house of taboos, those society imposes and perhaps our own illicit yearnings. It is often through intimate relationships that we come face to face with our own darkness. Here the client faces an opportunity to confront that part of himself which may need to change, an attitude or prejudice, that is no longer a viable part of his life. This may be referring to the 'transformation' associated with the eighth house in modern astrology.

This house reveals how far the client allows himself to become intimate with another person since intimacy can also be a form of death. Or does he choose a reluctant celibacy in order to keep his freedom? Here the client learns how to share himself and his resources with others. The sexual aspect of this house is not qualified by the fun and laughter supposedly experienced in the fifth house. Sex here may be representative of the never ending cycle of life and death.

Like its opposite house, the eighth also rules money but it is more likely to be unearned income and resources rather than what the client by hard work. These might include tax returns, inheritances, premium bonds and lottery stakes. Naturally, such luck is likely to be due to beneficial planets and the more favourable aspects. Otherwise with the malefics or outer planets placed in this house especially if receiving difficult aspects, financial loss and debt is likely to be experienced.

Spiritual

The pain often associated with this house is due to the struggle between the Soul and the Personality, or between the spiritual and the material life. The difficulties and obstacles that arise test the individual's strength and resolve under adversity. Through such trials he gains greater wisdom and understanding. He begins to see himself as he really is. Through loss he begins to see the transient nature of material life and so begins to explore the more subtle world beyond physical manifestation. This refers to the death of form and the freedom of the spirit, which is why this house is associated the occult and magic (and sex magic), black or white, depending on the evolutionary consciousness of the client.

The eighth house is also associated with Discipleship and contact with the Soul. The first sign of soul contact is usually through taking responsibility for others. This may be expressed in many ways as in voluntary work in a hospice perhaps or dealing with the deep psychological issues and traumas experienced by others. This is not a frivolous house, but it can ultimately bring rewards of a profoundly fulfilling nature. Rather than the pursuit of material resources, it indicates the gaining of resources of a more subtle, spiritual nature. It is possible that experiences gained at this time may create a new level of consciousness for the client and a feeling of rebirth.

Planets in the eighth house

Moon
Close intimate relationships are highlighted. Extreme sensitivity to prevailing undercurrents in relationships may however bring initial turmoil. Family squabbles involving resources tend to bring anxiety and anguish. The possibility of losing loved ones may lead to a deep feeling of loss and the client may have to undergo a period of mourning. A need to contact loved ones through some form of mediumship may be what the client is seeking in order to keep an emotional contact with the departed. Ultimately it will be necessary for the client to let go in order to move on into a new phase of living. This is a highly sensitive placement of the Moon.

Mercury
Superficial issues are no longer the client's concern. He delves into subjects that challenge his thinking. This may be in the field of psychology, the occult, detection, reincarnation and perhaps pondering upon the whole cycle of human existence. His investigative turn of mind encourages him to probe the mysteries of life and he becomes adept at ferreting out secrets. His attention may also be turned towards practical issues involving insurance, taxes and shared resources. Deep and prolonged research is a feature of life just now.

Venus
The usual equanimity of Venus is seriously challenged in the house of struggle. Feelings are aroused to a height that may seem alien to the client and so become hard to control. The strength of emotion threatens to overwhelm him and he may have to struggle with feelings of possessiveness, jealousy and even hate.

Battles arise in an existing relationship. A romance with an enigmatic partner with seductive appeal lures him into turbulent waters. Underlying everything is the fear of loss. The more the client tries to hold on the less he succeeds in doing so. He has to learn to give his partner more space.

Sun
Certain matters need to be confronted as it is no longer possible to avoid deep issues. Important future consequences could arise from finally dealing with a problem that has not gone away. Struggles with others over shared resources may be a feature of the life right now. There are many changes occurring and nothing remains as it was before. Power issues may be apparent giving rise to battles within intimate relationships. A test of strength occurs in all transactions, and there is a need to stand firm. Something is changing within the client that may effect all relationships. Interests develop along new channels which are quite different to the client's usual level of involvement.

Mars
This planet is associated with the eighth house because of its rulership over Scorpio, the eighth sign, indicating that courage and fortitude are qualities that must be developed at this time. It is possible that the client will be facing adverse circumstances. Contests of various kinds may generally be a feature of the client's life just now. There may be battles to overcome in the area of intimate relationships, sex and shared resources. Resentment and anger may be the emotions he has to face. Yet he seems to find the strength to deal with the difficulties that ensue. This may be a time of gain and loss in equal measure.

Jupiter
This may be a profitable time. Benefits could accrue through other people's generosity. Gains through lawsuits, insurance's, legacies and perhaps even the lottery may be made. Profits tend to be much more than one would expect. However, resources may become depleted at this time through the client's own overblown generosity. Interests could develop in the occult and spiritualism with efforts being made to contact the departed. Any crisis at this time is likely to be overcome by adopting a philosophical attitude. A time of growth in many directions.

Saturn
Associated with the eighth house through the Chaldean order of planets, Saturn placed here brings severe tests. The client may feel that the difficulties he now faces are insurmountable. It appears as if others deliberately put obstacles in his way. He experiences ill feeling everywhere he turns, and life seems like an uphill struggle. Intimate relations are likely to suffer most since affections may

cool and financial troubles loom. Yet there could be enormous growth at this time through developing patience, tolerance and perseverance. The client is likely to acquire great qualities of resourcefulness and attain greater maturity than hitherto before.

Uranus
Changes begin to occur which threaten to overturn the client's previous comfortable existence. There may at first be great resistance to these changes. But perhaps it is time to embrace new ideas and leave behind the cherished but outdated notions of the past. The debris of the past has to be cleared away before building a new foundation. A break in a relationship may occur as the shared interests of the past no longer seem viable. Resistance to these changes may only create the chaos the client desperately wants to avoid. It is a time to let go and detach from the present situation. Only in this way can an objective appraisal be made of the new changes. Ultimately, things should turn out for the better.

Neptune
The client becomes more aware of the subtleties of life and may be able to acquire consciousness on the two planes of existence. He can be used as the perfect medium. It is possible however, that he may, if dabbling with the occult, lose all sense of reality and experience a loss of power. He may find it hard to negotiate with others or get his opinions heard. There may be a lack of intimacy between him and loved ones. It might be difficult to understand what a loved one needs at this time. Ones own needs are not being met or so it feels. There may be a risk in starting any joint financial ventures at this time. Yet this could be a deeply enriching time if the client's mind turns towards sharing and giving and letting go of resentments of the past.

Pluto
An association with the eighth derives from Pluto's shared rulership of Scorpio, the eighth sign. Phenomenal changes occurring in the client's life leave him dazed and possibly confused for a while. He may find himself in a situation where he has to start afresh after the collapse of some project or relationship. Looking back at the past will serve no purpose as all that has gone before has outlived its usefulness and has little effect upon the future, except as wisdom through experience. The client may find a new direction in life especially if financial losses were involved. Possibly, all hindering factors to future progress are cleared away, allowing him to push ahead refreshed and reborn.

The Ninth House

Physical

The parts of the body ruled by this house tend to preside over movement. The legs carrying the weight of the body, are supported by the basin-shaped pelvic (hip) girdle which consists of two coxal bones. The hips also provide a surface for attachment for the muscles of locomotion, as well as protecting the organs in the pelvic cavity. This house also rules the thigh bone, or femur, which connects to the hip and is the longest bone in the body. The hamstrings, which flex and extend the thigh, also come under the rulership of this house as do the buttocks.

Psychological

Traditionally this is a very fortunate house perhaps because of its trine relationship with the first house as well as being the domain of God. Certainly devotional and religious matters come under its jurisdiction. This is where faith and optimism are found; the client's intrinsic belief system and his faith or religion is forged by experiences in this house. Planetary emphasis may bestow a positive outlook: no matter how bad things may appear at this time, better things are likely to happen in the future. It is not surprising therefore, that this is also the house of prophecy. Optimism keeps the organism intact if it can still look ahead to a future filled with joy. Many people who consult astrologers 'want something to look forward to'. However, malefics in this house can cause despondency, making the future look bleak and without hope. Paradoxically, the most fortunate of houses can breed despair at such times. It often falls to the astrologer to find 'meaning' for the client during these bleak moments as indeed the ninth does encourage the search for truth and meaning. Dreams, visions and divination are part and parcel of this house.

It is normally a house of joy and experimentation producing a great thirst for knowledge and a love of freedom. Emphasis on this house, therefore urges the client to find time and space in which to study and meditate - the main objective of those who retired into monasteries at one time. Monasteries of course, come under the ninth house banner. The first monks went into the desert to contemplate and meditate in an effort to seek a spiritual reality beyond physical manifestation. The freedom to search and investigate is an important aspect of the soul searching occasioned by this house. Monasticism is from the Greek word 'living alone'. Seeking truth in contemplation as well as in isolation was not only the domain of Christian monks. Monasticism also existed within the Islamic and Buddhist religions. An order of pagan hermits, the Therapeutae, was instrumental in promoting healing within monastic life, so besides becoming centres of learning, monasteries were also places where healing was sought. Spiritual healing may therefore be an aspect of this house.

Astrologically, the ninth is seen as the domain of the higher mind where intuition replaces logic. Psychologically a counterpart to this higher mind may be discerned in Sigmund Freud's *Super Ego*, the internalised representation of the values and morals of society. The main function of the Super Ego is to substitute moralistic goals for realistic gaols and inhibit the baser instincts such as sex and aggression. The ninth may also be represented by Roberto Assagioli's *Superconscious*, the source of higher feelings such as altruistic love, illumination or even ecstasy. The Superconscious evidently contains latent higher psychic functions and spiritual energies, as does the ninth.

The long voyages associated with this house may be illustrative of the sacred pilgrimages popular in the thirteenth, fourteenth and fifteenth century. Travellers undertook long and often perilous journeys to holy places either as an act of penance, thanksgiving or to seek supernatural aid. The client may now find himself on his own pilgrimage where he has to adopt a new philosophy by which he can live his life. This may derive through further studies or through travel to unfamiliar territories where he learns about cultures very different to his own.

The search for truth, which is analogous with this house, also brings within its domain the law, exploration, philosophy and publishing. The law seeks to govern society to control and prohibit unlawful behaviour in order to give freedom to others. Could this therefore, also be the house of conscience? Exploration, physical or metaphorical, grows from human curiosity, and encourages discovery, reportage and eventual aid to humanity. Philosophy, which from the Greek Philosophia refers to the love of wisdom, is derived from ninth house experience. Publishing and literature disseminates knowledge so that information can be a source of power to all.

The ninth is also the house of grandchildren, being the fifth from the fifth house.

Spiritual

This house creates the need to understand our relationship to the universe and discern and comprehend universal truths. Being the house of the higher mind malefics placed in this house can disturb the mental processes. It is interesting that mental aberration was once thought to be linked to the divine. The Akashic records, said to contain all the knowledge of the universe, are associated with this house. The ability to read them demands a mind of a very high order as well as a talent for clairvoyance which is untainted with astral desire, which apparently creates a fog over the truth. This suggests that the ninth house can hold esoteric truths accessed only through intuition and telepathy.

The ninth, therefore, places a strong emphasis on spirituality and spiritual law. It creates a need to understand the rights of others and adjust to ideas espoused by other races. The journeys covering long distances associated with this house are the physical expression of the later stages of the path (whereas the third house governs the early stages of the spiritual path).

This house is also connected with the building of the Antahkarana, the rainbow bridge leading from the Personality to the Soul. Discernment and wisdom gained from ninth house experiences can help in choosing the right metaphorical bricks in building the Antahkarana. The art of synthesis, making connections between symbolism and the material world, is seen as a creation of this house. Using symbols to provide an exact theory of logical deduction, not only gives an intuitive feel for truth, but also creates a talent for higher mathematics. Mathematics is now regarded as the science of relations, or as the science that draws necessary conclusions using symbolic logic.

Planets in the ninth house

Moon
The client seeks new areas of interest to fulfil his emotional needs. He adapts to changes in ways he once thought impossible. Tentatively he begins to explore new concepts of living and this may involve a temporary or permanent sojourn abroad. He begins to feel more comfortable with foreign ideas. Perhaps he develops an intuitive grasp of symbols and their meaning in his life. He begins to feel more certain about the future even if everything does not, as yet, run smoothly. Optimism and faith in a positive outcome to his problems will characterise his everyday affairs perhaps resulting in sudden good fortune. Idealistic aims however, do need to be grounded in practical work.

Mercury
A thirst for knowledge may encourage the client to take up further studies at this time. He may want to view the larger pattern of the universe in order to understand himself and his role in it. It may be a time to go back to college and retrain in totally different areas to that which interested him before. Material things may not be as important as a sense of inner fulfilment. A need for freedom and increasing restlessness may alienate loved ones if this new vision is not shared. Extended travel may also feature strongly. He may decide to take a sabbatical or a pilgrimage in order to find answers to some pressing questions. There may be interest or involvement in publishing, philosophy or the law.

The Consultation Chart

Venus
The sense of idealism pervading the client's thoughts and feelings right now may work along altruistic channels. Perhaps there will be an urge to take a convoy of food to a distant part of the globe through an urge to distribute love and compassion. There may even be a search for truth and deeper interests begin to grow in religion or ideologies. The client, open to a higher expression of love, sees virtues rather than faults in others and because of this, optimism and luck promised by this house may actually materialise. Even if a loved one falls far short of the ideals projected upon him or her, this may not cause a problem. Love and beauty may also be expressed in the arts particularly in painting and writing.

Sun
The house of the Sun's Joy indicates optimism and wide-ranging interests. The client has an inner urge to broaden his life perspective and find fulfilment in different ways. Many of his thoughts are concerned with things to come and he may spend a great deal of time making plans for what appears to others, to be a utopian vision of the future. Nevertheless it will be hard to dampen his optimism and anticipation of his destiny. He has a warmth and radiance that enthuses and inspires others. His idealism may make him lose touch with reality and quite possibly he forgets to live in the real world. This might cause problems if bills are left unpaid and commitments remain unfulfilled.

Mars
There is a fervour in the client's speech just now that impresses others. He is convinced that he has found the truth and the meaning of existence and refuses to be swayed from his point of view. Some of his views may be quite extreme and radical and alienation may result in halls of learning, ecclesiastical settings and perhaps also in the field of literature. Since self-expression is strong at this moment, there may even be a call to take up the pen that will to some extent, be wielded like a sword. A need for freedom may take the client far and wide in order to experience life more fully. Long distance travel may be a feature of these pressing and restive energies.

Jupiter
The association of Jupiter with this house is through the Chaldean order of planets as well as rulership of Sagittarius, the ninth sign. This may emphasise a great need for freedom in the search for knowledge. The mental and perhaps even physical restlessness that besets the client at this time highlights the limitations of his present path in life. He begins to plan distant travels perhaps without consciously realising why he needs to do so. He feels he needs to do something different to expand his knowledge or decides to follow some kind of

higher learning, education or retraining in order to expand his life. He becomes excited about the future and is able to say goodbye to the past without regret.

Saturn
This may be a time of depression, when difficulties appear inevitable. This is understandable as only obstacles and hardship seem to greet the client. There is no light or rainbow at the end of the tunnel, or so it appears. The path is a hard one at this time and it is easy to lose one's faith. The client may be feeling very constrained since he probably has to work within certain limitations. He finds it hard to think positively at this time and he needs to be reminded that this difficult period will pass. He has to be helped to see the bigger picture. Difficulties may be experienced in the field of travel and publications. Wisdom grows through struggle.

Uranus
There is a great need for change and expansion. New ideas and positive plans give the client the energy to face the challenges he once thought were impossible. He now sees that success is possible if he uses new skills and becomes more daring. Modern concepts in literature, the arts and education will be of interest as well as the field of technology. A sudden desire to travel may be quite uncharacteristic but this is expressive of his inner restlessness. The mind needs extra stimulation and ideas may be ahead of their time. There may be a new interest in prophecy, religion and philosophy. The meaning of life becomes an issue and personal concerns no longer seem so important.

Neptune
Plans tend to be of an idealistic nature right now and may need grounding in reality if they are to be accomplished. New ventures may ensure success if concerned with altruistic or humanitarian motives. This might describe giving aid overseas or becoming a leading light in some spiritual group. There is a danger of spiritual snobbery and hence becoming out of touch with people's real needs. The client may think he has found the truth behind existence. Rather the client should ask if truth is relative? Overseas voyages are likely but care should be taken if Neptune receives difficult aspects. There may also be danger of libel in publishing or scandal and deception as Neptune can distort the truth.

Pluto
There may be a reversal of views and general attitude to life at this time as the client may be facing great changes and upheavals. Enforced circumstances decree that he begins to think along different lines. He is therefore often found in hot pursuit of 'meaning' wherever it may be found. This may be in the halls

of learning as in further education or through extensive reading. It is possible that he will be able to influence others with his writings and oratory. Long journeys seem to beckon in his search for discovering hitherto hidden truths. Perhaps it is through the loss of friends or relatives that he begins to undertake a search for meaning in his life. He may take up studies in psychology or anthropology.

The Tenth House

Physical

The main area of rulership is the knees. It has been found within some healing systems that certain areas of the body correspond or reflect other specific areas of the body. The knee cap or patella corresponds to the elbow, therefore pain in one area my be reflected in the other. Tennis Elbow therefore, may be linked to Housemaid's Knee! The hamstrings seem to split rulership with the ninth and tenth houses. According to Cornell, planets placed in the tenth house have a powerful influence on health and disease, especially if they are of a malefic nature and are elevated above the Lights. The bones, overall, seem to be connected to the tenth house.

In decumbiture charts, the tenth house refers to the medicine/treatment/herbs that may be helpful in cases of sickness. Firstly, the planetary ruler of the tenth should be judged in terms of its strength and dignity. If it is debilitated, other planets placed there should be taken into consideration and judged in the same way. The relevant planet may suggest herbs or types of medicine conducive to helping the patient.

Psychological

This is the house of achievement and the fulfilment of one's purpose in life. Or in terms of the consultation chart, perhaps the tenth describes the chief purpose of the client at the present time. In terms of work, it is often confused with the sixth house, which deals with labour and service rather than the profession. Perhaps the sixth best describes the conditions of work whereas the tenth refers to a true vocation and the honours that may be achieved in that capacity. The sign on the cusp can describe the profession and whether fame and fortune beckon through one's deeds. It is the house that can put the client before the public in some way, especially if the Moon is involved either by placement therein or by benevolent aspect to the tenth house cusp.

Ultimately the tenth refers to one's reputation in society which may be the most important possession anyone can have. Psychologically speaking, therefore, to be accepted by one's peers and venerated for one's abilities can be a tremendous uplift to self-esteem. Validation of this kind will make the client feel that his decisions and what he has achieved have all been worthwhile. Well aspected benefics will help towards creating a good reputation, however, malefics with difficult aspects may 'cast man down from preferment', as Lilly says. He refers particularly to Saturn in the tenth house (C.A. Regulus, p.620), which was quite true in the case of Adolph Hitler and Napoleon Bonaparte. Oscar Wilde also had Saturn in the tenth and in his book De Profundis he says: "Certainly no man ever fell so ignobly, and by such ignoble instruments as I did" (Methuen, p.113). Not everyone with Saturn placed here will experience loss of reputation, especially if the old reaper is dignified. In Wilde's case for instance, his Saturn received the square from Neptune in the seventh and of course, it was through a relationship that Wilde fell from grace. If the client should experience such a calamity in his own life, it could be associated with a need to learn humility, hence the connection with the knees and the process of kneeling. Wilde seems to have realised this as he also says in De Profundis, p.25 "……..nothing in the whole world is meaningless, and suffering least of all. That something hidden away in my nature, like a treasure in a field, is Humility……It is the last thing left in me, and the best". The 'falls' associated with this house need not be metaphorical - they can be physical too.

This house also rules judges, royalty, politicians and all exalted personages. When emphasised in the consultation chart, it may suggest that the client is not only looking for a job or a profession that fits his temperament or gives him fulfilment, but also that he is ready to take on responsibility. It may be that responsibility is thrust upon him and there is nowhere to run and nowhere to hide. It is also the house of one of the parents, traditionally the mother. Modern astrology however, sees the mother ruled by the fourth house as does vedic astrology.

Spiritual

This house refers to true maturity and the opportunity of attaining full command of each and every situation. The client may arrive at a good social standing and the responsibilities that arise are dealt with efficiently and with ease. He develops the strength to tackle huge burdens that seem to defeat others and embraces rather than avoids responsibility. He accepts his mistakes and does not seek to blame others. Events arise which may put the client in authority over others but self aggrandisement is no longer his prime motivation. In all that he does, he is urged along by the idea of spiritual advancement. The kind of profession chosen is one that will benefit others since he has an inner desire to help humanity. A sense of purpose seems to guide him and he may develop a commanding presence and have great influence over others. This may sound quite splendid but in reality there is a great deal of hard work involved and sometimes little time for pleasure. The client does not shirk his responsibilities but they do sometimes feel like a heavy weight across his shoulders. Nevertheless he senses that his work is part of the spiritual will of the divine. Perhaps the lesson of the tenth house is to learn to stand alone and rely upon one's own counsel.

Planets in the tenth house

Moon
Success may beckon because the client is able to reflect public trends. Career prospects look good through knowing instinctively how to deal with people should the client find himself in a position of authority. Security and acquiring a good reputation is uppermost in the client's mind and this may mean changing certain attitudes to ensure promotion. Nothing is left to chance and confidence may grow with increasing success. It is also possible that family concerns put the client in a position of responsibility and everyone looks to him for sustenance and leadership. This may be an unsought honour. Ultimately the client learns that he has to depend upon himself. He must now take charge.

Mercury
Much thought is given to career issues just now and the ability to keep the mind steady and focused could bring rewards. There may be a great deal of scanning of papers and visits to job centres in an effort to find alternatives to present employment. It is a good time to put together a professional Curriculum Vitae which may be a necessary requisite for a future employer. An opportunity may arise in a career in communications such as telecommunications, publishing, the media or perhaps in teaching. The client's talents as an orator may be called upon and it may be a good idea to brush up on delivery and style.

Venus
Success in the career is possible since the client easily finds favour with people in authority. Doors open readily and opportunities arise more easily than before though hard work may still need to be part of the path to success. It is possible that the client's innate talents are being recognised at long last, which may be in the area of health, beauty and the arts. The promise of prosperity seems much more probable now though there might also be a tendency to rest upon one's laurels and expect the good luck to last forever.

Sun

The professional image becomes important and the focus is on succeeding in a career or beginning a new one. Much time is spent outside the home perhaps to the detriment of domestic matters. A single-mindedness of purpose exists which could ensure success. Certainly there is a need to show the world what the client is capable of just now. More than anything he needs to achieve. He cultivates a professional image that may well impress superiors and help him up the ladder of success. The Sun here gives a promise of longevity referring to health as well as business perhaps.

Mars

This is a strong placement for success since Mars is associated with the tenth through the Chaldean order of planets. There appears to be a great deal of energy at the client's disposal. He acts in a very single-minded manner because he becomes more highly focused. He develops foresight in planning and seems to know the right steps to take towards reaching his goals. He is unwilling to allow obstacles to stand in his way. Nothing seems to deter him from achieving his aims. His self assertion may be admired but there is a possibility that it may turn to ruthlessness. Certainly he knows where he is going and may not take kindly to orders issued by figures of authority.

Jupiter

Success and honours may come through the career. A period of professional luck is promised. Accolades seem to come the client's way at last. His talents and abilities are recognised and the time has come for him to be noticed and ascend some way up the ladder of accomplishment. He need no longer hide his light under a bushel. There now comes an opportunity for the achievement of status and wealth. Getting on well with people in authority helps to attain goals. He is likely to be a benevolent boss and finds employees amenable. There may just be a tendency to take on too much at times.

Saturn

An association with this house is through rulership of Capricorn, the tenth sign, yet the client is destined for a fall, literally or psychologically, according to Lilly (CA p.577). It is possible that this position suggests that now is a time when one gets all one deserves - a karmic handout perhaps. If Saturn is very afflicted the 'fall' may indeed be quite marked, otherwise it's possible that accolades and praise may be something to look forward to. This may in fact, be a time when all the hard work of the past is now likely to bring its rewards, though there may be more responsibility heaped on the client just now. There is no point in resting upon one's laurels, because there is still hard work ahead. There is a chance of reaching the top and staying there.

Uranus
Accolades may come for developing concepts that better the working conditions for others. New methods in management may at times upset those who cannot see future possibilities and for a while the client may feel that he is misunderstood. A new departure in the career almost seems inevitable. Certainly it is a time for change and this may mean leaving a secure and steady job that was hard won - yet security and remuneration no longer seem to be enough. A decision has to be made whether to stay with the familiar, or go for change. There are no guarantees of success except in the growth of consciousness and understanding.

Neptune
The client may be drawn to the healing arts, or artistic pursuits like music and dancing may attract. Depending upon the client's level of consciousness, he may be able to merge personal ambitions with those of a higher spiritual nature. He may begin to see his work as having spiritual meaning or seek employment that has a use for humanity and not just for personal gain. This may be in some healing field or perhaps even become a figurehead for good works as in the case of Princess Diana who had Neptune in the tenth. On a more practical level the client may seek work in a hospital, go to sea or find work on an oil rig. Neptune afflicted may describe subversive forces at work.

Pluto
Opportunities may come to achieve a powerful position either at work or in one's community. Others look to the client for leadership whether the client wants to take on that role or not. The test will come in how the client manages to handle such enormous power or whether he abuses his authority. Changes now have to be made in one's own life which may affect the lives of others. Sweeping changes may also occur in the career over which the client may have no control. These may take the form of company merges or redundancy. This can also signal that it is time to end one phase of life and begin another.

THE ELEVENTH HOUSE

Physical

The eleventh house rules over the calves and ankles. The bones included in this area are the tibia and fibula. Since Aquarius, the eleventh sign, has a connection with the blood circulation, the corresponding house may also have an influence in this regard. The eleventh house can also describe the partner's ability to have children since it is the fifth house from the seventh. Therefore, stepchildren also come under its domain. Malefics in either the eleventh or fifth limit or prohibit progeny. However, good indications in the eleventh can overcome any bad ones in the fifth house in relation to childbirth.

Psychological

This is one of the fortunate houses of the chart underscored by the fact that Jupiter has his Joy here. Jupiter's positive outlook is reflected by the eleventh and this augurs well for the formation of future plans. It is known as the house of good fortune. It personifies the kind of hope that once emerged from Pandora's box after all the other goblins had left. When the eleventh house is emphasised in a natal or consultation chart, there is an indication that despite misfortune in other areas of life, there is some goodwill towards the client arriving from some quarter. This may derive from the support of friends and peer groups, perhaps even wealthy and generous benefactors. It is the house of trust. A sense of faith begins to grow and a belief in the goodness of life ensues with an escalating feeling of confidence.

The house may show the praise the client receives from a job well done. As it is the second from the tenth house, it also shows the resources derived from the career. In the same way it describes the relationship with colleagues at work and the kind of teamwork that may be associated with the career.

The eleventh house is often referred to as the house of hopes and wishes indicating perhaps that these are likely to come true providing the benefic planets make a temporary sojourn there. Malefics may deny the fulfilment of the client's present hopes and wishes.

This is a very sociable house and emphasises groups rather than the individual. There is a meeting with like-minded people who share similar thoughts and feelings. Goals and objectives are likely to be of related interest. Emphasis on this house suggests that the client's social life is likely to improve and that the client feels accepted by his peers.

Spiritual

This house refers to the New Group of World Servers who look after the political, religious and educational fields of the human race. There may be an intuitive response by some people/clients towards involvement in concerns that effect better conditions for others. The development of group consciousness indicates that actions are undertaken for the good of the many rather than the benefit of the few. Former selfish objectives now begin to transform towards selfless actions.

A sense of brotherhood prevails and work and recreation is carried out with group purpose. As service has a humanitarian flavour, horizons begin to widen in thinking and feeling. International concerns may become more important and consciousness begins to expand through identification with common aims. Individual identity is retained but assimilated easily within the greater whole. Race or creed no longer acts as a barrier to brotherhood. Service on a wide scale may be expressed through charity work or within a business organisation that has wide ranging objectives and aspirations towards reformation. Friends and companions are now those who share a new vision. These may, though not always, be found in spiritual, occult or healing groups.

Planets in the eleventh house

Moon
The client may find himself in the company of relative strangers. As traditional bonds loosen, shared goals and similar ideologies take their place. Perhaps even humanitarian concerns become more important. New found friends seem like a family to him and the client becomes involved in a greater and improved social scene. Ultimately, the lesson may be in learning to tolerate and accept differences. The social scene may undergo much fluctuation before the client finds his proper niche.

Mercury
A social life that includes friends with the same attitude of mind becomes of increasing importance. This may include a gathering of friends with similar interests or sharing a common cause. Opinions expressed by others may influence the client's thinking. He may become the spokesperson of a group or help to organise activities and projects in some organisation. The emphasis is on teamwork now and working alone is no longer a viable option. Acceptance from peer groups may be important yet retaining a sense of individuality is still significant.

Venus
An urge to take part in the social scene dominates the client's life. He may decide that it is time to have fun and enjoy convivial company rather than spend too much time on his own. There is an opportunity to make new friends who seem to bring joy and laughter into the client's life. The need to be accepted by one's peers promotes a pleasing approach in dealing with others. The client courts popularity and this may be easy to attain for once. A friend might become a lover or a lover becomes a good friend. There might also be a natural inclination to take part in humanitarian groups.

Sun
The Sun is strong in this house since it is associated with the eleventh through the Chaldean order of planets. A need to implement long-standing hopes and

wishes ensues. Opportunities arise to break out of traditional patterns and rigid life-styles. A new path beckons and recently made acquaintances may prove influential in helping to create fresh opportunities. Friends may be more important than family just now and conflicts may arise if these two factions clash. The client may spend more time outside the home than within it. Humanitarian concerns may attract and a revolutionary and reforming fever may influence his attitude most profoundly. Fitting in with friends and peer groups becomes important.

Mars
Great organisational skills may be evident as well as leadership in teamwork. Career strategies are implemented, or humanitarian causes are espoused. Or perhaps there is simply more time spent in recreational pastimes. An energetic pursuance of a social life puts the client within groups of like-minded people. Being one of the crowd however, may conflict with a need for self-assertion. The emphasis on group activity just now will help him learn about sharing equally with others. This may be a time when he may have the opportunity to avidly pursue many of his hopes and wishes.

Jupiter
The house of happiness seems to be the natural domain of the benefic Jupiter since he finds his Joy here. Good fortune and contentment may be just around the corner since many of the client's hopes and wishes seem to be within his grasp. Perhaps good fortune comes about regardless of personal effort. Good communication with well-meaning friends proves helpful in so much as he gets to the know the 'right' people who give him a helping hand. He is likely to be warmly accepted by his peers and no longer feels like an outsider. He is aware of larger social issues and he may become significantly involved with philanthropic organisations.

Saturn
There is a association between Saturn and the eleventh house due to its traditional rulership of Aquarius, the eleventh sign. Hopes and wishes may be thwarted at this time if the old reaper is afflicted, but hard work may help the client attain his goals. It's possible that a relationship has terminated leaving him to re-enter the social scene once more. He may find it hard to fit into the social structure that has been familiar to him. He has fears starting anything new as he feels awkward and clumsy. Sometimes he feels like an outsider and perhaps even old friendships are no longer viable. He takes friendships seriously expecting others to be loyal and trustworthy and does not therefore, easily enter into new alliances. He may find that friends tend to put extra burdens upon him at this time. Difficulties may be experienced with stepchildren.

Uranus

An association with the eleventh is due to shared rulership of Aquarius perhaps suggesting a new departure in lifestyle. The client breaks away from the code of conduct he once shared with his friends and acquaintances. He no longer runs with the pack. Friendships are suddenly broken without apparent cause. In most cases he finds that they are in any event, no longer productive, yet the future remains uncertain as he wonders what will happen next. His actions appear rebellious and this tends to upset others. He may be labelled difficult or unpredictable. Changing attitudes may bring an interest in higher concerns and involvement in causes of a humanitarian nature. Resistance to change may bring tension and feelings of discontentment.

Neptune

The client begins to seek friends who are motivated by some spiritual goal. He may join occult societies that further his interests in reincarnation and the more subtle side of life. He begins to understand and tolerate people from different backgrounds and no longer feels threatened by differences. However, it is possible that misunderstandings may occur in existing friendships and perhaps there may even be a feeling of disillusionment. He finds himself cut off from people who once meant a great deal to him. It may be a time to develop greater tolerance of other people's weaknesses.

Pluto

It is possible that power struggles start to develop within existing groups and friendships. Harassment may come from unexpected quarters. Differences of opinion could arise threatening to annihilate carefully laid plans. A whole way of life might come to an end making the client feel deserted and even friendless. The client stands alone and has to depend upon himself in a challenging environment. The birth of a new set of values eventually sees the client in a totally new social environment. It is possible that some responsibility may be thrust upon him and he may have to take up the reins of leadership.

THE TWELFTH HOUSE

Physical

The Life Force tends to be somewhat diminished in this house and ill health may be a factor to consider from time to time. Physically, this may indicate the weakening of the immune system, the body's natural defence against all sorts of bacteria, fungi and parasites. The basic defence forces comprise the white blood cells containing antibodies which drain back into the lymph vessels, a network blood system connecting the lymph glands. The lymph glands are looked upon as the power houses of the immune system.

The feet are also targeted by this house. Within certain healing disciplines (such as reflexology) there are parts of the body that reflect in microscopic proportions the rest of the body. The feet (as well as the ears, hands and the iris) are one of these reflection points. Thus physical problems in other parts of the body will show up in the feet. This house may also signify impaired senses.

Psychological

The twelfth house, as well as the fourth and eighth, is one of the Terminal Houses, indicating a dissolution of energy. Also along with the fourth and eighth house it is forms part of the Occult Triangle and therefore becomes a house that favours mysticism. Associated with witchcraft, as well as other subversive forces such as treachery and espionage, it tends to rule all underhand activities. It does however, give the ability to sense the subtle side of life resulting possibly in clairvoyance, clairaudience and clairsentience.

Generally, the twelfth has a poor reputation since its main features seem to be unhappiness and sorrow usually through some sort of confinement. It is known as the house of imprisonment referring to both physical incarceration as well as mental bondage. This might be expressed as a feeling of loneliness, anxiety, entrapment, guilt, shame and seclusion. When this house is emphasised in a consultation chart, it suggests that the client probably feels weak and helpless and needs a great deal of encouragement. He or she may feel totally unsupported and seems to pursue a lonely path in life. This can however, augur a time of self-reliance and the development of self-sufficiency.

The twelfth rules large institutions such as grand companies and organisations where the individual merges unrecognised within the greater structure. Institutions also include prisons, hospitals and mental asylums indicating that the individual is under psychological as well as physical restraint. The volition to act and make decisions becomes difficult resulting in lack of motivation, apathy and despair. It is a house that confuses the boundaries between self and others, often resulting in a feeling of exploitation. Uncertainty about one's obligation to others creates a lack of confidence and perhaps even a crisis of identity. Excessive modesty and an unassuming nature inhibit awareness of personal talents and abilities.

The flow of natural energy is blocked in this house and difficulties arise in self expression creating a situation where emotional needs are often overlooked by others. The 'hidden enemies' associated with this house may be personified by outer oppressors or inner demons. Escape can be through drugs, drink, fantasy or even suicide.

Since the energies of this house tend to turn inward, much time may be spent in contemplation, often enriching the imagination. A positive expression may ignite the powers of some creative muse. Art, music, dancing, writing and mimicry are talents arising from this house. The ability to stand alone and spend time in seclusion, can often be a spur to creativity.

The twelfth does press strongly for the necessity to confront the demons of the past. It is a secret house and all things shameful, both real and imagined haunt the native. Scandals as well as family skeletons rattle the client. It is the house which bears the hallmark of his 'Achilles heel' (after all this house rules the feet!) Yet all such difficulties arise to offer an opportunity to face past mistakes, however painful, usually through atonement, forgiveness or forbearance. The sorrow allied with this house often spurs the individual towards a journey of self-discovery. As the small ego atrophies and 'merges with the whole' the client learns to understand others and develops compassion. Ultimately, an ability arises to alleviate suffering, one's own and that of others. Sacrifices are then made consciously and willingly. The healing aspect of this house should therefore, not be overlooked.

This house is also associated with the bedroom and large animals!

Spiritual

The house of constraint may limit the Soul's manifestation in the physical body by deprivation or obstruction of one or more of the five senses. This is the house of karma or the unredeemed past. Planets here typify the misused energies of past-lives which now need to be addressed once again and transformed. The twelfth represents a hard school of learning though ultimately there occurs a merging of the personal will with the divine will. A need emerges to identify or form a conscious relationship with the universal source of spiritual power. There may, however, be too much reliance placed upon gurus or teachers who promise enlightenment. A susceptibility to the influence of others may lead to possession by another's will and self-control may be lacking. The 'self-undoing' aspect of this house indicates problems and difficulties which are self-imposed.

This house refers to the unconscious mind, a repository of all past blunders and mistakes as well as dynamic and positive reserves. Through suffering and sacrifice, a more elevated state of consciousness is achieved which leads to a discovery of the essential spirit within. This can result in a more universal identity and an urge to 'save' others. The silence which is imposed through seclusion in either hospitals, prisons and other places of incarceration can lead to utter despair or aid in the search for inspiration and self-discovery.

Planets in the twelfth house

Moon
This house exacerbates the fluid nature of the Moon which leads to intense fluctuation of emotion. No one seems able to empathise with the client's unhappiness or cares less about what he feels, or so it seems. The client feels lost, vulnerable and unsupported during this time. This may be either real or imaginary and probably points to unfinished business with loved ones, notably family members. Still tied to family opinion, he allows them, albeit grudgingly, to encroach upon his generosity and time. He does this because he wants to be loved. A tighter sense of boundaries needs to be implemented and the willingness to let go of people, even those close to him, who exploit rather than love him. The care and concern he offers others may be through a sense of duty and he feels guilty if he puts his own needs first. Yet there is a possibility of developing strong mediumistic talents and tremendous perception.

Mercury
The mind becomes open to opinions and thoughts of others that can lead to a deeper understanding of life. Rational thought becomes less important and a search arises for the meaning of symbols which can lead to an interest in dreams, the occult and the arts. The imagination and intuition may begin to work on an almost psychic level leading to clairvoyant abilities. There may however, be a feeling of isolation and a sense of being misunderstood by others. Spending too much time alone may lead to feelings of distrust and suspicion. Fantasy is strong though also a possibility of losing touch with reality.

Venus
An association with the Chaldean order of planets strengthens the position of Venus in this house. The desire for personal fulfilment is now touched with a more spiritual understanding of love. This may be expressed through tolerance, forgiveness and acceptance of humanity with all its faults. Or at least this is the most noble expression of Venus when placed in the house of sorrow. Otherwise, personal love may be denied at this time and there may be a sense of isolation and lack of fulfilment unless there is a turning towards more altruistic forms of caring. Involvement with people who have special needs perhaps in some institution may be the keynote.

Sun
A period of solitude may be necessary or preferred rather than outer activity. This can be due to a number of reasons; loss of spouse, family member, job, etc. Illness and convalescence are not uncommon. A time for regeneration and relaxation may give an opportunity for contemplation and gaining new insights

into one's life. This may be helpful in forming future plans. An understanding of life and people deepens. Skeletons may possibly come out of the closet reminding one of past mistakes though an opportunity arises to deal with them. No time to harbour regrets. Anxiety may bring vulnerability but it is important for the client to forgive oneself for past blunders and stop dwelling on the past.

Mars
Difficulties with self-assertion may bring a period of isolation and impotence giving little scope in promoting ideas in the outside world or influencing others. Anger may be internalised resulting in frustration and depression. The inability to confront oppressors may result in manipulation or more positively, promote a more diplomatic expression of dealing with others. Self-sufficiency and relying upon one's own resources are qualities to be learnt at this time for future use. Through the suffering and pain an opportunity arises to direct resources in altruistic channels.

Jupiter
An association with Pisces, the twelfth sign, strengthens the position of Jupiter in this house. The ability to spend much time alone develops talent along creative lines. The imagination tends to be wide ranging and mystical and spiritual/religious tendencies may be evident. Isolation may be self-imposed in order to find time to think. Hobbies and recreational activity occupy the mind and there seems little need for the company of others. A temporary escape from society serves to regenerate energies. This is a time for contemplation and the synthesis of disparate strands of the client's life. There is usually a preference for exploring the inner life than dealing with the confusion and challenges of the outside world.

Saturn
Joy is experienced by Saturn in this house but Lilly says it is only because 'Saturn is author of mischief'. (CA p.56) The planet of karma in the house of karma suggests that life is tough and there may be a tendency to run away and hide. A compelling need for privacy may exist at this time. It may become necessary however, to confront difficulties rather than suppress them as this could result in illness. There may be an uncertainty with regard to boundaries resulting in psychological stress. A sense of being invisible and ignored creates low self-esteem. Difficult circumstances have to be evaluated objectively in order to promote a more positive attitude. There is a need to reconnect with others otherwise a feeling of loneliness may ensue.

Uranus
The expression of individual creativity and uniqueness may be thwarted. Being forced to conform to other people's views brings a feeling of frustration. This can lead to a breakdown of the usual life pattern and isolation may result. Feelings of resentment may lead to nervous problems, yet an understanding can grow of life's greater schemes and designs leading perhaps to the study of mysticism, clairvoyance and healing. Personal needs may be submerged in circumstances that promote the greater good. Yet this gives a chance to gain a panoramic view of the world. An opportunity also exists to push through new frontiers of art and healing.

Neptune
An association with this house occurs through the shared rulership of Pisces, the twelfth sign. This creates an extremely sensitive position making the client feel he is at the mercy of all and sundry. The client is very impressionable at this time and may be easily seduced into activities detrimental to his well-being. He lacks motivation and prefers to withdraw from life. This may even indicate a period in hospital. But it is also possible that the client adopts a more spiritual attitude and spends time in meditation or perhaps helping others in a healing sanctuary. Ego-dissolving episodes either bring despair or humility. He feels he is drawn into something bigger than himself. This could bring an interest in mysticism.

Pluto
Willpower may be lacking due to confrontation with oppressors in one form or another. Coercion into acting contrary to his own needs brings feelings of entrapment. Circumstances arise that are difficult to negotiate which can result in an explosion of temper. The necessity of dealing with immense challenges suggests that survival becomes an important issue ultimately creating an enormous reservoir of strength. Such force tends to remain hidden only surfacing when great difficulties need to be faced. A hidden power exists for good or ill. There is great insight into other people's motives which can be an excellent position for a psychologist or counsellor.

The Consultation Chart

CASE

HISTORIES

1. Career

The Consultation Chart

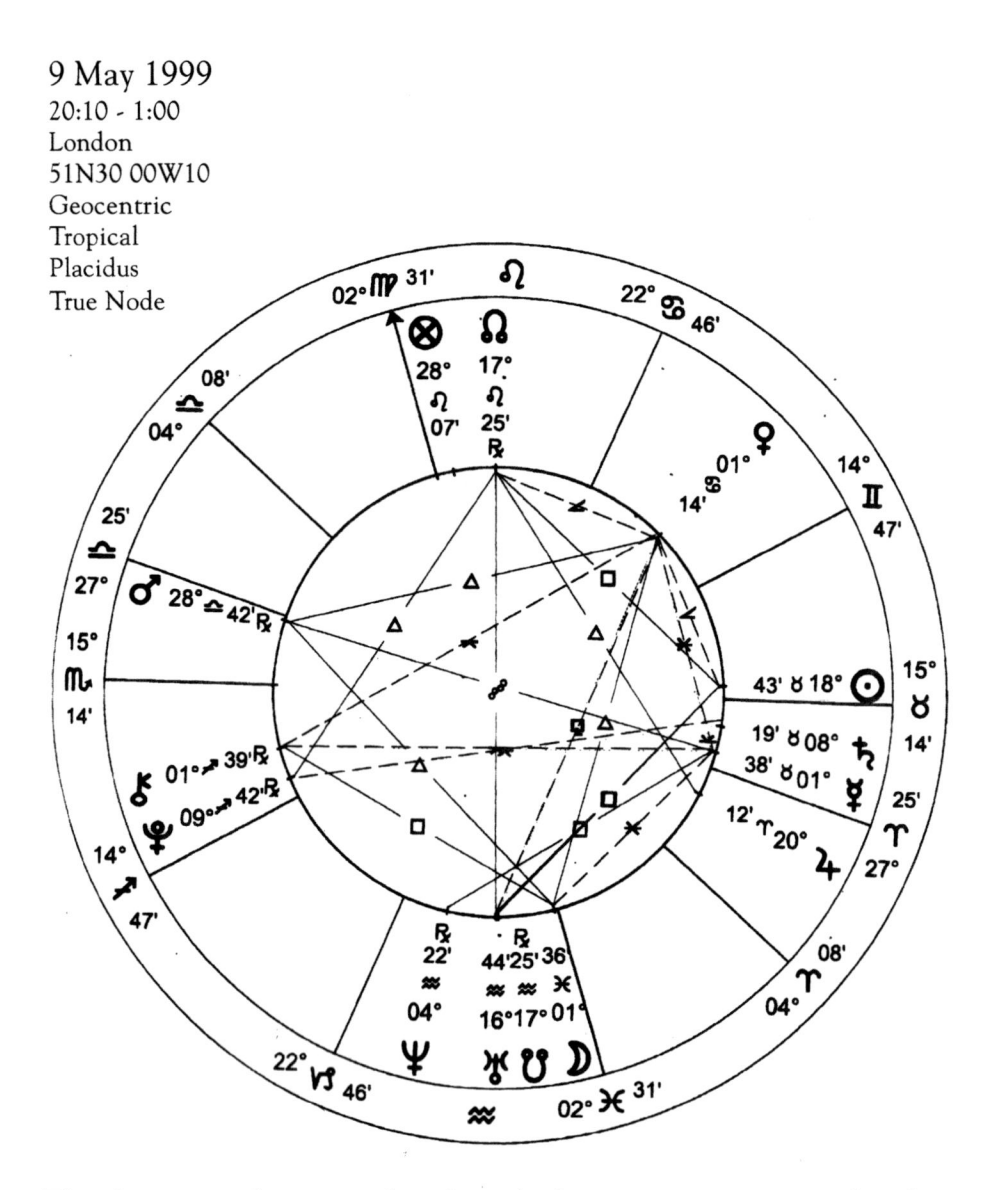

9 May 1999
20:10 - 1:00
London
51N30 00W10
Geocentric
Tropical
Placidus
True Node

The client came for a general reading. As Scorpio rises, it appears that she is facing upheavals and enforced changes in her life, perhaps not to her liking. This is confirmed by a debilitated Mars, the Ascendant ruler. Mars is in detriment, in the sorrowful twelfth house and retrograde. The client is obviously feeling very downcast and full of despair. Venus, ruler of the seventh house is separating from Mars by trine suggesting the end of the affair.

This is exactly what had happened and the client was feeling very unhappy. Her husband had left her for another woman although despite everything, the separation had been quite amicable (note that it is a peaceful trine separating Venus from Mars). What the client missed more than anything was the way they would discuss everything before coming to a decision, and she was finding it very hard to make her own decisions. Note that Mars is in Libra, a sign not noted for its rapid decision making qualities. I suggested that maybe she was now learning more about self-reliance (perhaps one of the good qualities granted by the twelfth house since it rules isolation).

The client's present mental state also seemed to be influenced by children and work, as Mars also rules the fifth and sixth houses. The client revealed she had just heard that the husband's girlfriend was pregnant and realised that the situation had reached a point of no return. Nevertheless, I tried to help her look with optimism towards the future as the offer of a new job promised a change of life-style. Mercury, ruler of the tenth house of career was actually separating from Mars by opposition, which seemed to indicate there had been a problem connected to her career. The client revealed that she had been offered a job but had turned it down because she had lost all her confidence. (The poor state of the Ascendant ruler was testimony to her feeling of despair). I suggested that she would probably have another chance to have a crack at the job if she wished. I thought this was likely because the Moon, also signifying the client, was applying closely to the sextile of Mercury. She seemed unwilling to believe this and thought my words were based on encouragement rather than astrology. The only way I could prove to her that I was using a method of prognostication was to describe the job to her.

This is what I deduced: Virgo on the cusp of the tenth house points to health and hygiene and Mercury, the ruler is in the sixth, giving further indications of health and hygiene as well as pointing to some kind of service. Since Mercury was placed in Taurus, it appeared as if food was connected to her work. The Moon in Pisces suggested compassion and caring and as it ruled the ninth house, education could be involved. The client cheered up considerably. Apparently, she worked in the food service industry and was offered a contract to go and teach different companies how to use new catering equipment!

I said that she would feel much more positive within a month (when Mars turned direct) and within two months she would feel even stronger and able to cope with everything that came her way (Mars entered Scorpio, its own sign). The client said she already felt much more encouraged to pursue this new career.

The Consultation Chart

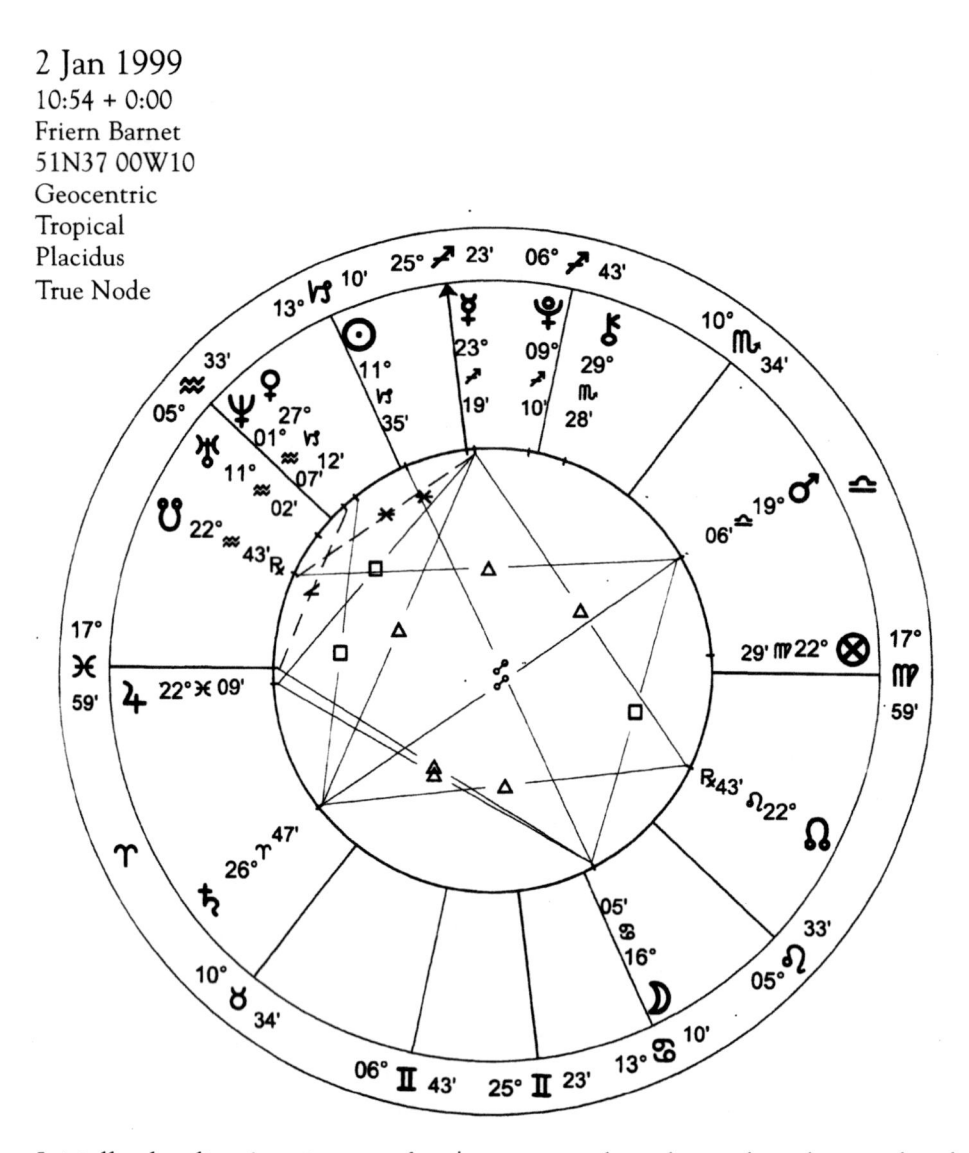

2 Jan 1999
10:54 + 0:00
Friern Barnet
51N37 00W10
Geocentric
Tropical
Placidus
True Node

Initially, the client's main area of concern was with a relationship - he wondered if there was still some hope for its continuance. Since Pisces (the last sign) rises, it suggests an end of a cycle. Jupiter rules the Ascendant, is extremely strong in its own sign Pisces and is placed in the first house, showing that the client is likely to be in an optimistic and hopeful frame of mind. This will no doubt help him face the disappointment which may lie ahead.

His partner is signified by Mercury, as ruler of the seventh house, and the planet is in its detriment in Sagittarius which shows a lack of motivational force. Mercury has also passed the square of Jupiter which indicates that they are parting and none too amicably. Neither does the Moon, also representative of the client, aspect Mercury, so there is no hope for the relationship. The client said that he did not really have any hope that it would continue since they spent most of their time arguing! He agreed that they were growing apart.

Since Jupiter also rules the ninth and tenth houses and is applying by square to the Midheaven, I asked if he were thinking of making changes to his career. He said he was. I asked him if he were particularly good at languages, since the ninth house rules foreign travel and this is further emphasised by Sagittarius - the sign of adventure - on the cusp. Could he indeed be thinking of teaching languages abroad? He revealed that he had recently visited a friend in the East (Fire signs rule an easterly direction) who taught English abroad. He said that he had in fact been thinking of doing something similar but he was also very much tied to his home and was in conflict about this. Since the debilitated Mercury also rules the fourth house, and is in a separating aspect with Jupiter, I said he would find the strength to leave his home behind. Also, if we take the Moon to represent the client and Jupiter ruling the ninth and tenth houses, the applying trine between them augers well for a trip and employment abroad.

The client said that this had given him the encouragement to look further into the possibility of a career change.

The Consultation Chart

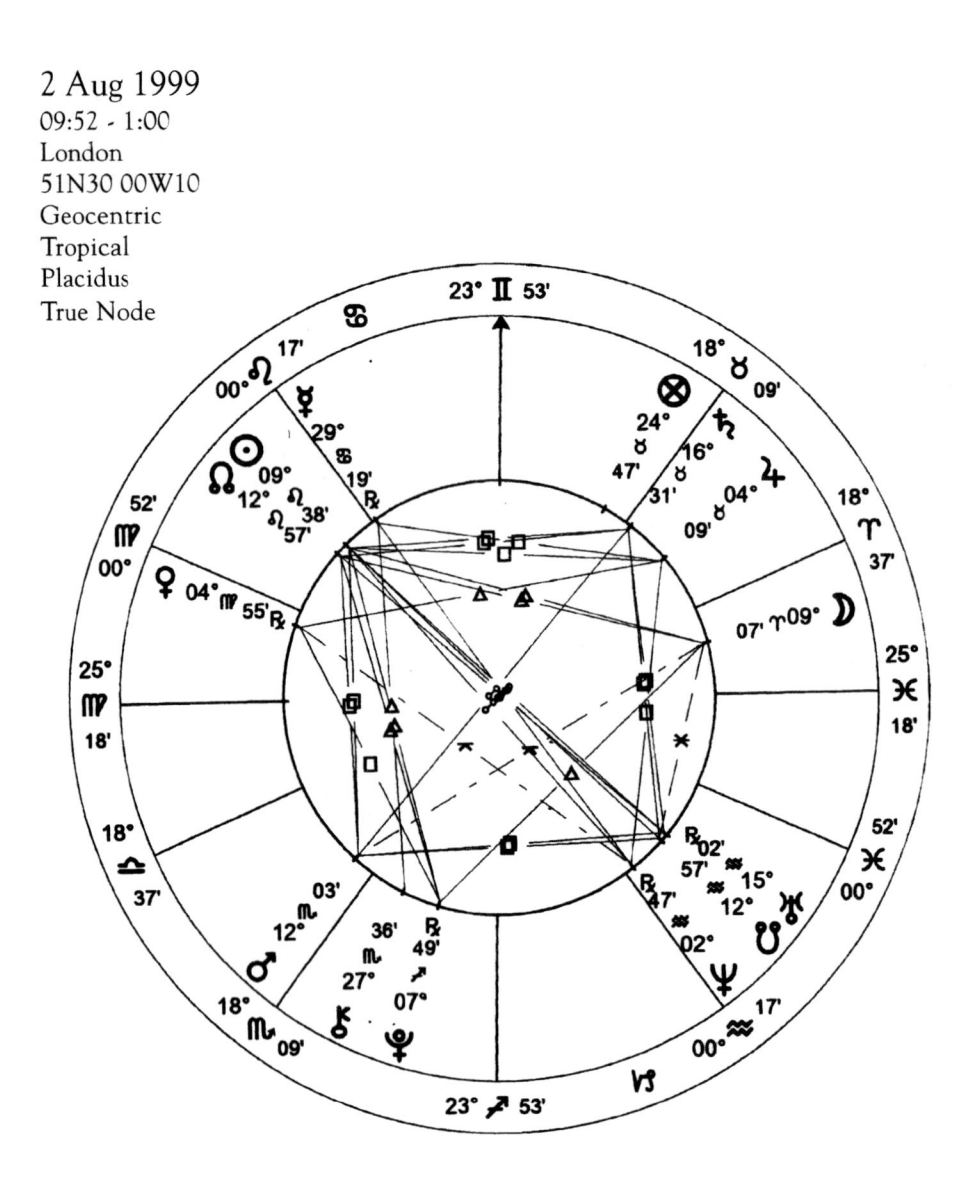

2 Aug 1999
09:52 - 1:00
London
51N30 00W10
Geocentric
Tropical
Placidus
True Node

Virgo rises, indicating that this may be an issue concerning either work or health or perhaps both. Since Virgo also rules the difficult twelfth house, the client may not feel strong enough to cope with her various problems. Mercury rules the Ascendant as well as the tenth house, which begins to suggest that the main area of interest does lie within her career structure. Mercury is at the last degree of the sign indicating that the client has come to the end of a cycle. However, it is retrograde, suggesting she finds it hard to come to a final decision with regard to issues connected with her career. Could it be that she knows it is time to move on but cannot make up her mind whether to stay or go? This feeling of indecision is compounded by the fact that Mercury is in Cancer, a sign that needs to feel safe and secure in familiar surroundings. The fact that Mercury is on the cusp of the eleventh house indicates that the client is involved in teamwork at work, and perhaps feels sorry to leave her follow workers.

Mercury is separating from the trine with Chiron in the third house, suggesting that the client probably worked in some caring capacity, perhaps with people who had special needs. Mercury is also applying with an opposition to Neptune in the fifth indicating work with children.

It transpired that the client was very keen to work with children who had special needs. She was a nurse by profession and had actually been working with older people. She confirmed that whilst she wanted to leave, she was in fact quite fearful of stepping into new territory and was in a state of indecision just at the present time; she was also unhappy about leaving her colleagues behind. Since Mercury would turn direct in a few days time, I said she would be feeling more positive within a week and be better able to make up her mind.

The Consultation Chart

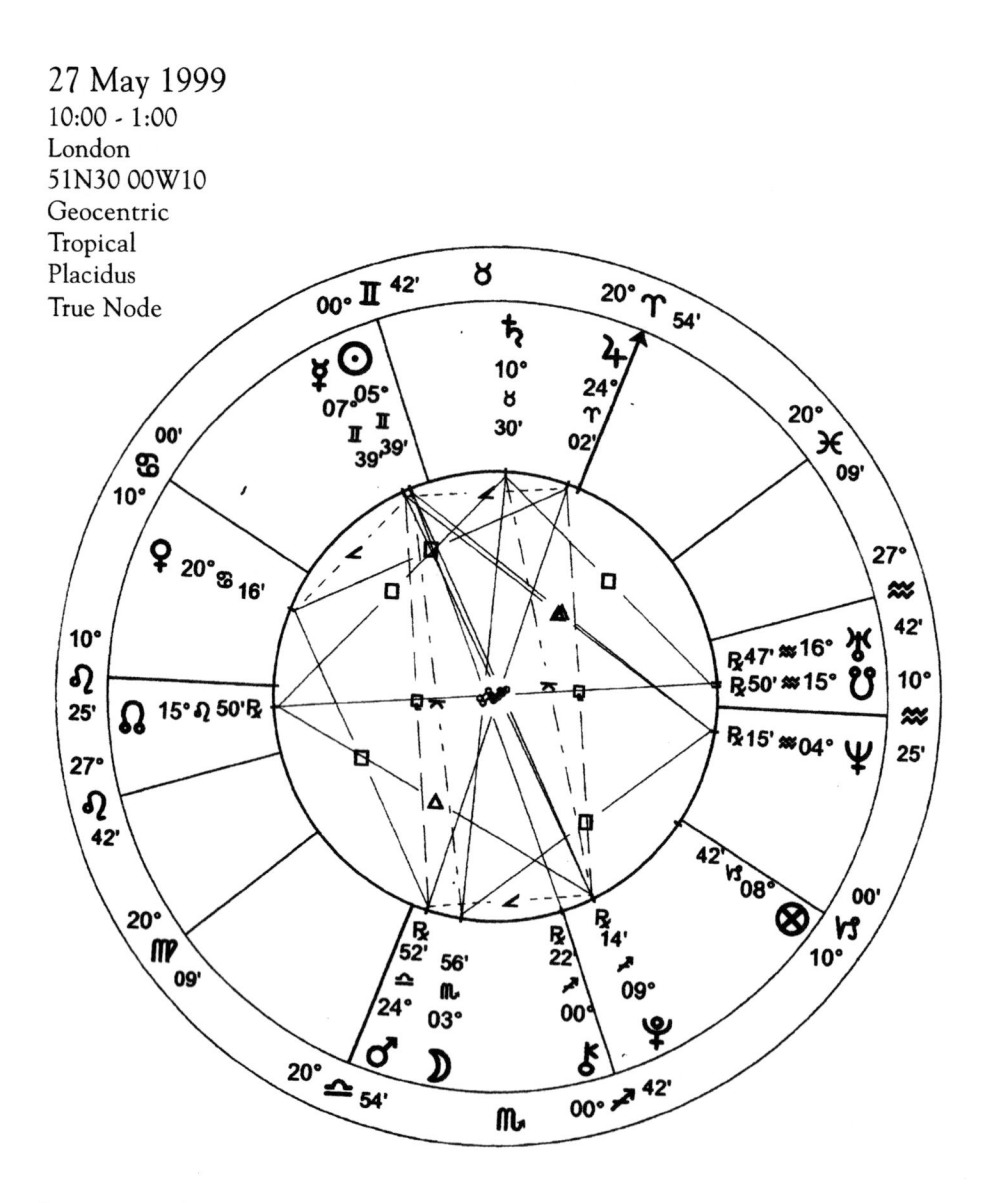

27 May 1999
10:00 - 1:00
London
51N30 00W10
Geocentric
Tropical
Placidus
True Node

Leo rises indicating that the client was preparing to assert her individuality and organisational skills within some area of her life. As Leo also rules the second house this suggests that her organisational and leadership skills were probably connected to finance. The North Node in the first house indicates that she feels strongly about the path she has chosen, whatever that may be. However, Uranus conjoins the South Node in the seventh, suggesting that her new project or goals are likely to disrupt her marriage or partnership. Uranus in its highest expression intensifies the urge for humanitarian reform though its action is likely to disturb existing structures.

This was indeed what was happening at the present time. The client had become so enthused with a new fund-raising project that it had caused problems within her marriage.

The Sun, ruling the Ascendant, is in Gemini in the eleventh house, describing involvement with large groups of people with the emphasis on communication. The Sun puts Mercury, ruler of the eleventh house, into combustion indicating problems with interaction, possibly causing arguments with her peers. Note that Mercury also rules the eleventh house of groups as well as the third house of communication. Since Mercury is separating from the Sun, the problems are fast receding, fortunately. The Sun and Mercury also oppose Pluto, indicating the possibility of power struggles within the group. The client revealed that some of her peers seemed jealous of the success she had achieved at fund raising and this had indeed caused a few arguments; however, communication was slowly improving. She felt that she might have been a little high-handed in her approach and was now willing to reach a compromise.

The Sun is trine Neptune in Aquarius in the sixth house, indicating service to some benevolent cause. This is also suggested by the Sun's half-square aspect to Venus which has its Joy in the twelfth house, and together with its sign placement, shows a very caring and compassionate nature. Venus is however, in a T-square with the two most angular planets in the chart, Mars and Jupiter. Mars rules the MC and Jupiter conjoins the MC which refers to the client's career/goals. Jupiter rules the ninth and fifth houses, with the focus upon education and children.

The client finally revealed that she had become involved in a fund raising activity on behalf of a new educational set-up for gifted children. There were many communication problems with other people involved in the project but she was fast overcoming them. She also foresaw difficulties with the project as a whole and felt that it would indeed be a long road to success. Her new found assertiveness had brought difficulties in the marriage and disruption within the home. Further change within the home were indicated by the aforesaid Sun's approaching opposition to Pluto, co-ruler of the fourth house indicating that outside forces would unsettle the family structure. The client was obviously worried about this. The Moon, also representative of the client, was in the fourth house and in its fall in Scorpio, suggesting emotional discord. The Moon's opposition to Saturn, ruling the seventh shows further confrontation with her husband, with the possibility of emotional alienation. The client realised that her new and exciting project could bring severe marital discord unless she was able to balance these two areas of her life.

2. HEALTH

The Consultation Chart

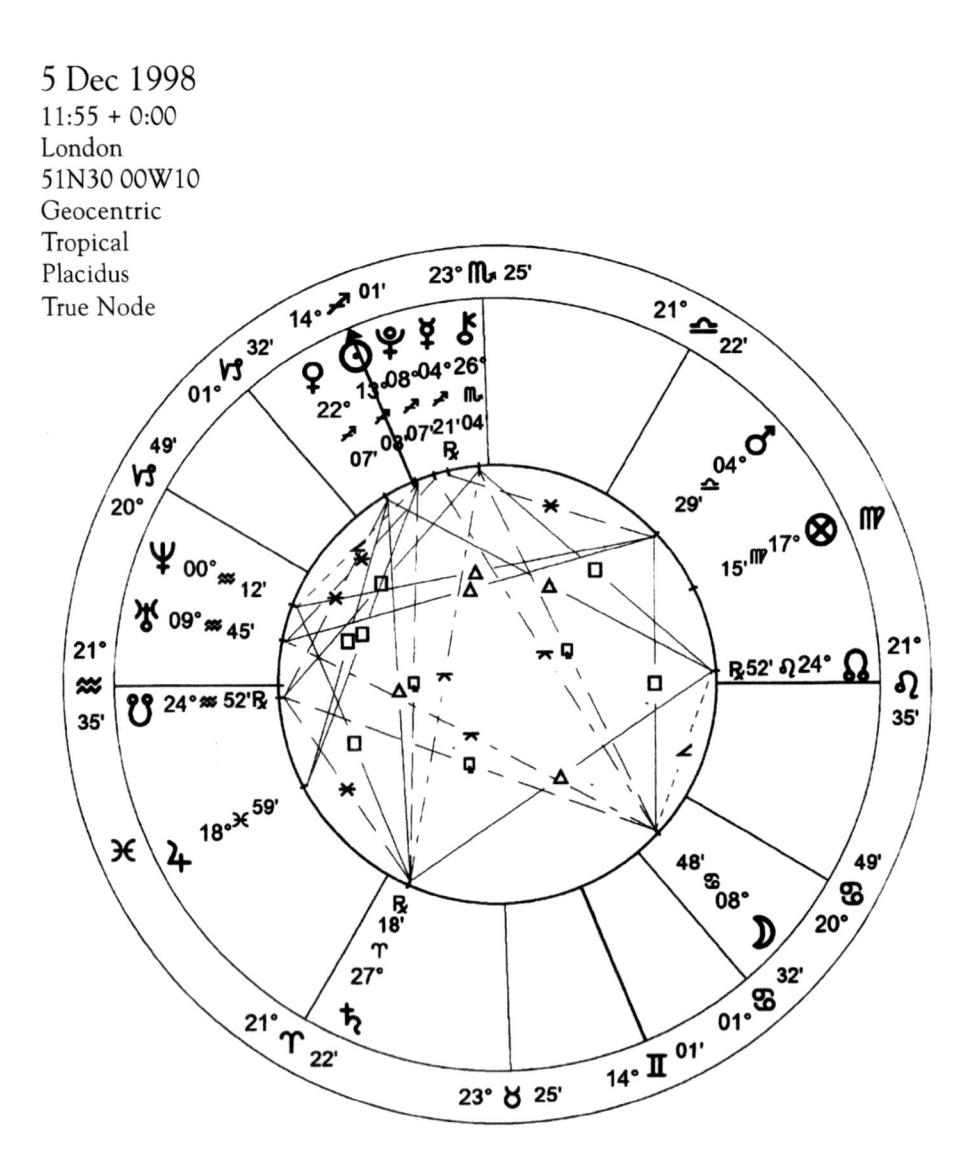

5 Dec 1998
11:55 + 0:00
London
51N30 00W10
Geocentric
Tropical
Placidus
True Node

The client wanted to know about her general health. Aquarius/Leo span the horizon putting an emphasis on the circulation. Saturn, ruling the Ascendant is in fall and further debilitated by retrogradation. This suggests a weak constitution, albeit temporarily. Within the second house, Saturn puts a block on the flow of energy or Prana. It is sesquiquadrate the Sun blocking out the vibrant Solar rays and in square to Neptune indicating weakness. To compound the situation, Saturn is inconjunct Chiron - certainly the health suffers. The one fortunate aspect is the trine Saturn receives from Venus in the tenth, known as the house of medicine.

Further indications of ill health will be shown by the sixth house and its ruler. With Cancer on the cusp and the Moon strong in its own sign, it looks as if the disease, whatever it may be, has a strong hold. The Moon's last traditional aspect was a square to Mars, which happens to be the dispositor of Saturn, the client's significator. Mars in Libra indicates the kidneys and I wondered if the client had had problems in this area. Since the Moon separates from Mars by just under four degrees, I wondered if the trouble with the kidneys was in fact a past illness of either 3 months or 3 years previously. She confirmed that she had an operation on her kidneys some 3 years back but that was no longer the problem. This was good news for the client but not so for the astrologer. Where was the disease?

The problem of illness is often indicatedby the sign on the sixth house cusp and its ruler. Cancer and the cool and moist Moon pointed to the chest area and the square to hot and dry Mars indicated a problem of inflammation. Heat and breasts seemed to tie in together. I mentioned this to the client and she said that her problem was 'burning breasts'. She wondered whether this could be a side effect of Hormone Replacement Therapy (HRT). She had spoken to her doctor but had received no help she said, and thought that an astrologer might throw some light on the problem. Naturally, I said that I could not take the place of her doctor but would try to give her some cosmological guidance. The malefic Mars appeared to be the afflicting planet. It rules blood and its position in the seventh house pointed to the womb and a square suggests excess. I said that it was possible that HRT was at the basis of her 'burning breasts' because the administration of oestrogen may have increased the blood flow to the breasts. Breast tenderness can be a possible side effect of HRT.

Since the Moon was next applying to a strong Jupiter, placed in its own sign, I felt that the client's problem would eventually desist. Not only is Jupiter a benefactor and protector, it also rules the tenth house of medicine, indicating that she would get beneficial treatment for her condition. I suggested that she ask for a second opinion and that it was likely that she would get the help she was looking for. The Sun signifying the physician, as it rules the seventh house, is also in the tenth house suggesting that a physician would eventually come to her aid.

The Sun's square to Jupiter does not counteract this advice since it is nullified by the swifter Moon applying to Jupiter before the Sun.

The Consultation Chart

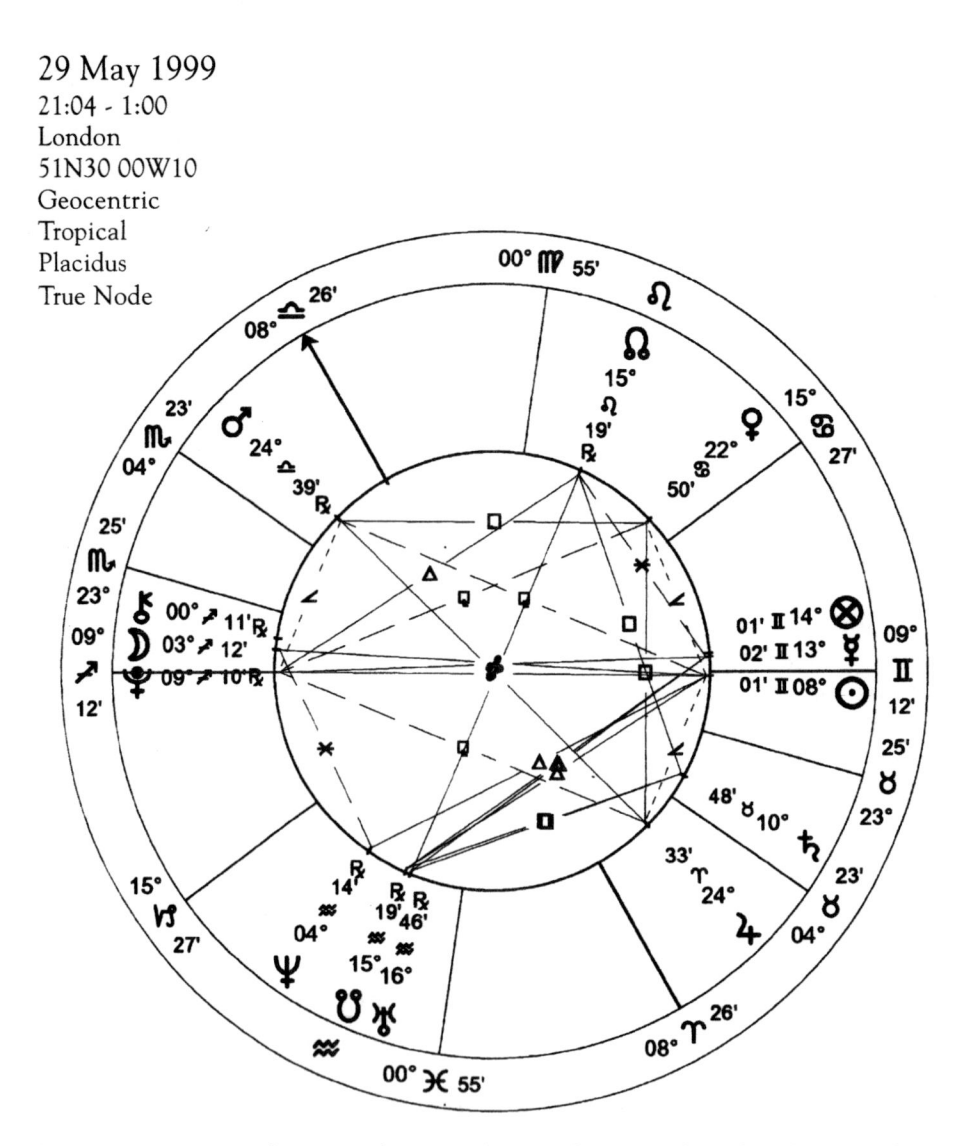

29 May 1999
21:04 - 1:00
London
51N30 00W10
Geocentric
Tropical
Placidus
True Node

Sagittarius rises in the consultation chart indicating that the client seeks to expand her life through the pursuit of new horizons. Jupiter, her significator, is in Aries confirming her urge to enter some new field. Placed in the fourth house and also ruling the third, she seems set to take up new studies which she will carry out from home.

The client confirmed that she was indeed thinking along these lines, but as yet, nothing tangible had occurred. Jupiter is afflicted due to its involvement in a T-square with Venus and Mars; certainly the client is beset by problems and no doubt very stressed. But why?

164

Case Histories

The sesquiquadrate between Jupiter and Pluto placed on the Ascendant looks uneasy. Could it be that the answer lies with the lord of the underworld? Some outside factor has entered her life putting a halt to her plans. Antares, that malevolent fixed star also rises with the Ascendant - bad tidings beckon it would seem. Pluto's association with Scorpio connects the planet to the eleventh and twelfth houses and I wondered if the client's present circumstances were influenced by the plight of a friend. A connection with hospitals seemed likely due to the twelfth house influence as well as the tenancy of the Moon and Chiron in the house of confinement. The Moon was close to Full and ruling the eighth house of death. Someone was seriously ill.

The client then confirmed that she had indeed spent much time in hospital comforting a friend - but it was the friend's husband who was ill, the client said. Nevertheless, we can see that the friend is in no fit state to cope on her own. Traditionally the friend is ruled by Mars, as ruler of the eleventh and Mars is in a sorry state. It is in detriment, retrograde and in the friend's twelfth house if we turn the chart (the Radix tenth). My client confirmed that the friend was distraught and quite unable to cope, hence my client's involvement.

Naturally, my client wanted to know what could happen to the friend's husband. He is signified by the Radix fifth house, it being the seventh house from the eleventh. Saturn is placed therein, which is not good for health. Further Saturn is square the Nodes and Uranus, indicating a very difficult situation. The Radix fifth house rules the heart and liver which my client confirmed were the offending organs. The husband had cancer. The course of the illness will be seen by following Venus, ruling the husband's first house. Venus is part of the T-square noted earlier and it is now evident that each planet involved in this configuration rules the three players in the chart. Venus rules the husband, Mars the wife and Jupiter my client. However, in the turned chart read for the husband, Mars also rules death as it governs his eighth house (the Radix twelfth). Unfortunately, Venus applies to Mars by square, suggesting that he and death will meet up.

I told my client that her friend's husband would possibly die in about two weeks - there were about two degrees separating Venus and Mars. I left it to her to decide whether she thought it wise to impart this information to her friend, or not; some people do of course, like to be prepared for the appearance of the grim reaper. The client did not inform her friend of the possibility of death, but the knowledge helped her deal much better with the friend's bereavement. The husband died just over two weeks later.

Much later the client was able to get on with her plans to study for a new career.

The Consultation Chart

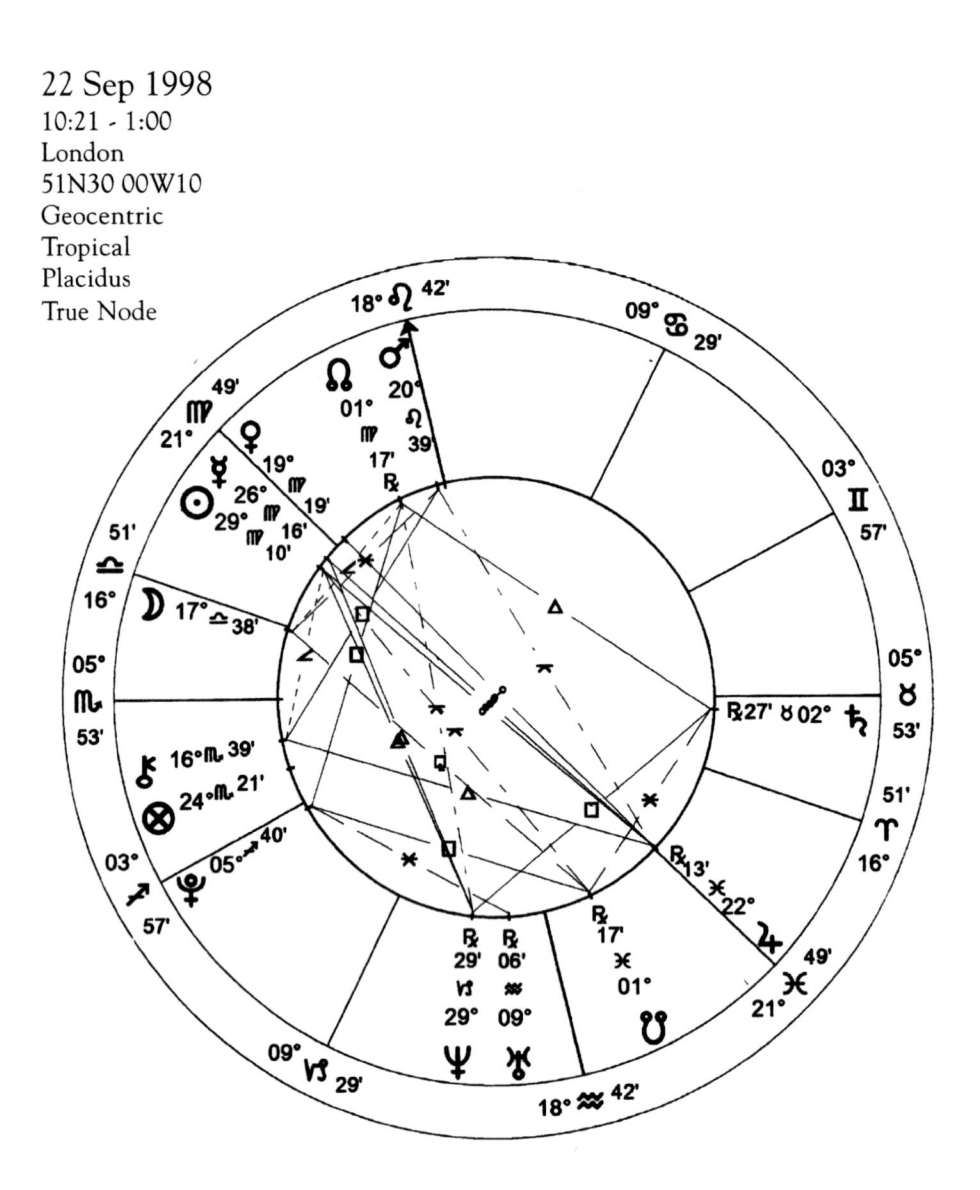

22 Sep 1998
10:21 - 1:00
London
51N30 00W10
Geocentric
Tropical
Placidus
True Node

The client did indeed ask a question: she wanted to know whether she would become pregnant in the very near future. Scorpio rising suggests changes and upheavals as well as focusing upon the reproductive system. The Ascendant ruler Mars is in Leo, a barren sign, and fails to aspect Jupiter (by traditional aspect), the ruler of the fifth house of children. Neither does the Moon, which also indicates the client or querent, aspect Jupiter. Therefore, it was unlikely she would conceive in the very near future. In order to comfort the client, however, I suggested she was fertile and could still become pregnant in the future - fertility is suggested by the strength of Jupiter's position in its own sign

Pisces, a fertile sign. She said the two children she already had were testimony to her fertility! An aspect does of course, exist between Mars and Jupiter, though considered ineffective in traditional astrology since it is a quincunx (150 degrees). It often refers to ill-health, and I followed this line of thought since the hot and dry Mars (representative of the client) is in Leo, a hot and dry sign as well; possibly the client was 'burnt out' through overwork. Note that Mars also rules the sixth house of ill-health and work and is placed in the tenth of career. In short, I suggested that she was exhausted and not really in the right frame of mind or physical condition to conceive. She agreed that was exactly how she felt. She had been extremely busy looking after the family business and was in fact tired and worn out.

To judge how the business was likely to fare, I examined the Sun, which rules the tenth house. Placed in Virgo and the eleventh house of groups, it appeared as if there were several people involved in the business. Well of course - the whole family! The exact trine to Neptune, a benevolent aspect, seemed to pose little threat. Nevertheless, Neptune was involved in a square with Saturn, creating an unstable situation. Saturn opposing the Ascendant described obstacles to be faced and overcome. I suggested that the client had experienced deception from a neighbour (Neptune in third). This was verified by the client who said that a jealous neighbour had complained to the authorities about the family business, making false claims. Since both the Sun and Neptune were at the last degrees of their respective signs, I said that the matter would soon be resolved and the neighbour would be discredited.

The client informed me that is exactly what happened.

The Consultation Chart

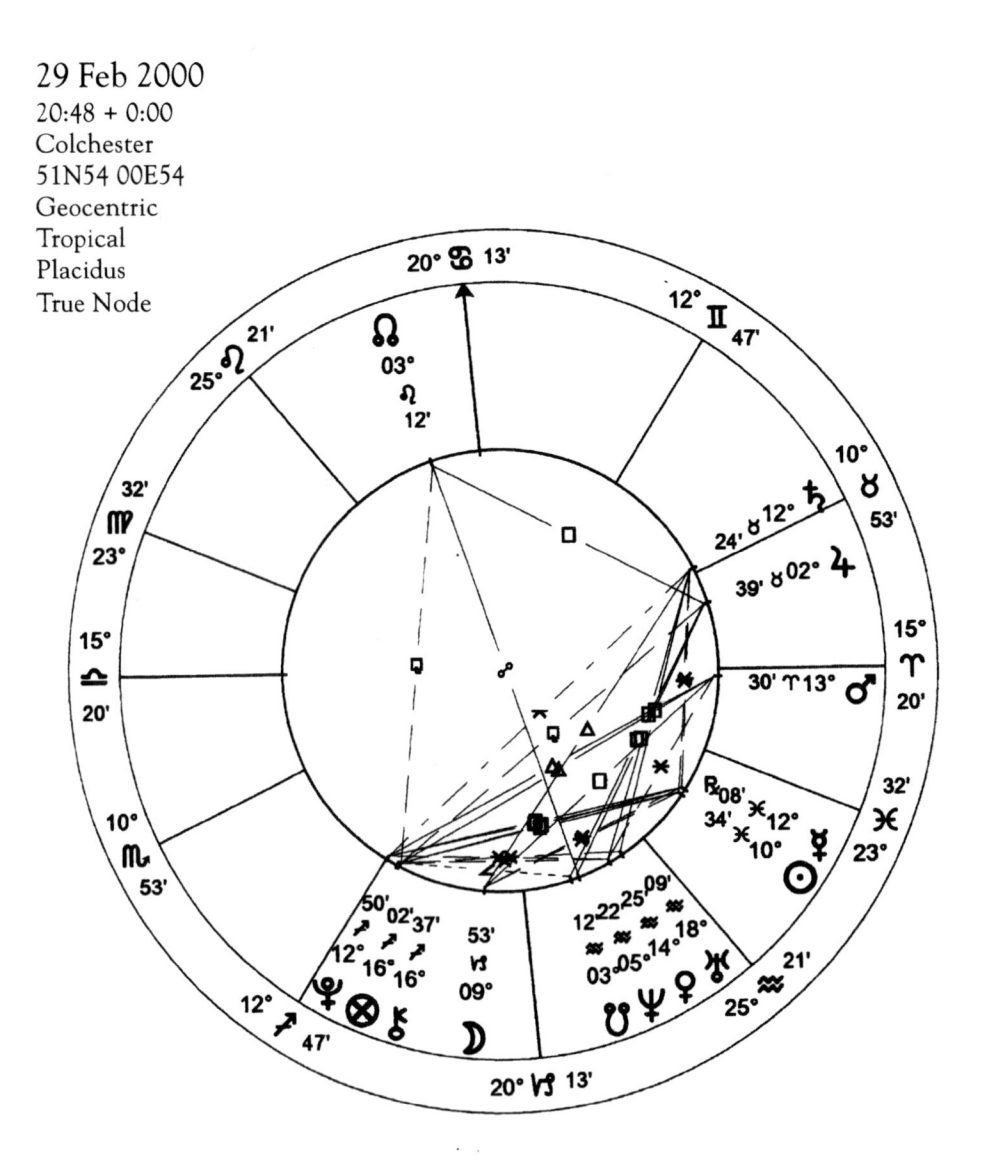

29 Feb 2000
20:48 + 0:00
Colchester
51N54 00E54
Geocentric
Tropical
Placidus
True Node

The client wanted to know the significance of the rash around her neck. She had a doctor's appointment but wondered if an astrologer could pinpoint the cause.

The sixth house of illness has Pisces on the cusp with its ruler Jupiter in Taurus. This confirms the part of the body afflicted by the rash, since Taurus rules the neck. As Jupiter is in the seventh, this of course, points to another party. Jupiter also rules the third house of communication, and its square to Neptune, the Nodes and sesquiquadrate to Chiron suggest confusion and pain.

I asked if she and another party had been in some kind of argument recently? She replied that she had, with her partner, and that is when the rash began, or shortly after. The end of the relationship is signified by Venus, ruling the Ascendant which separates by just *one* degree from a sextile with Mars, ruling the seventh house. I asked if they had broken up *one* month ago, and the client confirmed that they had.

Venus (the client) in Aquarius and the fourth house is besieged by two outer planets. This described the client as withdrawn and unable to act, as if overwhelmed by events. Furthermore, Venus had only shortly separated from the square of Saturn, and since the planets are still in orb, the unhappiness of the parting persists and so does the rash. The client said that she did in fact feel churned up and unable to let go. I encouraged her to voice her emotions, which were: *betrayal, unhappiness, stabbed in the back, loss of trust*. Saturn is in the eighth house where it delights of course, and is quite capable of promoting the betrayal and unhappiness described by the client.

I remembered that Jupiter (ruling the affliction) was in square to the Nodes, indicating a persistent and familiar situation. The Nodal line crosses the fourth and tenth axis, which suggests a connection to the parents and early home life. Were those feelings of betrayal and unhappiness something she experienced with her parents? She agreed that these were feelings that were all too familiar to her. I suggested that maybe this was an appropriate time to deal with these feelings, and perhaps the argument with her partner had brought them to the surface. I then asked her an obvious question as I wanted her to seek answers for herself. What colour was the rash I enquired? She said that it was red, of course. I asked her to tell me what the colour red meant to her - and she said it spelt danger. I asked her if the argument with her partner made her feel she was in danger. *Yes, he had grabbed her by the throat and had started to strangle her!*

I suggested that the shock of that incident was still with her, hence the rash, and she was right to seek treatment. Besides seeing her G.P., I suggested she might try one of the complementary therapies, like massage or shiatsu, which would help re-align the body's energies and chakras.

The client seemed satisfied that we had uncovered the cause of the persistent rash.

The Consultation Chart

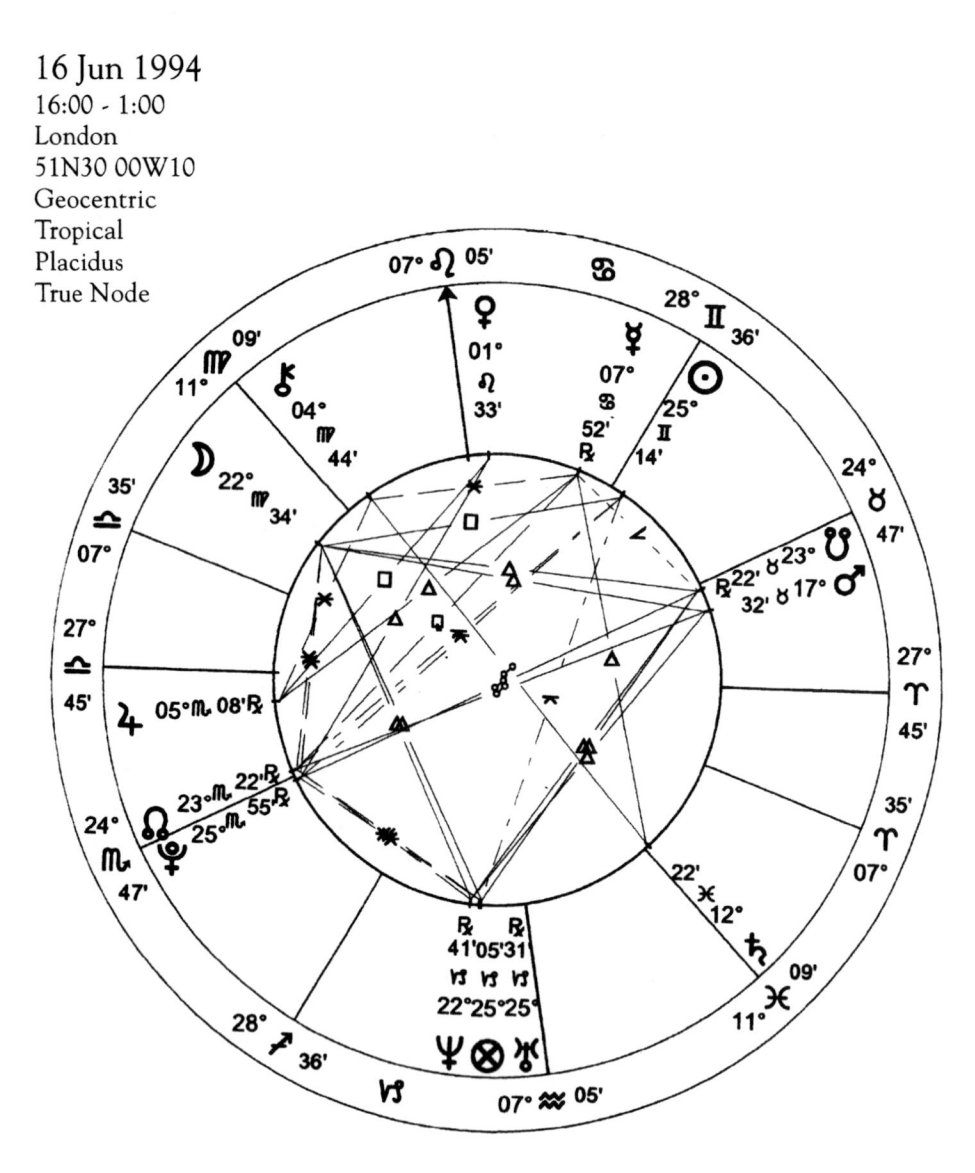

16 Jun 1994
16:00 - 1:00
London
51N30 00W10
Geocentric
Tropical
Placidus
True Node

A decumbiture chart can also be a consultation chart. Decumbiture was the form of astrology used by astrologer/herbalists, particularly in the 17th century, to determine the cause of sickness. The word decumbiture derives from the Latin *decumbere*, meaning to lie down. A chart was therefore set up for the moment the patient first took to his bed upon becoming ill, or failing that, for the time the patient took his urine to the physician. It was also acceptable to erect a chart for the first meeting or *consultation* between patient and physician/astrologer.

In my practise as an aromatherapist, I customarily took the time of the first arrival of each client. If the client's condition proved to be a challenging one, I would set up a chart to throw further light on the situation both from a medical and psychological viewpoint. The following is a consultation decumbiture.

My client, Meg, aged 50, had been suffering from severe headaches located just behind the eyes for around 6 years and the condition was getting worse. The pain tended to increase at the onset of menstruation. Medical checks had shown a hormone imbalance but the medics had not indicated if this was linked to the headaches. Meg's neck and shoulders became swollen at the end of each day. She felt bloated, especially after drinking milk and suffered with water retention, lethargy and insomnia. Her GP had organised tests for her with an eye specialist, and when nothing was found to account for her headaches he suggested she try aromatherapy massage to lessen her anxiety.

During treatment, I noticed that the reflexes on her feet pertaining to her sinuses were very painful. She had not mentioned problems in this area during the consultation, but admitted that she suffered terribly with blocked sinuses. (The sinuses are cavities in the bones just under the eyes either side of the nose; they reduce the weight of the skull and add resonance to the voice.) She then mentioned that whenever the sinuses 'unblocked', her nose would start running and her headaches lessened. I asked if any doctor had suggested that her sinus problem might be connected to her headaches. None had.

In the consultation/decumbiture chart, Libra rises and signifies there may be a problem with the homeostatic function within the body. This is confirmed by the placement of Venus, a cold and moist planet and the ruler of the Ascendant ruler, in Leo, a hot and dry sign. The contrast in temperature was an indication of the client's uncomfortable feelings. Venus rules hormones and glands and is square to the ascending degree, and Jupiter in the first house has an effect upon the general constitution. It rules the lungs and liver and is relatively weak through retrogradation. In Scorpio it highlights the reproductive system and the nose. Scorpio has co-rulership with Aries over the nose, which sign is actually on the sixth house cusp of illness. This shows that the difficulty lies in the head - ruled by Aries.

    The ruler, Mars, is in Taurus and weak through detriment. Taurus rules the throat as well as the naso-pharynx, a passage-way which connects the back of the mouth and nose with the larynx, the voice box. Mars is in platick (in aspect by sign) opposition to Jupiter, which connects the nose, throat and reproductive system through the Taurus/Scorpio axis. Therefore there did seem to be a connection between the headaches, the blocked sinuses and menstruation. It seemed like a problem of elimination since Scorpio is a sign of elimination as is the nose and menstruation. Remember that the headaches would ease when the nose 'unblocked'.

'Medicines' are ruled by the tenth house, where we find the sign of Leo. The ruler, the Sun, is applying by trine to the ascending degree suggesting that Sun-type medicines would probably help. My 'medicines' were in the form of essential oils since this was an aromatherapy consultation. Essential oils are extracted from plants and have a powerful effect on both mind and body by ingestion through the pores of the skin (massage) and inhalation. I chose Rosemary, Frankincense and Juniper, all Sun-ruled plants/oils. Rosemary is well known for its cephalic (head clearing) properties. It is also diuretic (releasing water) and a liver decongestant. Frankincense helps to clear the lungs, deepens breathing and helps to release phlegm. Juniper helps to balance water in the body and encourages detoxification.

After a few treatments spanning a month, the client's headaches become less intense and less frequent. Her sinuses were much less painful and her nose was unblocked most of the time. Her next period was less painful and her shoulders ached less. She was also sleeping much better; only later did she mention her chronic constipation - once that had started to improve! The decumbiture/consultation chart had indeed pointed to the difficulty lying in the process of elimination, as both the bowels and the nose are ruled by Scorpio.

Case Histories

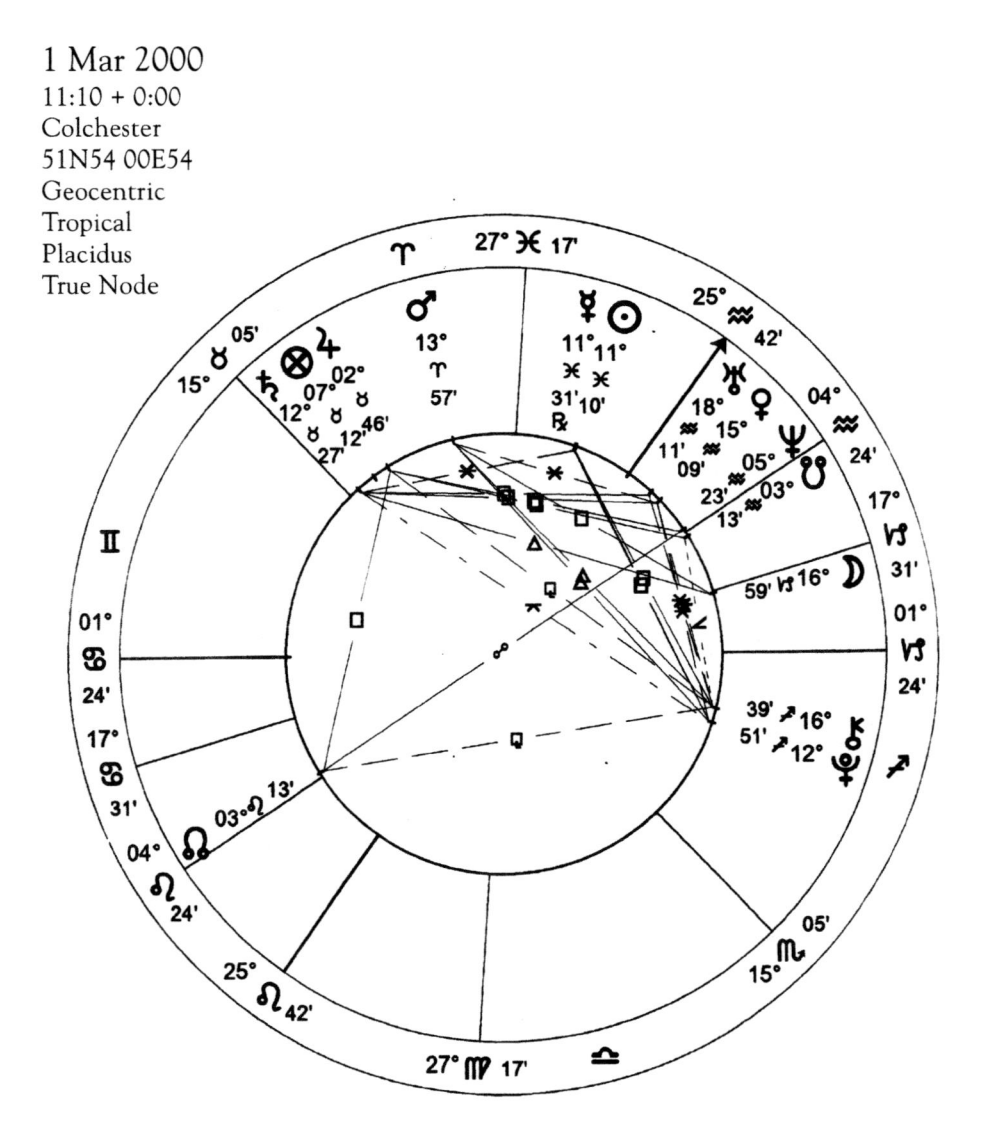

1 Mar 2000
11:10 + 0:00
Colchester
51N54 00E54
Geocentric
Tropical
Placidus
True Node

Certain rules and regulations effect the horary chart which rather inhibit the astrologer in judging a chart. Some of these rules are 'strictures', others are 'considerations before judgement' and if too many of them apply to a chart, then it is unlikely the chart is radical. Does this mean that the client is turned away because the heavenly umpire does not want to play dice with the cosmos? Ultimately perhaps these 'strictures' and 'considerations' are really there for our own good, because what we delineate or judge may not be correct, should they go unheeded. Do we also look upon the horary chart (or almost any chart for that matter) as a means of prognostication only, or is it also a tool for counselling? After all, we are dealing with a real live person who would not

The Consultation Chart

understand being turned out of the consultation room because the planets at the time of the question were not quite in alignment with traditional rules and regulations.

According to traditional rules I should not have given this chart another glance after realising that an early degree was rising and that the Moon was Void of Course. Please check statements in 'Christian Astrology' by William Lilly (p.122) which exhort us to run hell for leather in circumstances such as these. But when the client asked me to say something about her health, I could hardly leave her stranded. Well, health questions are a bit tricky anyway, so perhaps most sensible astrologers would have declined to delineate. If I had been looking at the chart purely from a predictive point of view, there really wouldn't have been much to say; after all, the Moon *was* Void of Course, so nothing was likely to happen. Also, the early degree rising was shouting that 'it was too early to say'. Rubbish. There was nothing *early* about the client's situation.

Cancer rising indicated that some emotional and domestic matter had put the client/querent into an unhappy frame of mind. The Moon, representing the client, was in its detriment giving her little to laugh about. It was separating from a square to a hot little Mars in Aries, indicating an inflammatory condition. Mars is also the ruler of her sixth house of ill-health. The Moon in Capricorn rules bones and I suggested arthritis, which the client confirmed. Arthritis is a disease where the joints become affected by inflammatory or degenerative changes causing pain and stiffness. So okay, the prognosis tends to be poor though perhaps much better today than in former years - perhaps the chart was screaming loudly that nothing could be done about the client's illness. Could psychological insight do something where steroids only stem the tide? Let's see.

The Moon separates from Mars by three degrees and I asked if the condition had been around for three years. The answer was in the affirmative, but why hadn't I said three days rather than years, since both planets were in cardinal signs (C.A.p.267)? I'll be honest, I don't know, it just felt right at the time. Perhaps it has something to do with *'mixing art with reason'* as Lilly would say. Also, I wondered if the onset of the arthritis had occurred due to some difficulty in a relationship. Note the Moon is in the seventh house. The client said that it was the greatest difficulty of all: her husband had died the same year as the arthritis reared its ugly head. Turning the chart, we see that the husband's sixth house (radix twelfth) has Taurus on its cusp and Gemini intercepted therein, indicating the throat and lungs. Saturn is poised on its cusp indicating blockages. I wondered if her husband had had trouble breathing. The client told me that he had suffered from pulmonary emphysema, which is characterised by distension of the air sacs (alveoli). The husband's illness had lasted for a long time, causing the client a great deal of heartache. She had nursed him, dutifully, as we can see from the Moon's separating trine from Saturn, but my goodness wasn't she angry with him too! (Moon square Mars is anger after all). There were more floods of tears now because that was exactly the case. She said that she had become exhausted from looking after him and never had a moment to herself. Of course, her grief was great at his death, but she also felt relieved. I suggested that the root of her problems was the guilt. Saturn disposes of the Moon and poised on the twelfth house cusp suggests sorrow and guilt, but also a total repression of feelings which are not socially acceptable; she could hardly show her relief openly. Socially she could not be stigmatised, but her body was burdened with these repressed emotions.

Now she could at least speak of them, giving such taboos an airing to someone who would not judge, and then feel free to get on with her life. I don't know what happened after that, but I'd like to think that some chink of light entered her mind after our conversation and maybe, just maybe she felt better.

3. Relationships

The Consultation Chart

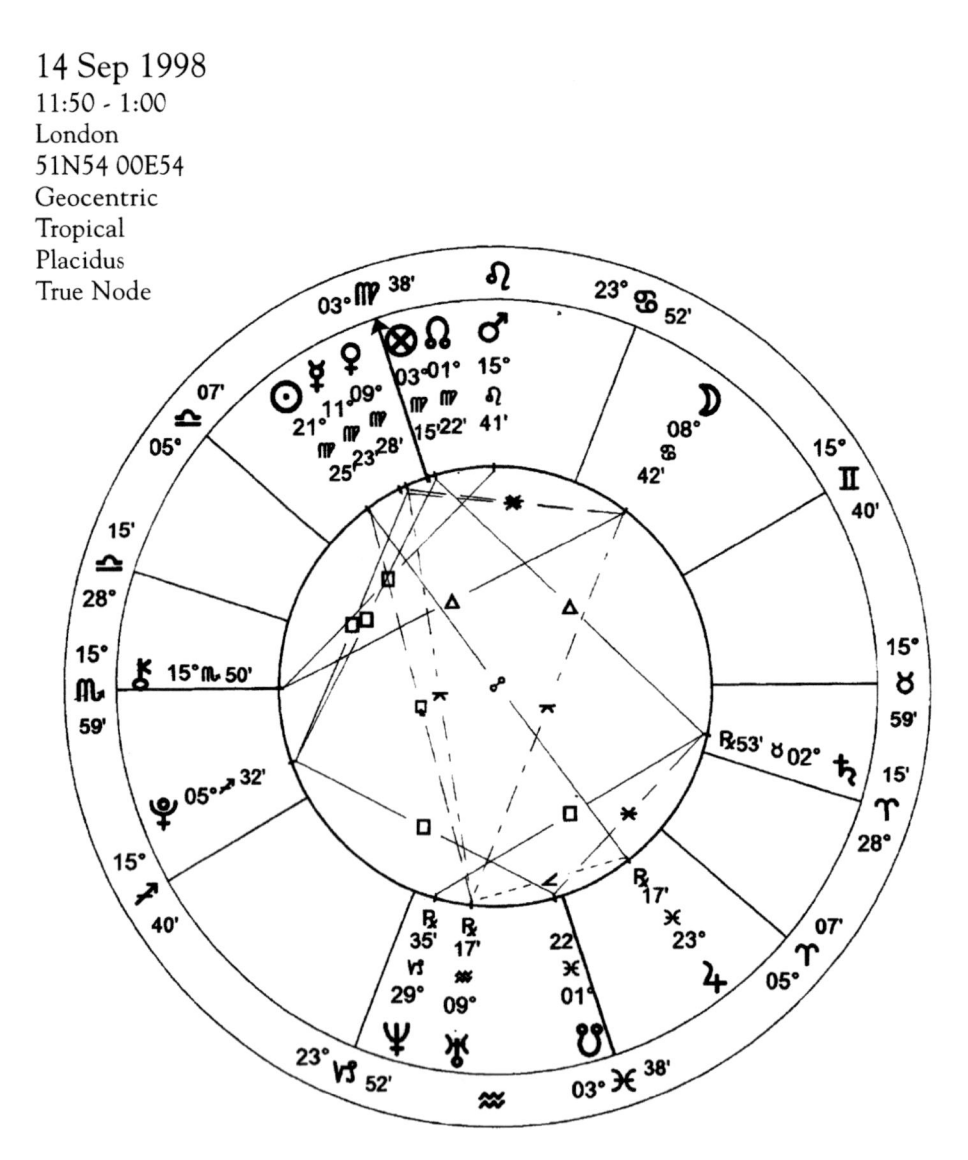

14 Sep 1998
11:50 - 1:00
London
51N54 00E54
Geocentric
Tropical
Placidus
True Node

The client wanted to know if she would have a relationship. I would obviously look for an applying aspect between Mars and Venus as rulers of the first and seventh houses respectively. Since there was none I examined the Moon, also representative of the client, and found that it was indeed applying by an unimpeded sextile to Venus. Yes, I said, there would be a relationship. The client was crestfallen. Somehow this news did not please her as the object of her affections was married, she said, and so was she! I asked her if her implied question was: *if we have a relationship, will he leave his wife?* Yes, she said, that is what she hoped for. I did not feel that the man would leave his wife by virtue of the following reasoning: Venus, his significator, is in its fall and therefore weak and it is also conjunct Mercury which represents both his wife (planetary conjunction can represent an interested party) and his home. Both planets are in the fourth house ruled by Mercury, which disposes of Venus and is of course, extremely strong in its own sign. The wife and his home still have a strong pull on his affections, so I said that it was highly unlikely this man would leave his wife.

As Venus, his significator, was in the client's tenth house, I wondered if he was connected to her place of work: she confirmed that he was. Since Virgo was so prominent I asked if he were involved in health matters, which indeed he was. Since the Moon was in Cancer, it was obvious she also worked in a caring capacity, possibly as a nurse. It seemed as if this was a hospital romance. It was. Although the Moon is strong through placements in its own sign, it is in a form of besiegement, because it stands between the two malefics, Mars and Saturn. It seemed to me that she was very unhappy and suffering through the constraints of some emotional situation since the Moon is in the eighth house, indication of emotional turmoil. Chiron on the Ascendant suggested she was a wounded soul.

It appeared she was extremely unhappy in her marriage and a discussion ensued about this. The upshot of the consultation was that the client decided she would try to sort out her problems with her husband and seek counselling.

The Consultation Chart

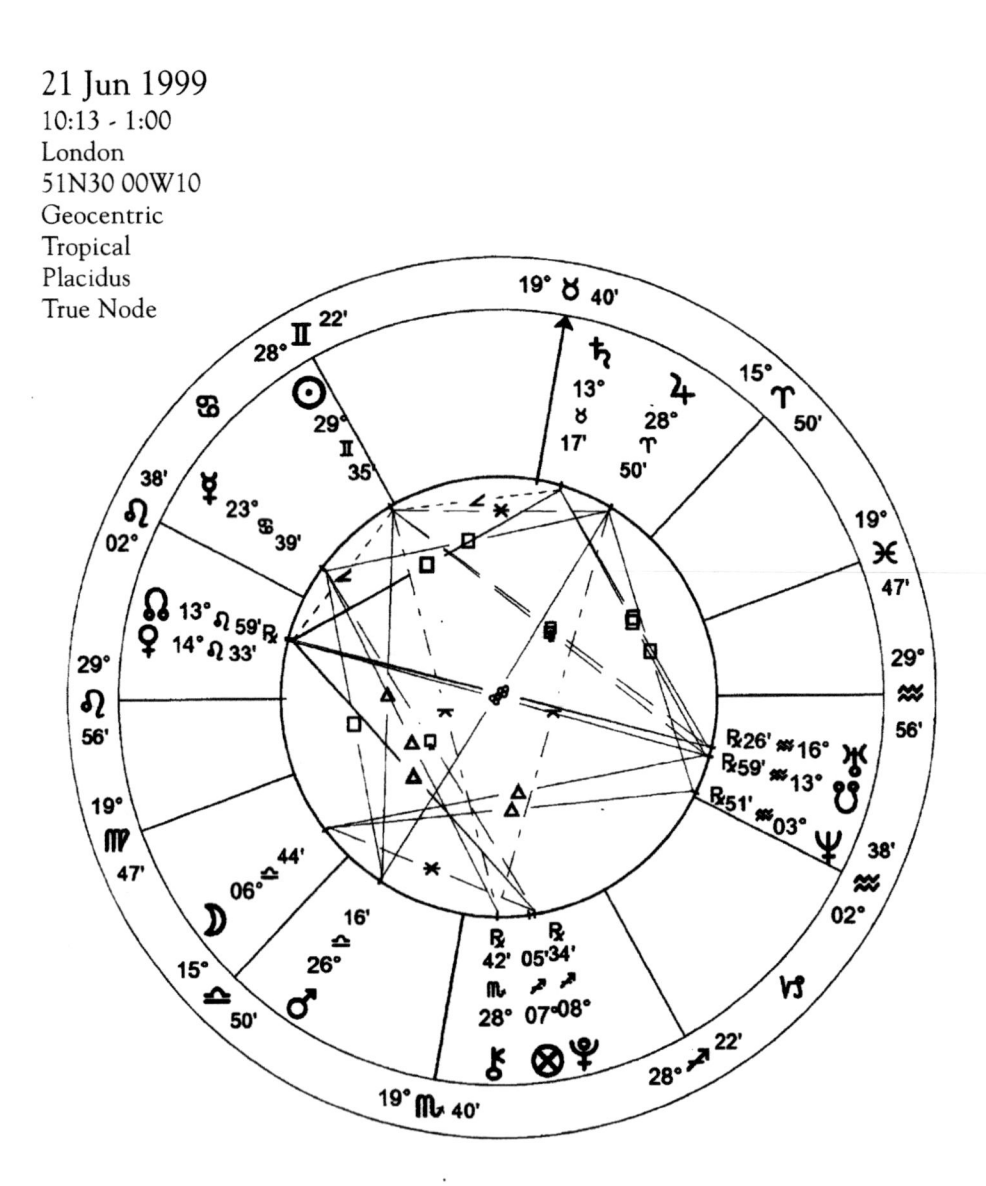

21 Jun 1999
10:13 - 1:00
London
51N30 00W10
Geocentric
Tropical
Placidus
True Node

As Leo rises, it appears that the client is ready to flex her creative muscles as well as her skills at organisation. The Sun, the Ascendant ruler, is placed in Gemini and the eleventh house. It may be safe to predict that there is a busy time ahead with much communication amongst large groups of people. Quite possibly her social life will improve, yet she seems to be coming to the end of a cycle as the Sun is at the last degree of the sign, as is the rising sign. One phase of her life is ending and another beginning. The Sun is separating from the sextile of Jupiter which is placed in the ninth house of legal matters, and rules the eighth house of joint resources. It appears that the client has been sorting out financial matters probably through the courts. The sextile indicates that it was a good settlement. The Sun's semi-square aspect to Venus, the North Node and Saturn however, indicates that she probably feels quite sad: she may be saying goodbye to someone she loves as Saturn rules the seventh house. It looks as if love has cooled. I felt that work was involved in this situation, since Venus rules the tenth house. The Sun is also separating from the trine of Mars which is in the third house and rules the fourth, indicating that she has received a communication from someone from her past.

The client explained that she was going through a divorce and sorting out the joint finances between herself and her husband. The settlement had been to her advantage. The marriage had broken down because they no longer loved each other - he had in fact proved very difficult and had made trouble for her at work, much to her embarrassment. She did indeed feel that one phase of her life was coming to an end and another beginning and she was in fact looking forward to increasing her social circle. A boyfriend from the past had contacted her. In this consultation, prediction was not part of the equation, since the Sun, the client's ruling planet, would not aspect another planet before leaving the sign, and the Moon's next aspect to Venus was quite wide. It would be tempting to say that 'nothing would happen' but of course, that was not quite right, since the client was about to enter a new phase in her life. She would eventually be making new friends and the 'romance' with the old boyfriend would continue for a while (until the Sun and Mars were no longer in the moeity of their orbs). It gave the client some encouragement to know that the cosmos mirrored her situation so precisely!

The Consultation Chart

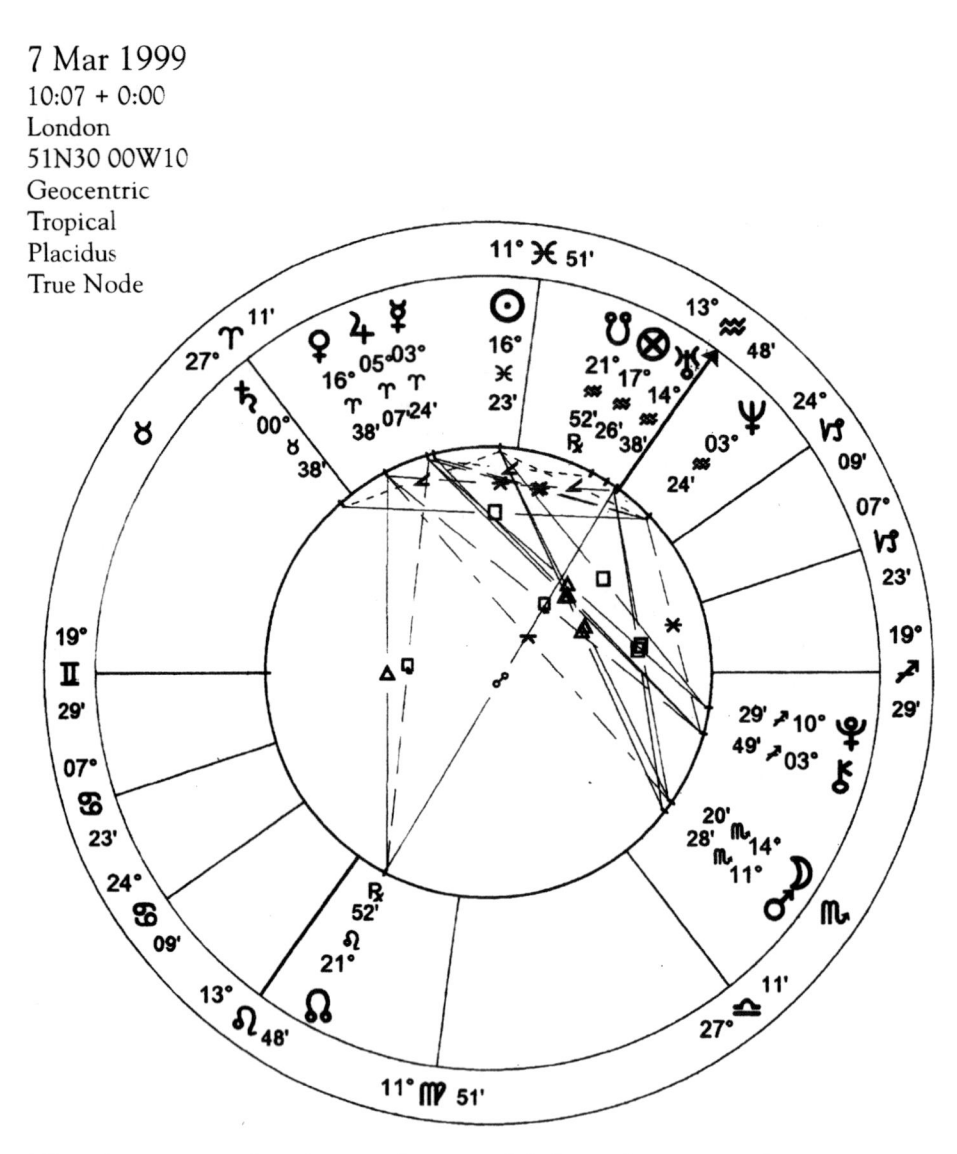

7 Mar 1999
10:07 + 0:00
London
51N30 00W10
Geocentric
Tropical
Placidus
True Node

The client wanted to know what was likely to happen within an existing relationship. Gemini rises indicating that the client was probably undecided about her present situation, yet with the Ascendant ruler Mercury placed in Aries, she was quite keen and probably somewhat impatient to come to some kind of understanding with her partner. It appears that Mercury will soon conjoin Jupiter, the ruler of the seventh house, her partner, and that the client will be safely in his arms.

Not so, unfortunately!

Mercury will turn retrograde on 10th March - an example of *refranation* - before it reaches Jupiter's degree. I said she would probably walk away from this relationship. The client then asked if her partner had another woman. As Venus was so close to Jupiter I said it looked as if there had been someone else on the scene, quite recently, perhaps a few weeks previously (when Venus and Jupiter had been conjunct). I didn't think it had been anything serious because Venus was weak through detriment and was separating from Jupiter. The client confirmed that was around the time she suspected that there had been someone else on the scene. She had indeed thought that her lover had been unfaithful.

In a relationship matter, the swifter planet often shows the keener of the two and as the client is represented by Mercury, she is obviously fonder of him than he is of her. With this in mind I said that it looked as if her relationship had been floundering long before the other woman came on the scene. It turned out that he was married anyway and this other woman was probably catalytic to their break-up.

The client was very hurt and said that she was very tempted to take revenge on the man, his wife and the other woman. This seemed rather descriptive of the Moon's fall in Scorpio, also representative of the client. Since Mars conjoined the Moon and being much stronger, placed as it was in its own sign, I said she herself would suffer most by any actions of revenge. Whenever the Moon and Mars are conjoined, the Moon seems to gets hurt. Mars also influences the sixth/twelfth houses, the axis of victimisation (Mars is in the sixth, rules the twelfth). The client felt exploited and hurt and wanted to hit back. Fortunately she decided against plotting revenge as I felt it would backfire. The next aspect of the Moon was the square to Uranus on the tenth house cusp and I advised her to concentrate on her career, as I could see she was planning a change. She said she was indeed and agreed to put her energies in that direction.

The Consultation Chart

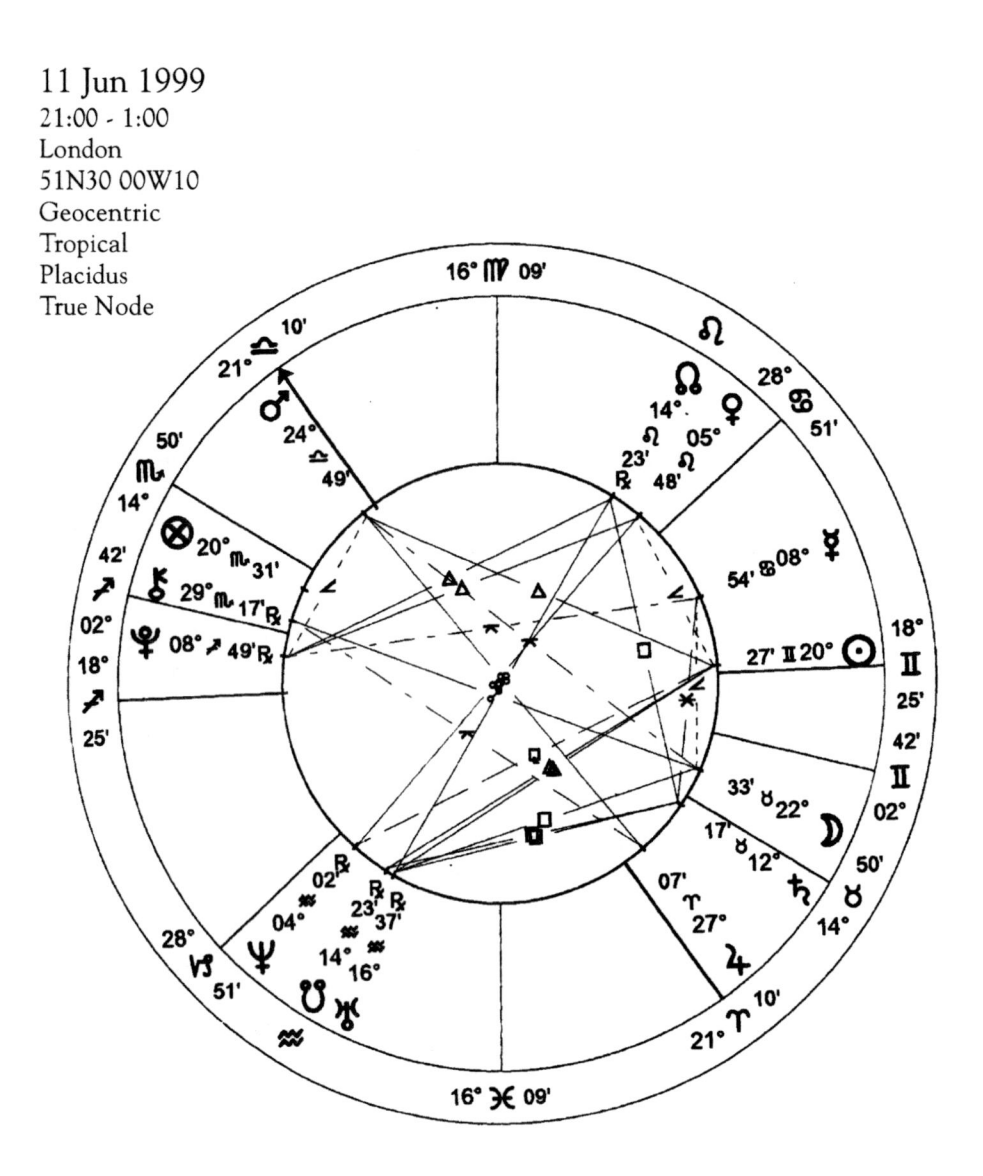

11 Jun 1999
21:00 - 1:00
London
51N30 00W10
Geocentric
Tropical
Placidus
True Node

Initially the client wanted to know more about the state of her health but her concern transpired to be symptomatic of a deeper emotional problem. Nevertheless, I examined the sixth house to ascertain what health problems existed, if any.

Gemini cusping the sixth house pointed to the chest, while its ruler Mercury was in Cancer, indicating the breasts and stomach. The Sun, which rules the heart, opposes the Ascendant. I asked the client if she had any pains in her upper torso, avoiding actual diagnosis. She said that she was indeed troubled by pains in her chest. Mercury, ruler of the sixth, applied by sextile to Saturn in the fourth, almost fifth house, and by semi-square to the Moon in the fifth. The focus did appear to be on the heart, the domain of the fifth. I naturally advised her to contact her doctor for a check up as this would put her mind at rest.

Of course, there need not be a physical cause to illness - her chest pains could have been symptomatic of some deep emotion connected to the heart chakra. I suspected this to be the case since Mercury ruled the seventh house as well as the sixth and was placed in the seventh. This suggested that a relationship was in some way connected to her feelings of ill-health. I ventured to ask if she might be concerned over a partnership question. She revealed that an old boyfriend had recently appeared on the scene and this had reactivated old emotions; in fact she felt disoriented and out of control. I asked if her chest pains coincided with his appearance. She suddenly realised that she had indeed begun to have these pains soon after he had re-entered her life.

Mercury's inconjunct to Pluto may well point to a health problem, as it is an aspect of ill-health, but Pluto's position in the twelfth house also shows a lack of willpower. Was the client unable to express her innermost needs? Was there some kind of 'unfinished business' in the client's life which the ex-boyfriend somehow represented? The relationship itself was unlikely to resume since there was no aspect between Mercury and Jupiter, the Ascendant ruler. The client said she had not expected a reconciliation.

I asked the client to describe the feelings she associated with her boyfriend. She said he had made her feel 'warm, loved and connected'. I then asked her to go back to a time in her life when she felt the opposite, that is 'cold, unloved and disconnected'. She revealed that she had always felt unloved by her parents and excluded from their lives. Note that Jupiter, her ruler, is actually in the fourth house in opposition to Mars in the tenth, which actually rules the fourth. It appeared as if she were in conflict with one of her parents at this time, and she confirmed that she was in dispute with her mother. The client said that it had always been a difficult relationship and it had recently become worse. Her mother was dominating and unreliable.

I suggested that the pains in her chest were in some way connected to her lack of nurturing, perhaps brought on by the recent altercation with her mother and the ex-boyfriend's sudden appearance on the scene. He was a reminder of the love she once had which contrasted so starkly to the lack of love from her mother. Although this was a painful time, it also represented an opportunity for her to reconnect to the expression of love.

The Consultation Chart

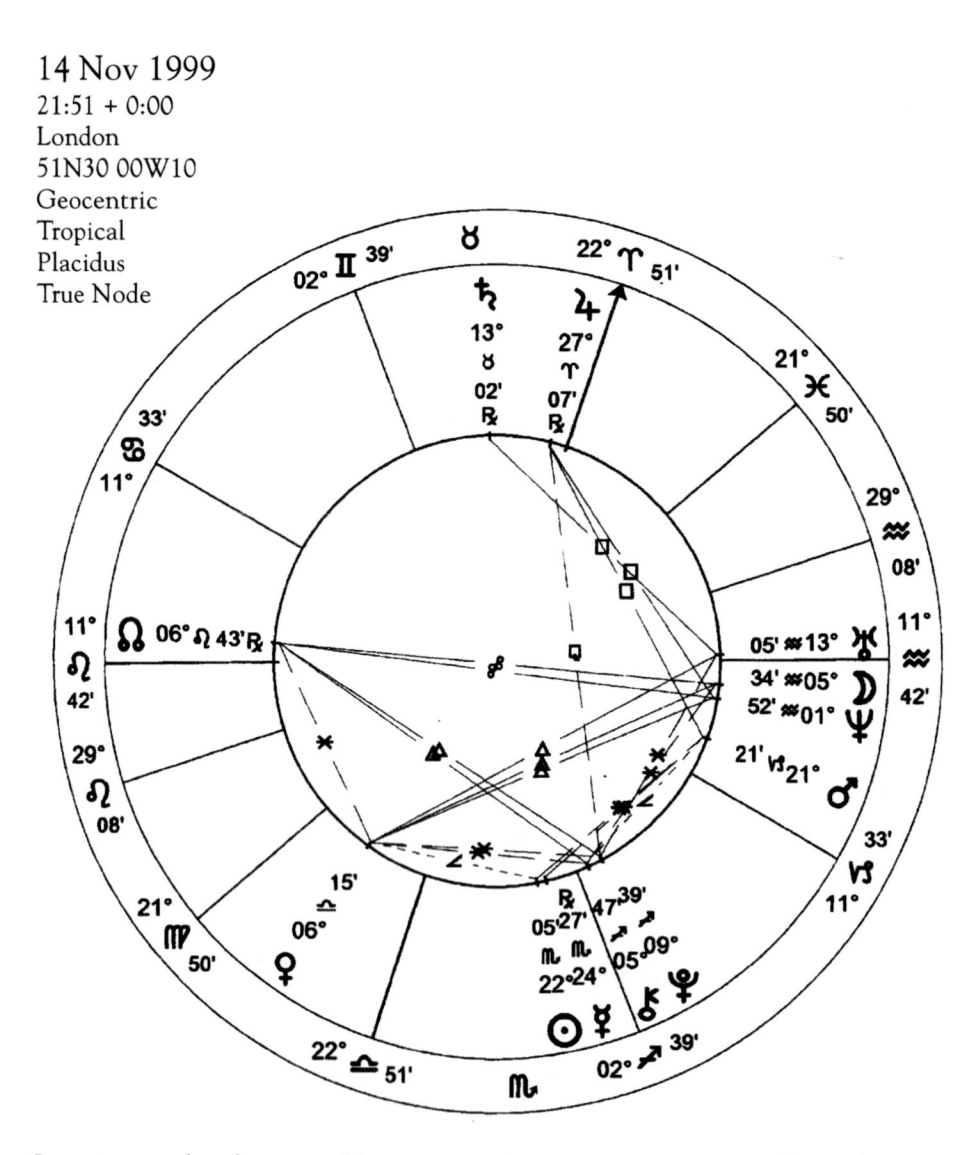

14 Nov 1999
21:51 + 0:00
London
51N30 00W10
Geocentric
Tropical
Placidus
True Node

Leo rises and indicates a blossoming of new activity, or an affair. The Sun, ruling the Ascendant is in Scorpio, intercepted in the fourth house. The client is in turmoil and unable to express her needs. The Sun has passed the sextile with Mars by one degree. Mars in Capricorn is strong by exaltation and placed in the sixth house as well as ruling the tenth, which seemed to point to work and career. The client was only mildly interested in this aspect of her life, though she was facing changes in this area.

The Sun had recently passed the opposition of Saturn, which rules the sixth, seventh and eighth houses, indicating a change of circumstances in a relationship: the client was all ears and wanted to know what would happen next. Was there a chance for the relationship still? Obviously not, as the Sun and Saturn were not meeting up again. Would the Moon, also ruling the client or querent, contact Saturn? The Moon is indeed applying to a square of Saturn, but could this combination point to a happy, go-lucky, successful and warm relationship? Quite unlikely. I told the client that she would never be happy in this relationship. Not only does the Moon contact cold Saturn, it is also besieged. The Moon leaves the conjunction of Neptune and applies to a conjunction of Uranus, the planet of separation, which is in the seventh house. There is no chance for this relationship to prosper - I felt that her partner had probably walked all over her as the Moon had after all just left sacrificial Neptune.

Apparently that was the case. The client had given up everything to be with her partner; she no longer saw her friends because she thought that just having each other would be enough. It wasn't and her partner left. The client didn't think the relationship was going anywhere, in fact it had finished, but she wanted confirmation. I was able to give it.

Not wanting to part on a dismal note, I wanted to find something in the chart to cheer her up. I noticed that the Moon's next application would be to the trine of a rather strong Venus in the third house. Surely the placement of Venus in its own sign of Libra would suggest artistic activities? The client confirmed that she was actually thinking of signing up for an art class but wasn't sure. I said she would, and discover unsuspected talents. She did.

The Consultation Chart

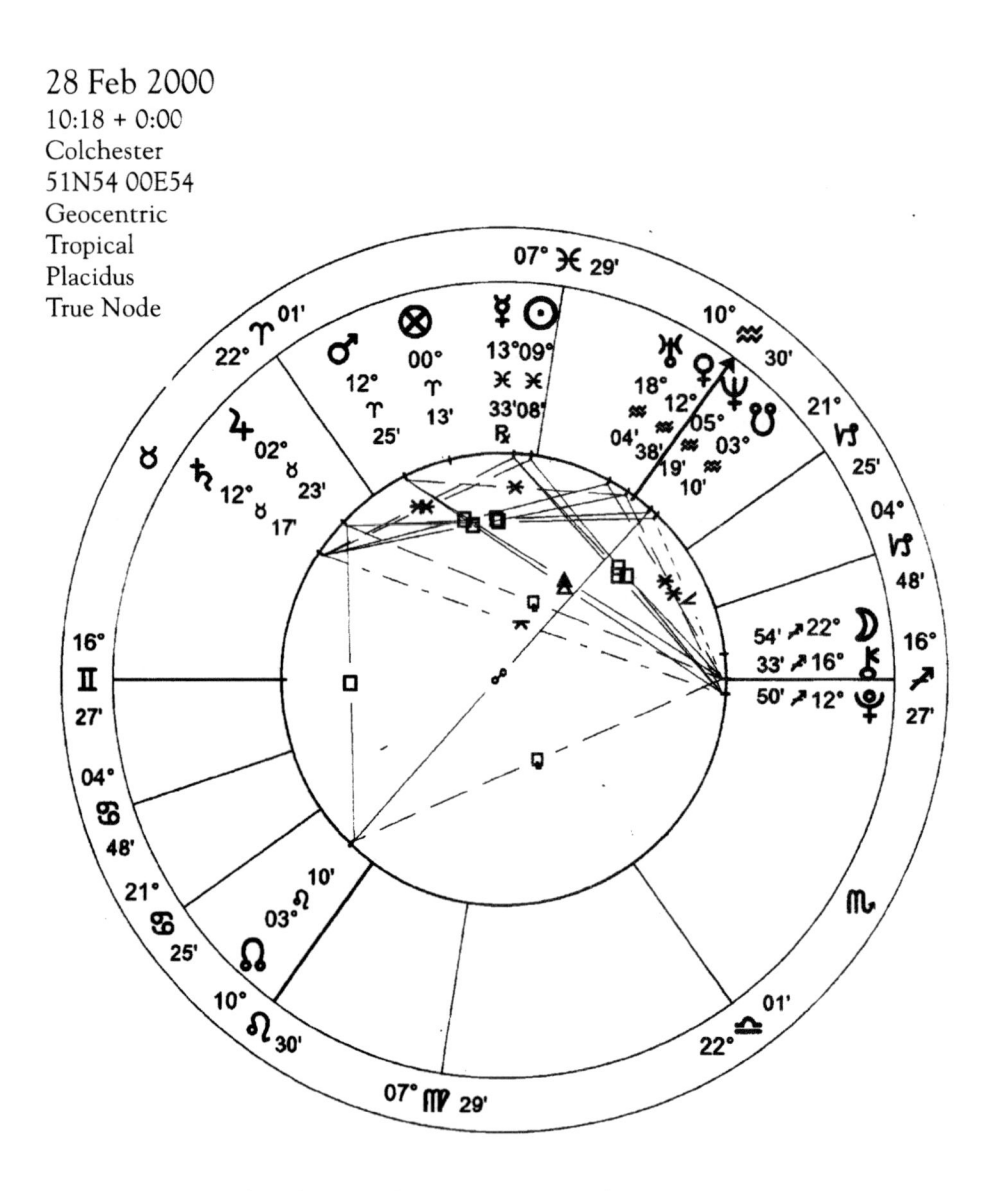

28 Feb 2000
10:18 + 0:00
Colchester
51N54 00E54
Geocentric
Tropical
Placidus
True Node

Gemini rises in this chart, indicating that the client was in two minds about a particular situation. The Ascendant ruler, Mercury, is in its worst possible position since in Pisces it is both in its detriment and fall, as well as being retrograde and combust. It was evident that the client was feeling very unhappy and totally powerless to influence her present situation, whatever that might be. Mercury, her ruler, had been moving away from a sextile with Saturn and a square with Pluto, but was now retrograding back to them. Whatever pain she had suffered was not over, unfortunately. Saturn and Pluto are inconjunct each other, suggesting sacrifices to be made in a relationship; Pluto is on the cusp of the seventh house and the Lord of Karma is in the twelfth, where he rejoices. This looked very much like a painful renunciation, as in fact turned out to be the case.

The client was distraught due to the ending of a relationship and realised there was little hope of its continuance, but wanted confirmation from an astrologer. Saturn actually rules the eighth, ninth and tenth houses, indicating perhaps that the problem had existed within the physical/sexual side of the relationship and this had dashed her hopes and future goals. This described the situation perfectly: there had been a lack of physical intimacy and all the dreams she had of a fulfilling relationship had been dashed.

It appeared that her partner was beset by emotional problems which he would need to deal with, and was in no fit state to be involved in a loving relationship. Together, the Moon, Chiron and Pluto on the seventh house cusp indicate emotional pain of an intense kind. His ruler, Jupiter, was in his sixth house (the radix twelfth), suggesting sickness, and his lack of mental clarity is indicated by Jupiter's square to Neptune and the Nodes in his third house (the radix ninth). The involvement of the Nodes in the square suggested that his problem was of long-standing origin (the Nodes are linked with karma) probably connected with his parents. Note that the Nodes are closing upon the fourth/tenth house axis in both the radix and the turned chart, and are in the signs ruled by this axis.

The client confirmed that this did indeed describe her partner. He was confused and felt totally lost and unable to make any kind of decision. He was also still very much under his parents' influence, although an adult and she said that he had had many problems with them in his childhood. She said he was unable to face his problems and had started sleeping rough. He was not looking after himself and did not want to communicate. Despite the fact that Mercury, her ruler, was retrograding back to Jupiter, her ruler, it seemed that little encouragement could be given for the continuance of the relationship. Mercury was, as noted, in a very weak position, and the client was unlikely to influence her partner. The client agreed there was little hope. Since the two planets would perfect the sextile, I said they would not lose contact just yet. Indeed this was the case, but the relationship did not prosper.

4. Spooks

The Consultation Chart

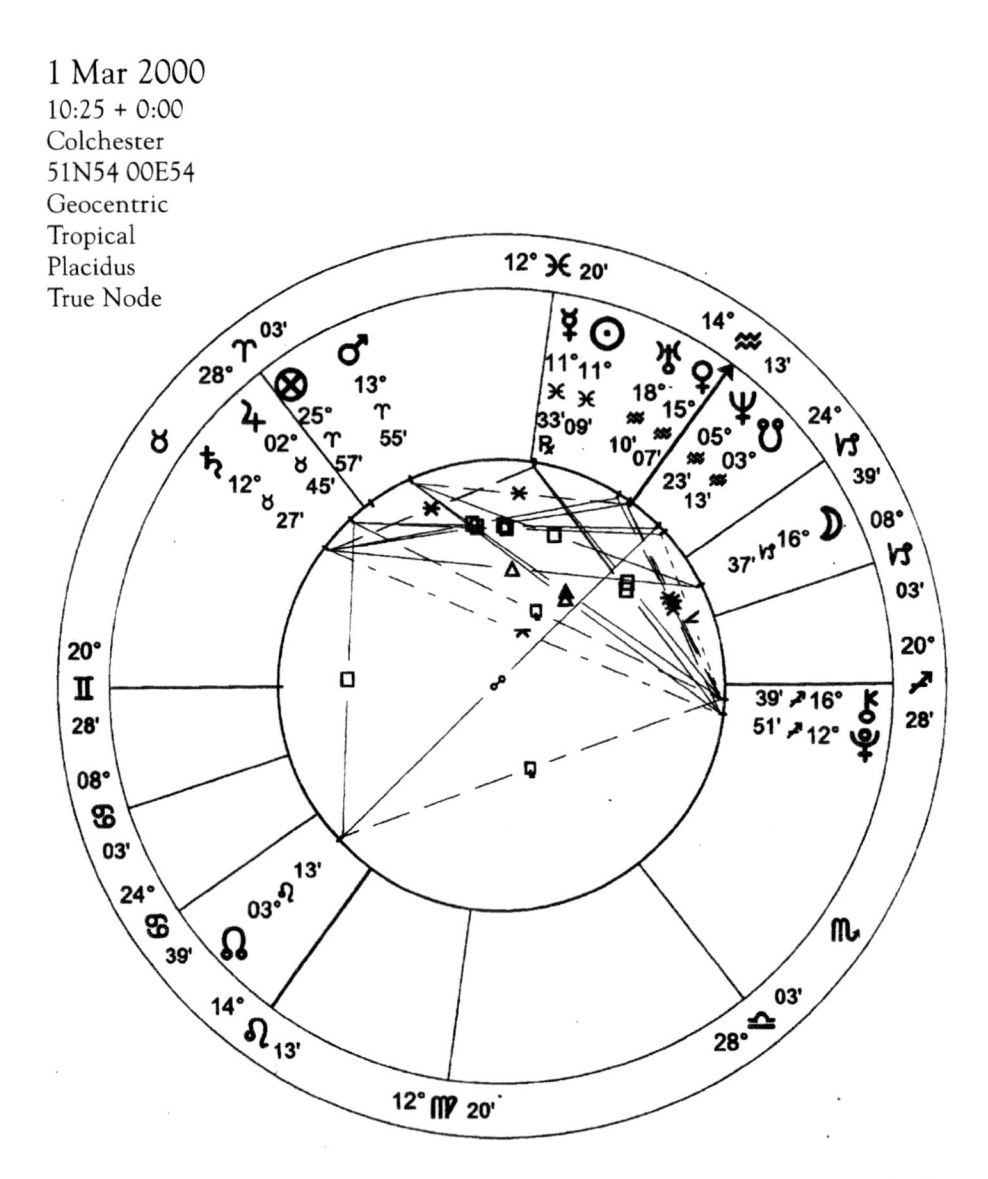

1 Mar 2000
10:25 + 0:00
Colchester
51N54 00E54
Geocentric
Tropical
Placidus
True Node

The astrologer's case load can be very strange indeed. Certainly he or she has to be prepared for anything as this consultation chart seems to suggest.

Gemini rises, possibly indicating an unstable situation, or that the client is in two minds about something. Certainly she is exhausted and lacking direction as she is represented by a very debilitated Mercury in Pisces - the messenger is having a very hard time indeed. He is in its detriment and fall, as well as being retrograde and combust. It is obvious that the quality of the client's life is very strained and she is totally dis-empowered, further suggested by the combustion.

The client confirmed she was at a very low ebb indeed and felt she had no voice in her present circumstances - after all, Pisces is a mute sign. What was it that was taking away all her willpower and motivation? We have to follow the route of the Sun since it dominates the messenger. As the Sun rules the fourth house it was obvious that family matters had brought her so low. Could it be that her father was over-riding all her wishes? Maybe it was also something to do with the family home? The client confirmed that the matter concerned the family home, and the father-in-law was a real nuisance. She and her husband owned a shop and had been trying to sell it for 7 years. Prospective buyers came to see the property, and were always very enthusiastic about it, but they never came back.

I pressed home my point about her father-in law. Was he interfering in any way? She was quite convinced he was, at least his spirit was since he had died several years ago! The client felt that her father-in-law had never left the property and was interfering with prospective buyers. Apparently, he had been adamant that the family should stay together, that they should not move - all the family had lived together.

Strictly speaking of course, her husband's father would be ruled by Saturn in the turned chart, since the radix tenth house is her husband's fourth house, which refers to his father. My attention now turned to Saturn, which is with Jupiter, her husband's significator in radix twelfth house - perhaps suggesting secret and unconscious processes. I asked if her husband had been very much under his father's influence and that perhaps the real problem was with her husband I suggested. The client said that he had been, and she felt that he was still very much under his father's influence even though the old man had long since died. I suggested that if she really felt the old man's spirit was still around, perhaps she ought to see a medium who might be able to tell him to move on. Sometimes spirits do get stuck between the two worlds and need to be informed that they are dead and need to go into the light. Certainly if the client felt he was still around, perhaps some kind of ceremony with a medium who was able to release his spirit would in turn release the psychological hold on the family. It was more important of course, that her husband should realise he was free of his father's influence. Unfortunately the story ends here as the client did not report back. Since the chart has a Void Moon, perhaps nothing more happened. The Moon does eventually aspect the Part of Fortune however, but with a square, so resloution of the situation would probably not go smoothly.

The Consultation Chart

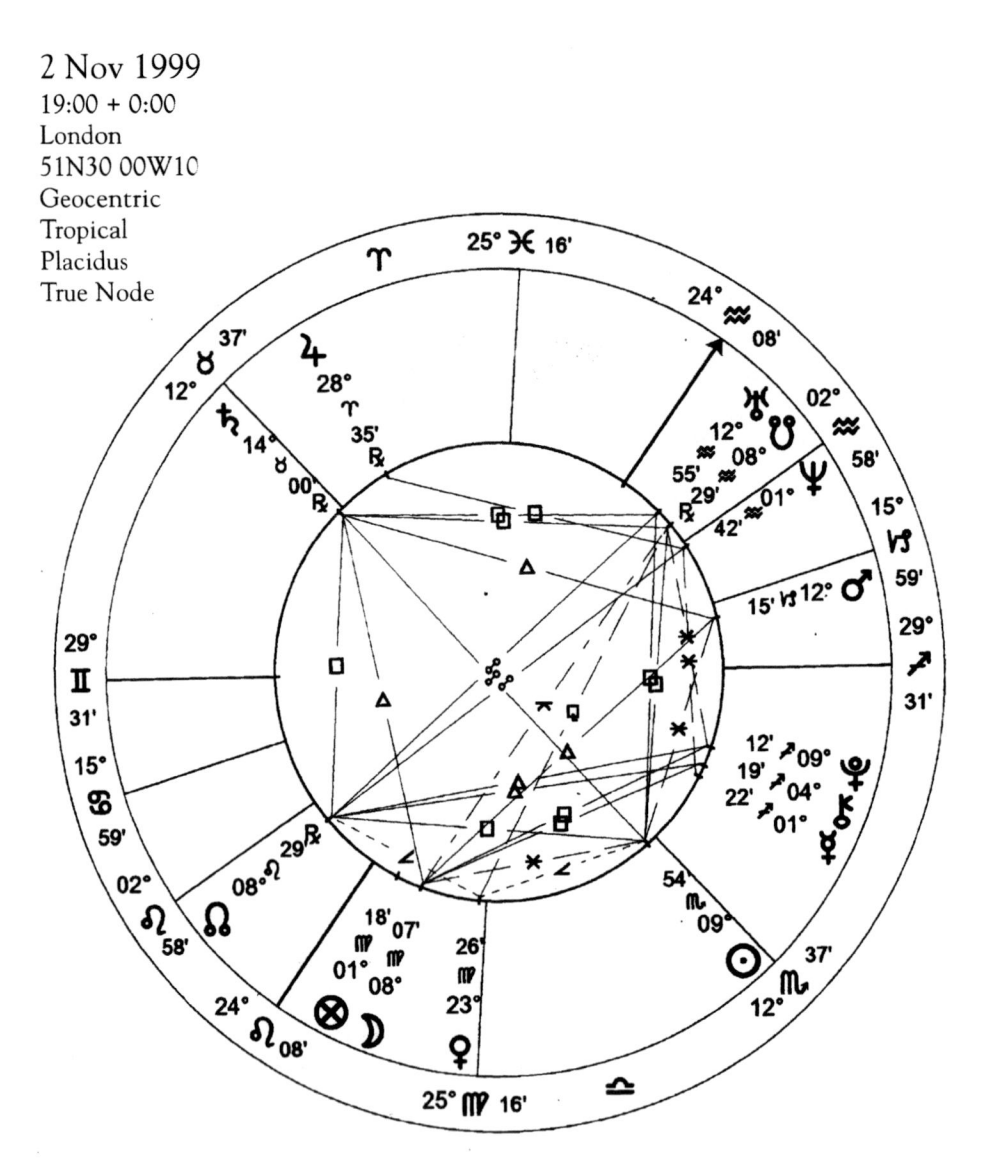

2 Nov 1999
19:00 + 0:00
London
51N30 00W10
Geocentric
Tropical
Placidus
True Node

The client wanted to know how her mother fared in the spirit world. Obviously I didn't want to disappoint her, but I wasn't sure if I had the means to contact the spirits. Not to be outdone, I looked at the tenth house (the mother) to see what it would reveal. Aquarius is on the tenth house cusp with Saturn ruling. The old reaper is placed in the mother's third house (the radix twelfth), which immediately suggested the mind and confinement. Further, Saturn is set in a Grand Cross formation since it opposes the Sun, and is in square to Uranus and the Nodes across the mother's sixth/twelfth house axis (the radix third/ninth). This looks like a situation indicative of tension and stress primarily on

194

the mental level. I said that it looked very much as if her mother had suffered with her nerves prior to her death, and quite severely too. The client revealed that her mother had had Alzheimer's disease, presenile dementia, which is a slowing of mental processes, forgetfulness and irritability. There is no cure at present, though vasodilator drugs are prescribed to improve blood supply to the brain.

No wonder the client wanted to know how her mother was getting on in the spirit world. Life had obviously been difficult for her on this side of the grave. I like to leave a client with some kind of hope, so I looked for more cheerful aspects to Saturn (the mother's significator). I found a trine to the Moon. I asked if she could possibly be with a small child as the Moon rules childhood. The client said this was probably her young nephew. Since the Moon was in Virgo I wondered if he had a problem with his intestines. Apparently he had had a heart condition, but had been fed through the abdomen (Virgo). The client wanted to know if there were other people supporting her mother in the spirit world. The trine Saturn received from Mars pointed to a male, possibly a soldier (having the warlord's fighting spirit in mind). The client said she did not know who that was because there had been so many soldiers in the family! I could not supply her with a name of course.

We now came down to earth as the client asked about her husband's illness - he was still alive. As Gemini rises, Sagittarius on the seventh house cusp and Jupiter would represent her husband. Jupiter in Aries, at the end of the sign, shows that the husband is near the end of treatment or illness but recovery is slow because Jupiter is retrograde. The client confirmed that he was undergoing chemotherapy and this was now coming to an end. Note that Jupiter is square to Neptune, which probably rules chemotherapy. What was the disease? The husband's sixth house in the turned chart is the radix twelfth, ruled by Taurus and Venus. Venus is in Virgo, so the abdomen is pinpointed again and the client confirmed that was where the disease was. Saturn in sixth house also shows slow recovery.

I am not a medium and I was only reading the chart, but it revealed the mother's illness and described her companions in the spirit world. The client felt comforted because a stranger had pinpointed the situation so accurately, even though the chart described nothing more than what the client already knew!

The Consultation Chart

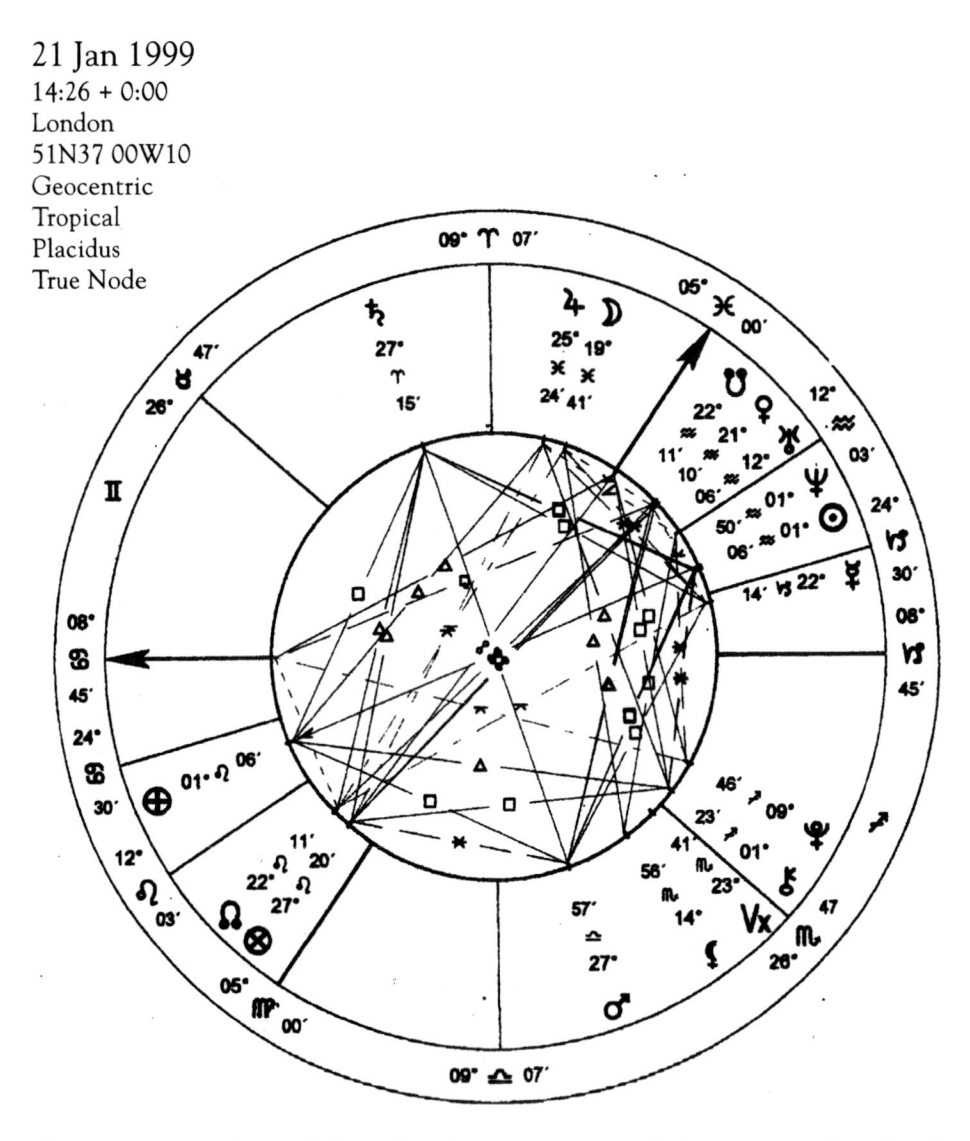

21 Jan 1999
14:26 + 0:00
London
51N37 00W10
Geocentric
Tropical
Placidus
True Node

Cancer rising indicated that the client was particularly interested in family issues but with the Moon as ruler of the Ascendant placed in the tenth house, I wondered if she also had her mind on career issues. Regardless, the family were playing an important role in her goals, since the Moon's next application is a sextile to Mercury which rules the fourth house. Mercury rules an intercepted Gemini in the twelfth house, suggesting that the client is facing rather frustrating circumstances in connection with her home and family. The client said she was waiting to hear about the home of her dreams, but not much was happening - Mercury's T-square formation with Mars and Saturn compounds the frustration. The Moon, representing the client, would complete the sextile to Mercury before Mercury arrived at the squares to the malefics, so the house situation looked promising. After Mercury, the Moon conjuncts Jupiter, the king of the gods, which rules the tenth house and is in the tenth house itself: as I had thought earlier, she was indeed thinking of her career. The client said she was thinking of turning her domestic skills into a kind of cottage industry, but what she really wanted to know was how her father was faring in the spirit world. No surprise as the Moon's next application was to Mercury, the ruler of the fourth house of fatherhood. With my new status as a medium, I decided to face the challenge of speaking about the deceased's present state of health!

I had noted earlier that Mercury was in the 'T' square formation with Mars and Saturn, which of course described a very frustrating and debilitating state of affairs. I didn't stop to consider the aspects in terms of application and separation, I just looked at the symbolism. It seemed to me that her father had suffered a great deal before his death, particularly in connection with his family circumstances where some separating influence had been operating (Mars and Saturn often point to separation). Had he lost someone he loved? The client revealed that her mother had left him about six months prior to his death. As Mars rules anger and Saturn resentment, I wondered if her father had died an angry and resentful man. This was apparently the case and the reason why the client was particularly worried about her father. I could understand her concern because this is usually the basis of karma; it is the thoughts and feelings that we take with us into the world beyond which help to construct the basis of the next life. Perhaps Mercury's application to the malefics indicated he was taking his anger and resentment with him. Since Mercury would actually contact Jupiter first - and by a helpful sextile - I said it was possible that her father was now learning about forgiveness and compassion. Note that Jupiter is in Pisces, the sign associated with these two qualities. The client seemed relieved. Becoming quite involved in my new work as a medium, I also suggested that the father had a large family pet by his side. The daughter was delighted and thought this to be a large dog belonging to her father who had died shortly before he did. My reasoning for the animal's presence was the dissociate conjunction between Mercury and the Sun, which in the turned chart rules the father's twelfth house (the radix third). The twelfth house rules large animals!

The client wanted more information from the other side and asked me to say something about her daughter (who is still alive) in relation to her father as the two had been close. Her daughter is ruled by Venus, lady of the fifth house and is in Aquarius, the ninth house. I felt stumped and wondered what to say as there was no connection between Venus and Mercury, the father's (now grandfather's) ruler. The client was waiting with bated breath and so as not to disappoint her, I bent traditional rules and looked upon Uranus as also having track with grandfathers. (He was the grandaddy of the gods after all!). I suggested that her daughter and her father were extremely alike, so much so that they had a similar birthmark on their calves. (Both Venus and Uranus are in Aquarius which of course rules calves). The client replied that she was not that familiar with her father's anatomy, but she could testify that her daughter certainly did have a birthmark on her calf!

5. Using the Consultation and Natal Charts Together

The Consultation Chart

Consultation Chart
2 Jun 1999
19:49 - 1:00
London
51N30 00W10
Geocentric
Tropical
Placidus
True Node

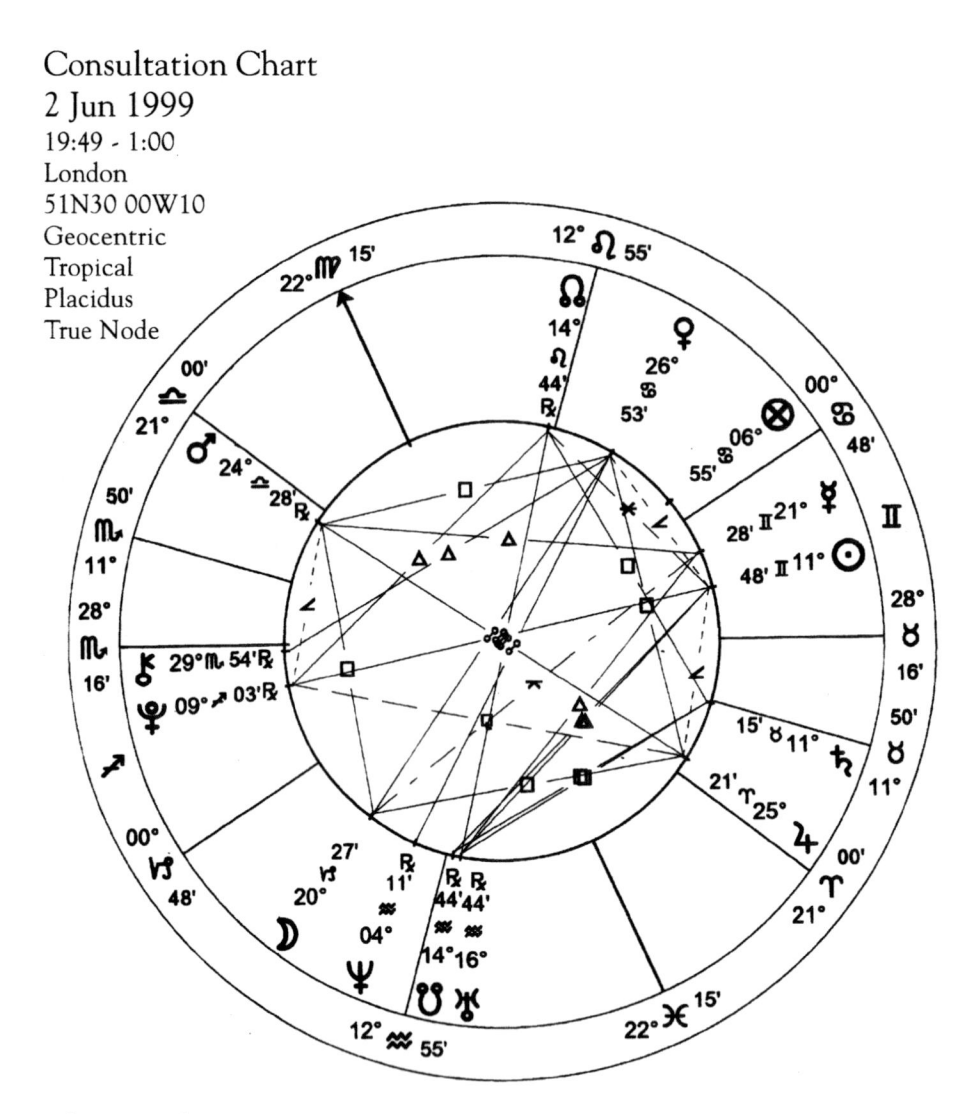

The Consultation Chart

Scorpio rises in this consultation chart indicating that the client is undergoing enforced changes. Chiron so close to the Ascendant shows she is feeling very hurt, or perhaps dealing with some deep wound. This is confirmed by the plight of Mars, the Ascendant ruler, as it is in its detriment in Libra and retrograde. Mars also rules the twelfth house suggesting that the client feels isolated, lonely and unhappy. The cause of her sorrow lies with Venus, the planet of love and ruler of the seventh house of relationships in the chart, separating from a square with Mars; this suggests the end of a relationship. In fact, she and her partner were still together, she said, but only just, and she was wondering if she should give up on the relationship altogether. Venus, her partner's significator, separates from a square with Jupiter, which rules the partner's tenth house (the radix fourth). I asked if he had he taken a new job. Apparently that was the crux of the matter: he had just been offered a new job that would take him overseas and away from home, effectively putting an end to the relationship. She was obviously feeling lonely, depressed and deserted having to face the fact that the relationship was reaching its end. The client went on to say that she was particularly distraught because, at her partner's insistence, she had given up a job she really enjoyed. No sooner had she complied with his request, than he told her he was leaving. This was a very distressing situation because it was a repeat performance of an earlier relationship where she had also given up enjoyable work to please a former partner. The first partner subsequently disappeared from her life as the current one was about to do.

The good news was that she would be employed again. This was suggested by Mercury, ruler of her tenth house, applying by trine to Mars, her significator. Since Mercury was in Gemini, it appeared as if her work would involve communications and possibly travel. She agreed that this was a strong possibility as she had already heard from some former colleagues that they were starting up a new business involving travel. Apparently they would be contacting her with a view to new employment.

In spite of the confirmation of good news, her distress understandably centred around the relationship. I had already confirmed her feelings that the relationship was on the rocks, but perhaps the most interesting point in this situation is why had she so *readily* renounced two jobs she loved to please partners who promptly rejected her? I felt that renunciation had probably played a big part in her life and I wanted to trace the root cause.

The Natal Chart
The signs of renunciation are Pisces and Virgo, which in the consultation chart are on the cusp of the fourth and tenth houses, emphasising the career axis. However, this is also the parental axis, so I wondered if 'renunciation' stemmed from experiences in her early life that had subsequently set the pattern. Moving on to her natal chart (see next page) it was no surprise to see Virgo and Pisces across the horizon. Renunciation was in her blood. This was confirmed by the debilitated state of Mercury, which as the Ascendant ruler represents the client. It is in combustion and is also overshadowed by a strong Venus, ruler of the third house. Mercury's position in Scorpio suggests her thoughts turn inwards, and placed in the third house it indicates that the client is unable to make her wishes heard. The client had no voice, metaphorically speaking.

Transiting Saturn from the ninth house would have opposed the planets in the third house recently, suggesting that the client was unable to

The Consultation Chart

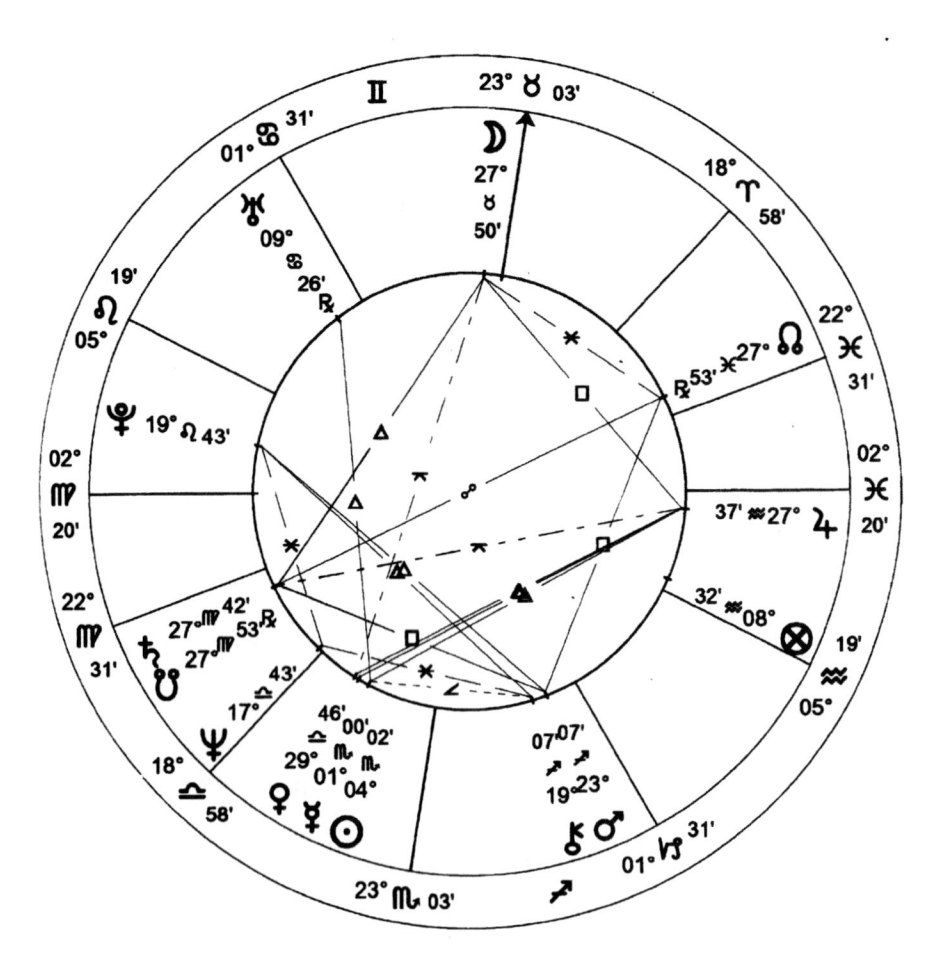

Natal Chart details withheld by request

communicate her needs. The present situation was probably a replay of much earlier wounds connected to her siblings, which are of course ruled by the third house. I noticed that the strong Venus would have perfected the conjunction with Mercury by Solar Arc progression within a year of the client's birth. It appeared as if a sibling had been born around that time and the client's light may have been obscured by his/her birth, because Venus is so much stronger than Mercury. The client revealed this was precisely what had happened. It transpired that her mother had never wanted her but had idolised her brother, who was born when the client was about one year old. Personified by Venus in Libra, he must have been a charmer - which he certainly was, according to the client, who said that everyone loved him and ignored her. With so much emphasis on the third house I wondered if she had other siblings and perhaps felt a little left out. The client was indeed overshadowed by her stronger siblings, and her habit of always giving in to them became an established pattern. She continued to give into people throughout her life in the belief that she would be liked if she remained amenable and compliant. In reality the opposite occurred and people used her and ignored her. The client agreed it time to get on with life without seeking other people's approval. She had to rediscover her own needs and willpower.

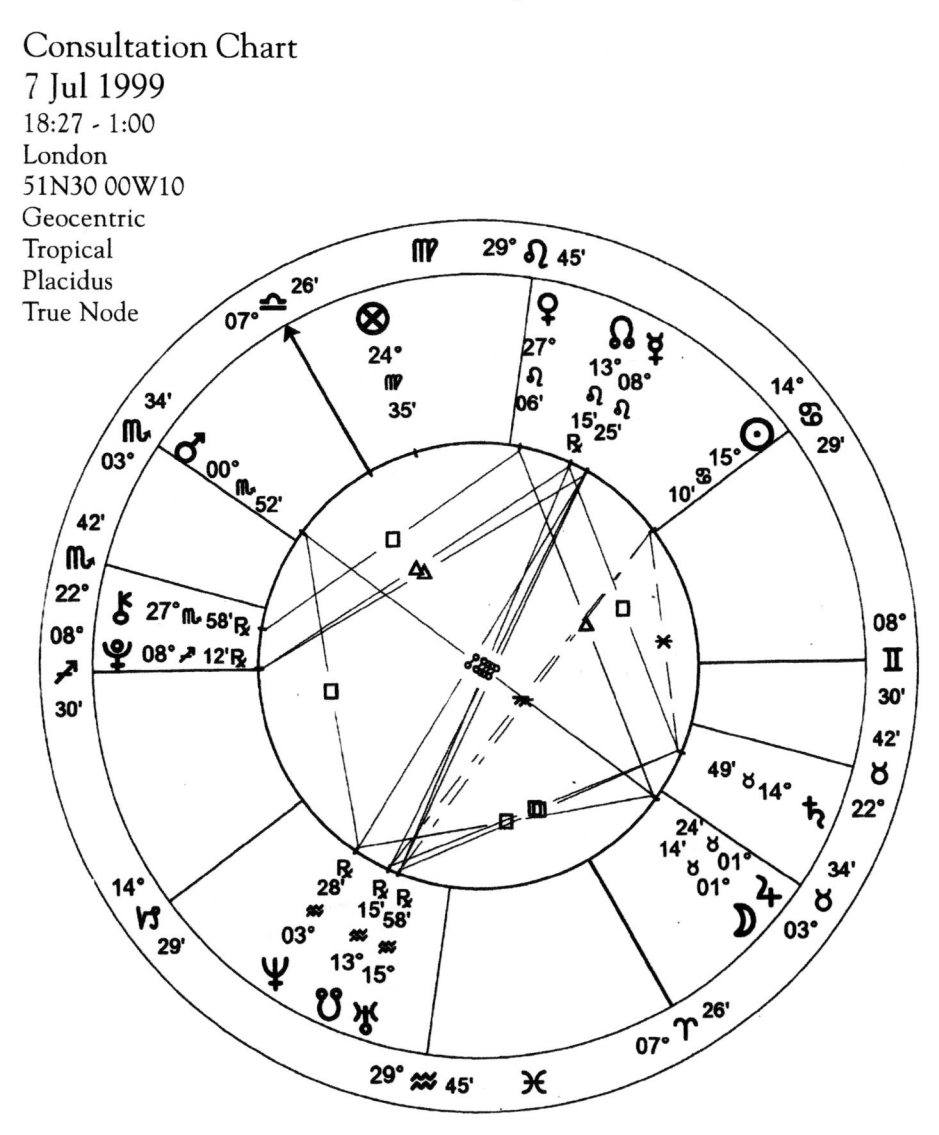

Consultation Chart
7 Jul 1999
18:27 - 1:00
London
51N30 00W10
Geocentric
Tropical
Placidus
True Node

The Consultation Chart
The client arrived for a general reading. Sagittarius is rising in the consultation chart, indicating expansion and adventure, but the client is held back by difficulties emanating from the past. This is seen by the position of Jupiter, the

The Consultation Chart

Ascendant ruler, in the fourth house relating to the home and past, and further emphasised by its conjunction to the Moon - also connected to the past. The Moon rules the eighth house, indicating deep family issues. Furthermore, Jupiter is in a T-square formation with Mars and Neptune. The opposition from a strong Mars in Scorpio suggests sexual issues, and the square from Neptune seems to dissolve the power of the Mars/Jupiter opposition.

Mercury ruling the seventh house is separating from a square with Jupiter, and its position in the eighth indicates that a relationship is at an end. The client confirmed this was the case. Since Pluto is conjunct the Ascendant and co-ruling the eleventh and twelfth houses, I wondered if there were indeed deep problems of a sexual nature influencing her ability to relate to others. However, I suggested that maybe it had been some kind of inhibition which had affected the relationship. The client said that this was the case exactly,

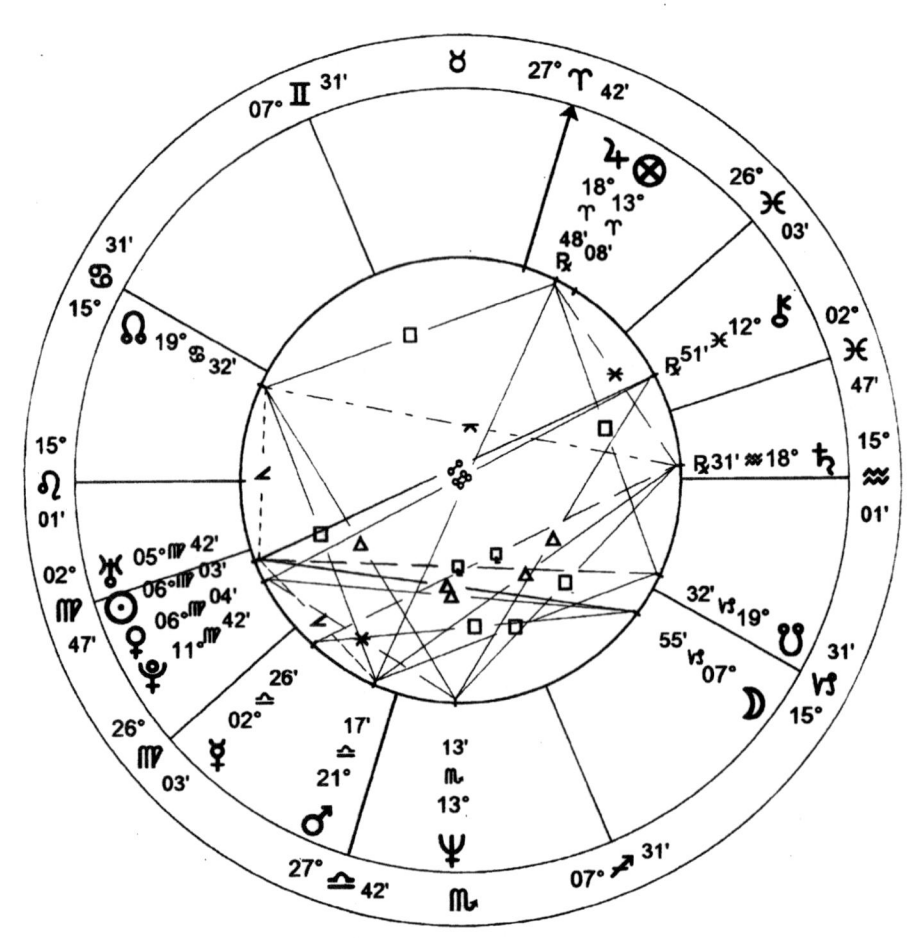

Natal Chart details witheld by request

and she felt it had been her inability to relate on a deep sexual level that had caused the problems in the relationship. I wondered if perhaps the natal chart would furnish a broader perspective on the problem.

The Natal Chart
At the time of the consultation, transiting Saturn was in Taurus passing through the tenth house, in square to the horizon and approaching the square of natal Saturn on the Descendant. Transiting Saturn had recently opposed natal Neptune, activating the natal T-square between the horizon, Saturn and Neptune; this indicated an unstable situation with regard to relationships and the home. Transiting Uranus in Aquarius also activated this T-square, suggesting the present situation would be overturned.

The natal square between Saturn and Neptune is separated by around five degrees, and this would have formed an exact square by Solar Arc at the age of five years. Neptune in the fourth house suggests that the early home life appeared to have been unstable. Neptune's association with the eighth and ninth houses pointed to a lack of boundaries within the sphere of sexuality and religion. The chart was suggesting some kind of abuse, but I allowed the client to relate the incident pertinent to that early age. I did not feel it was right for me to suggest it. The client admitted she had been sexually molested at the age of five. She agreed this had probably affected her ability to enter into intimate relationships and that she lacked confidence in her relationships with people generally.

I could not see an easy resolution to her present relationship and suggested she may need to seek therapeutic help with her sexual problems. She said she was actually in therapy and these issues were being addressed.

It is possible that the transiting Uranus to Saturn and the T-square generally was breaking up the difficult pattern of the past, and that the client would have the opportunity, through therapy, to change her future approach to relationships.

6. The Turned Chart

The Consultation Chart

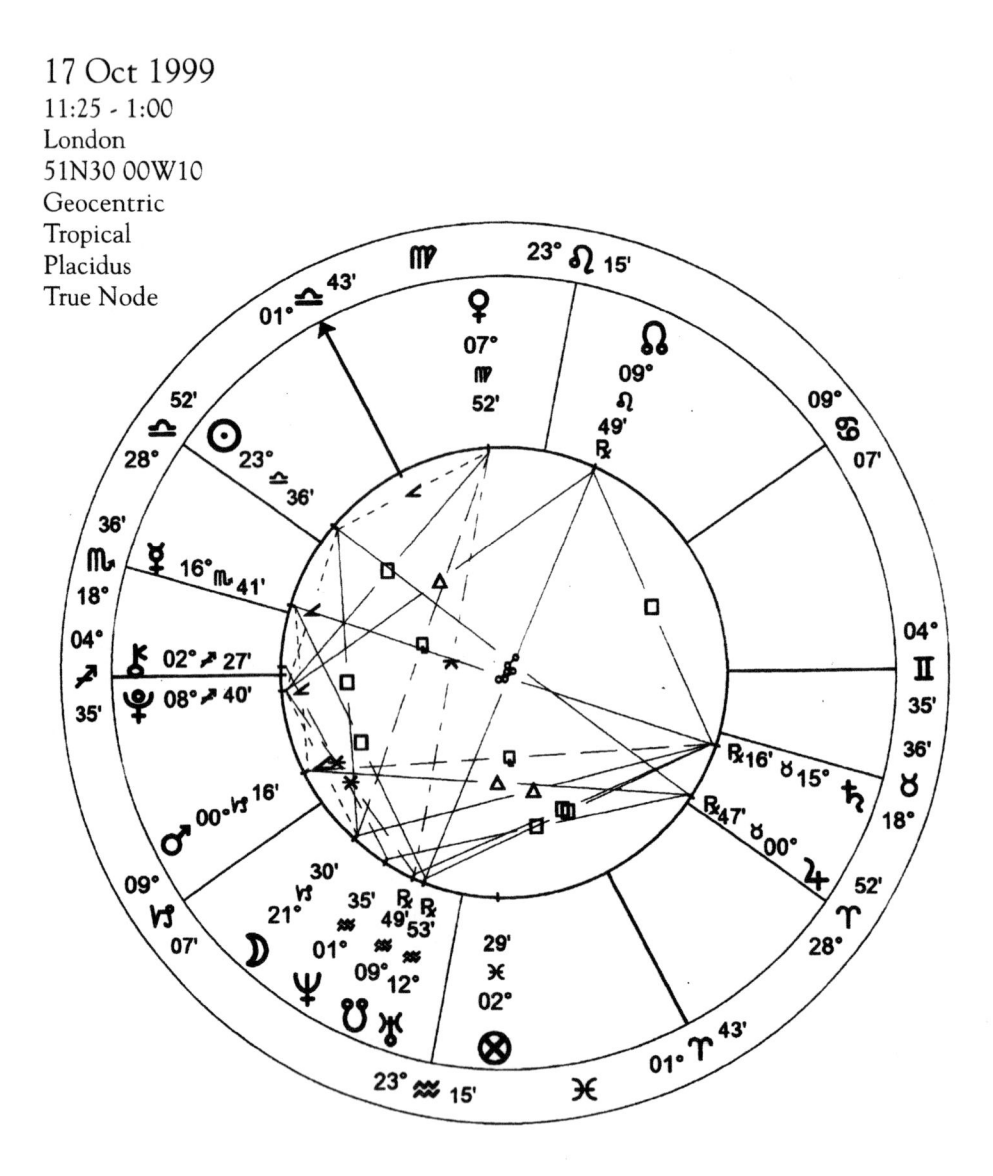

17 Oct 1999
11:25 - 1:00
London
51N30 00W10
Geocentric
Tropical
Placidus
True Node

The client was concerned about her daughter and asked me for help. She volunteered no other information so I examined the fifth house, which of course rules children. Aries is on the cusp with Mars strong in Capricorn, its sign of exaltation. It seemed that the daughter was in a powerful position to handle her difficulties, whatever they may be, and the client agreed. I suspected that the daughter had problems with her own child. This I deduced firstly because Mars receives a semi-square from Mercury ruling Virgo, intercepted in the daughter's fifth house (the radix ninth). It is the plight of the messenger that suggests a problem: it is in Scorpio, the sign of turmoil, and placed on the cusp of the radix twelfth house of confinement. Furthermore, Mars is sesquiquadrate Saturn, placed on the cusp of the radix sixth house in Taurus. Mercury and Saturn are in opposition across the difficult sixth/twelfth axis suggesting blocks in the flow of energy or vital force.

In the turned chart, that is using the fifth house as the daughter's first, we see this opposition across her second/eighth house axis, which relates to vital force and its dissolution. In the daughter's turned chart, Mercury also rules the third house of communication and speech (radix seventh). It appears that it is the daughter's child who has the communication problem. I suggested to the client that the child may have learning difficulties. The client confirmed that this was in fact the case, since the child had recently been diagnosed as dyslexic. This as most people know is difficulty in understanding the written or the spoken word.

However, it was not this particular daughter's problems that the client had in mind at this point in time! The radix fifth house had described the eldest daughter. The client revealed that she was particularly interested in the welfare of her *third* daughter. Seen from the perspective of the parent, I view each succeeding fifth house from the fifth, as describing the children in succession. Therefore, the client's *second* daughter would be ruled by the ninth house (fifth from the fifth) and the *third* daughter would be ruled by the Ascendant (fifth from the ninth). Therefore, the third child and the client were both ruled by the Ascendant. Some astrologers believe that the second child is ruled by the Radix seventh house, it being the third from the fifth. This might be the case if we wanted to discern how the child ruled by the fifth *perceived* her sibling, but here I was looking at the third child from the mother's perspective.

As the Ascendant represents both mother and daughter I said that they were probably very alike and she wholeheartedly agreed. They were more like twins, she said, similar in build and with the same taste in clothes; they even dressed alike. Jupiter rules the Ascendant and its placement in Taurus in the fifth house seems to keep the emphasis on children. I asked if she were actually concerned about her daughter's children. The client revealed that she had lost contact with her daughter and missed her and the grandchildren terribly - she was desperate to see them again. I thought that it was highly likely that a reunion would occur. I deduced this from the applying trine between Mars (ruling children in both the radix and turned charts) and Jupiter, ruling both client and third daughter. Unfortunately, I cannot verify that this actually happened as the client did not contact me again but it seemed highly likely. Nevertheless, I did manage to ascertain the cause of their estrangement.

As Jupiter rules both mother and daughter, it suggests that a mutual experience may be at the root of their problem. Jupiter is square to Neptune creating misunderstandings, especially as Neptune co-rules the third house of communication. Jupiter is also in opposition to the Sun, ruling the ninth house. Could there be a legal problem involved? The client revealed that she was actually divorcing her husband at the present time. I was not sure how relevant this was to the rift between daughter and mother and the client did not elaborate just then.

More clues were gleaned from the Ascendant since it represents both women. Pluto in the first house conjoins Chiron, suggesting that both women felt wounded by something. The association of Pluto with the twelfth house indicated repression and sorrow. Pluto is square Venus and semi-square the Moon signifying depth and intensity in the expression of love. Pluto is also midway between the Sun and the Moon, intersecting the male and female energies. By now I had a good idea what had caused the rift between mother and daughter but the situation needed to be handled with extreme care. It looked very much like sexual abuse since the main myth connected to the lord of the underworld is of sexual violation. I tentatively asked if some difficulty had arisen between her daughter and herself over the father, the client's husband. She replied in the affirmative, but said little more. I described the husband as a powerful and demanding person (Pluto) who may have hurt his daughter in some way. The client finally revealed that her husband had sexually abused her daughter and that was why she was now divorcing him.

It transpired that the daughter had never revealed the abuse to her mother. It had finally been brought out into the open the year previously and the news had naturally devastated the client. Mother and daughter had been extremely close but the revelation had driven a wedge between them. The daughter felt that she could not forgive her mother for not having been aware of the situation. The mother said she had never suspected that this had occurred. She said that she and her daughter had not been speaking since the revelation, and she was very keen to see her again. I can only hope that with the aforesaid application of Mars to Jupiter that this would happen.

The dynamics within this family graphically reflected the myth associated with Pluto and Persephone. The seduction of Persephone and her subjugation in the underworld reflected the daughter's own rape and years of silence. When the daughter had finally told her mother of the abuse, it was as if Pluto had removed his helmet of invisibility and unveiled the full horror of the situation. The mother in this consultation chart is like Ceres, who in the myth yearned to see her daughter once again. Ceres had consulted Jupiter (Zeus) hoping he would intercede on her behalf and the modern mother consulted an astrologer to give her some guidance for the future.

Conclusion

My use of the consultation chart has evolved through many years of both telephone and face-to-face consultations, and I have come to see it as an incredibly powerful way of getting to the heart of the client's situation. I find the consultation chart indicates just how the client is dealing with their problem right now and what sort of information they need in order to successfully handle it and then move on. The Ascendant and the position of its ruler is particularly helpful in ascertaining the client's state of mind and the way they are coping with the situation.

In a sense, this chart is like Pandora's box: everything is in it, including Hope at the bottom. It opens the lid on the present, bringing the difficulties to light, yet still retains hopes for the future. Many things may come to the surface that would not otherwise have come up in discussion.

People often come to an astrologer as a last resort, hoping for a miraculous solution to their problems. Miracles are not usually possible but I like to think that the client will leave the consultation feeling that there is at least some light at the end of their tunnel.

My hope is that the information in this book will encourage you to explore the possibilities of the consultation chart with your own clients, and even for yourselves when you need to clarify a situation. The same delineations can be used to understand the natal chart in much the same way. The deeper you delve into the consultation chart, the more your intuition will grow.

Wanda Sellar
December 2000

BIBLIOGRAPHY

Alice Bailey, *Esoteric Psychology I*, Lucis Publishing Company, 1936
Alice Bailey, *Esoteric Psychology II*, Lucis Publishing Company, 1942
Alice Bailey, *Esoteric Astrology*, Lucis Publishing Company, 1951
Alice Bailey, *Esoteric Healing*, Lucis Publishing Company, 1953
Olivia Barclay, *Horary Astrology Rediscovered*, Whitford Press 1990
C.E.O. Carter, *Essays on the Foundations of Astrology*, Theosophical Publishing House, 1947
Dr H. L. Cornell, M.D.,LL.D. *Encyclopaedia of Medical Astrology* 1933, 1977
Dr. David Frawley, *The Astrology of the Seers*, Passage Press, 1990
Jane F. Gardner, *Roman Myths*, British Museum Press, 1993
Michael Grant & John Hazel, *Who's Who in Classical Mythology*, Weidenfeld & Nicholson, 1973
Robert Graves, *Greek Myths*, Penguin 1955
J.S. Gordon, *Astrology of the Path of Return*, Orpheus Publishing House, 1998
A.R. Hope Moncrieff, *Classical Mythology*, Studio Editions, 1994
Deborah Houlding *The Houses: Temples of the Sky*, Ascella Publications, 1998
Erminie Lantero, *The Continuing Discovery of Chiron*, Samuel Weiser, Inc 1983
David Levy, *Skywatching*, Harper Collins Publishers, 1995
William Lilly, *Christian Astrology*, Regulus
Bernard Lovell, *In the Centre of Immensities*, Hutchinson & Co, 1979
A.T. Mann, *The Round Art*, Dragon's World Limited Imprint, 1979
David McNab and James Youger, *The Planets*, BBC Worldwide Ltd 1999
A.G.S. Norris, *Transcendental Astrology*, The Occult Book Society
Alan Oken, *Soul Centred Astrology*, Bantam Books, 1990
Haydn Paul, *Revolutionary Spirit - Exploring the Astrological Uranus*, Element Books, 1989
Ptolemy, *Tetrabiblos*, Harvard University Press, 1940
Jane Ridder-Patrick, *A Handbook of Medical Astrology*, Arkana, 1990
Howard Sasportas, *The Twelve Houses*, The Aquarian Press, 1985
Michael Stapleton, *A Dictionary of Greek and Roman Mythology*, Hamlyn 1978
Komilla Sutton, *The Essentials of Vedic Astrology*, The Wessex Astrologer 1999
Errol Weiner, *Transpersonal Astrology*, Element, 1991

ACKNOWLEDGEMENTS

Grateful thanks to *The Traditional Astrologer* for Ptolemy's table. Published by Ascella. Visit their website at www.astrology-world.com/ascella_books

ASTROLOGICAL SCHOOLS AND ORGANISATIONS

This is by no means a definitive list, and apologies to any organisation that feels they have been missed out. It is however a good starting point for anyone thinking of studying astrology.

The Astrological Association
Lee Valley Technopark, Tottenham Hale, London N17 9LN.
Tel: 0208 880 4848, Fax: 0208 880 4849,
email: astrological.association@zetnet.co.uk.
website: www.astrologer.com/aanet
The AA publishes a bi-monthly Journal and runs an annual conference which is attended by astrologers from all over the world. Its main objectives are to facilitate the exchange of information within the astrological community, and promote the good name of astrology in general.

The Astrological Lodge of London
50, Gloucester Place, London W1H 4EA
website: www.astrolodge.co.uk
The Astrological Lodge holds regular classes in London. It supports all branches of astrology, whilst encouraging the study and understanding of the philosophical, historical and symbolic aspects of astrology. Its magazine, The Astrological Quarterly, is free to members.

British Association for Vedic Astrology
19, Jenner Way, Romsey, Hants. SO51 8PD
Tel: 01794 524178
email: bava@btinternet.com
website: www.bava.org
BAVA runs regular classes in London, and an annual conference which attracts speakers from all over the world.

British Astrological and Psychic Society
Robert Denholm House, Bletchingly Road, Nutfield Surrey, RH1 4HW
Tel: 0906 4700827
email: baps@tlpplc.com
website: www.bapsoc.co.uk
BAPS runs certificate courses in astrology, tarot and palmistry. It also provides a register of members, with details of local courses and discussion nights.

The Centre for Psychological Astrology (CPA)
Box 1815, London WC1N 3XX
Tel: 0208 749 2330
email cpalondon@aol.com website: www.astrologer.com
Director: Liz Greene PhD, DFAstrolS, Dip Analyt Psych. The CPA is the outstanding centre in the world for the study of astrology in relationship to depth psychology. It runs regular courses and seminars in London and occasional additional seminars in Zurich. The CPA 3-year Diploma seminar programme, based at Regent's College in London, is

also open to members of the public. High quality books presenting seminar material by CPA tutors are available from the CPA Press via Midheaven Books (tel 0207-607-4133) where Apollon, the quality Journal of Psychological Astrology, can also be ordered.

The Company of Astrologers
PO Box 3001, London, N1 1LY
Tel: 01227 362427
email: admin@coa.org.uk
website:: www.hubcom.com/coa
The Company is the home of divinatory astrology. It runs certificate courses as well as seminars and an annual conference.

The English Huber School of Astrological Counselling
PO Box 118, Knutsford, Cheshire, WA16 8TG
Tel/Fax: 01565 651131
email: huberschool@btinternet.com
website: www.ncsa.es/eschuber.sch
The English Huber School provides correspondence courses and workshops for all levels of astrology.

The Faculty of Astrological Studies
BM7470, London WC1N 3XX
Tel: 07000 790143
Fax: 01689 603537
email: info@astrology.org.uk
The Faculty provides tuition at all levels of astrology, through home study courses, evening classes in London, seminar tapes and annual summer schools in Oxford.

The Mayo School
Alvana Gardens, Tregavethan, Truro, Cornwall, TR4 9EN
Tel: 01872 560048
website: www.astrology-world.com/mayo.html
Founded by Jeff Mayo, the school offers correspondence courses at certificate and diploma level and issues a list of their qualified consultants who have gained the diploma.

The London School of Astrology
BCM Planets
London WC1N 3XX
Tel: 07002 33 44 55
Website: www.londonschoolofastrology.co.uk.
Founded by Sue Tompkins and Christine Tate in 2000, the school has a holistic approach to astrology. It offers beginners classes and monthly seminars in London.

The Mountain Astrologer Magazine

Widely acknowledged as the most intelligent English-language astrology magazine in the world

- Western and Vedic articles in every issue
- A detailed, user-friendly forecast section
- World-class writing on a wide range of astrology topics, from writers such as Donna Cunningham, Bill Meridian, Rob Hand, Steven Forrest, Bruce Scofield, Dana Gerhardt, Gloria Star, and many others
- Something for everyone — beginner to professional

— **Available at finer bookstores and by subscription** —

In Europe and the British Isles contact:
The Wessex Astrologer, Ltd.
PO Box 2751
Bournemouth BH6 3ZJ, ENGLAND
Phone/Fax: +44 1202 424695
info@wessexastrologer.com

In Australia and New Zealand contact:
Spica Publications
FREE 1800 626 402
e-mail: spica@world.net

In the U.S. and elswhere in the world contact:
The Mountain Astrologer
PO Box 970
Cedar Ridge, CA 95924 U.S.A.
Phone: (800) 287- 4828
Fax: (530) 477-9423
subs@mountainastrologer.com

INDEX

C

case histories 207
   career 151
   health 161
   relationships 177
   spooks 191
   the turned chart 207
   using the consultation and natal charts together 199
Chiron 91
collection 17
combustion 18
considerations before judgement 18

E

early or late degrees ascending 19
eighth house 126
eleventh house 140

F

fifth house 111
first house 96
fourth house 107
frustration 18

J

Jupiter 61
   astrology 62
   astronomy 61
   esoteric view 63
   in Aquarius 66
   in Aries 63
   in Cancer 64
   in Capricorn 66
   in Gemini 64
   in Leo 64
   in Libra 65
   in Pisces 67
   in Sagittarius 66
   in Scorpio 65
   in Taurus 64
   in Virgo 65
   mythology 61

M

malefics in the first house 21
Mars 52
   astrology 54
   astronomy 52
   esoteric view 55
   in Aquarius 58
   in Aries 55
   in Cancer 56
   in Capricorn 58
   in Gemini 56
   in Leo 57
   in Libra 57
   in Pisces 59
   in Sagittarius 58
   in Scorpio 58
   in Taurus 56
   in Virgo 57
   mythology 53
Mercury 30
   astrology 31
   astronomy 30
   esoteric view 32
   in Aquarius 36
   in Aries 33
   in Cancer 34
   in Capricorn 35
   in Gemini 33
   in Leo 34
   in Libra 35
   in Pisces 36
   in Sagittarius 35
   in Scorpio 35

in Taurus 33
in Virgo 34
mythology 30
Moon 23
  astrology 24
  astronomy 23
  esoteric view 25
  in Aquarius 28
  in Aries 25
  in Cancer 26
  in Capricorn 28
  in Gemini 26
  in Leo 27
  in Libra 27
  in Pisces 29
  in Sagittarius 28
  in Scorpio 28
  in Taurus 26
  in Virgo 27
  mythology 23
  void of course 19

N

Neptune 80
  astrology 82
  astronomy 80
  esoteric view 83
  mythology 81
ninth house 131
North Node 89

P

passage of the moon 19
peregrination 17
Pluto 84
  astrology 86
  astronomy 85
  esoteric view 88
  mythology 85
prognostication 16
prohibition 18

R

refranation 18
rising sign 1

Aquarius 9
Aries 2
Cancer 4
Capricorn 8
Gemini 3
Leo 4
Libra 6
Pisces 9
Sagittarius 7
Scorpio 7
Taurus 2
Virgo 5

S

Saturn 68
  astrology 69
  astronomy 68
  esoteric view 70
  in Aquarius 74
  in Aries 71
  in Cancer 72
  in Capricorn 74
  in Gemini 72
  in Leo 72
  in Libra 73
  in Pisces 74
  in Sagittarius 73
  in Scorpio 73
  in Taurus 71
  in Virgo 73
  mythology 68
second house 99
seventh house 122
signification of forthcoming events 16
signposts to delineation 10
sixth house 116
South Node 89
split rulership 1
Sun 44
  astrology 46
  astronomy 44
  esoteric view 47
  in Aquarius 51
  in Aries 47
  in Cancer 48

    in Capricorn 50
    in Gemini 48
    in Leo 49
    in Libra 49
    in Pisces 51
    in Sagittarius 50
    in Scorpio 50
    in Taurus 48
    in Virgo 49
    mythology 45
sunbeams 18

T

tenth house 136
third house 102
translation 17
turned chart 15
twelfth house 144

U

Uranus 76
    astrology 77
    astronomy 76
    esoteric view 79
    mythology 77

V

Venus 37
    astrology 39
    astronomy 37
    esoteric view 39
    in Aquarius 43
    in Aries 40
    in Cancer 41
    in Capricorn 43
    in Gemini 41
    in Leo 41
    in Libra 42
    in Pisces 43
    in Sagittarius 42
    in Scorpio 42
    in Taurus 40
    in Virgo 42
    mythology 38
via combusta 20